The Intelligent Layman's Book of

Jewellery

Jack Ogden

For my daughters Carita, Theodora and Alexia who enjoy jewellery, for the curators and historians who enjoy sharing their knowledge of jewellery, and for the fakers and forgers who make jewellery and prove that none of us enjoy infallibility.

© The Intelligent Layman Publishers Ltd.
Thornton House, Thornton Road
London SW19 4NG

Jack Ogden asserts his moral rights to be
identified as the author of this book.

Printed in Slovenia by MKT Print on
behalf of Compass Press Ltd.

ISBN 0947798358

December 2006

Contents

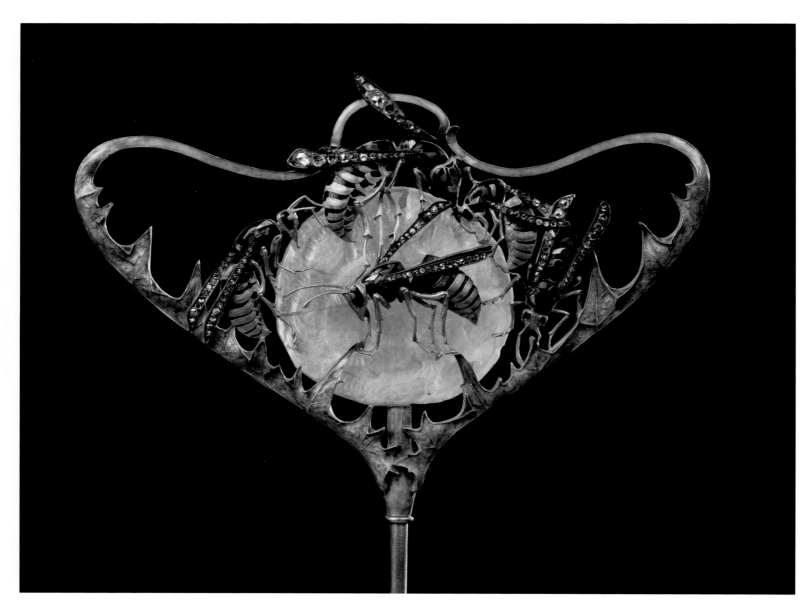

Fig.298: Wasp pin in enamelled gold with a large opal and diamonds.
René Lalique, Paris ca 1900. (Danish Museum of Decorative Arts, Copenhagen)
Danish Museum of Decorative Arts, Copenhagen

Introduction   I

Introduction

This is a book about 5000 years of jewellery from many parts of the globe. Much of this jewellery is pleasing to look at, and its technical precision can be astounding, but there is more to it than that. The preciousness, beauty and intricacy of jewellery stimulate public attention, and fund excavations, fill exhibitions and help to sell books such as this one. But jewellery also provides knowledge about people and societies in the past, about their interconnections, economics and trade; about their technologies and about their beliefs and hierarchies. This is the realm of the jewellery historian.

The job of the jewellery historian, like any art historian, is to ask questions of jewellery. It is little use to tell our audiences what we think of the jewellery. Too many catalogues of jewellery go into rapturous, almost poetic, descriptions of the jewellery, but do not stop to ask or explain the basic questions: who? how? why? with what? There must be both subjective and objective observation. Considering materials and techniques might seem to strip the artistic soul from jewellery, but these practical factors had a very significant affect on jewellery assembly and thus on forms and thus on fashion. Throughout history, there was a symbiotic relationship between craftsperson and patron. New materials and techniques allowed new approaches to construction and assembly, and these interacted with the prevalent art styles and fashions to allow new styles of jewellery. Monarchs, mistresses and ministers throughout history led the way in establishing jewellery fashions, sometimes lionising individual makers, but the materials and techniques that tickled the patrons' imaginations and permitted those fashions were worked and developed at the bench. The magnificent engine-turned gold box flourished by a late eighteenth century grandee would have been impossible without the developments in steel production within the noisy, sooty factories of the industrial revolution.

It used to be a complaint in Britain that school history was simply a list of the dates, deeds and misdeeds of kings, and that the lives of the common people were ignored. We might level the same criticism at jewellery history since so much seems to focus on the treasures of the elite, from Tutankhamen to the Czars. This is unavoidable, it is in the very nature of the materials that the richer or more powerful you were, the more you could own and appropriate, and even be buried with. Concepts of preciousness, of course, changed from period to period and from place to place. Indians in Ecuador made fish hooks of platinum gold while just a century and a half ago Napoleon III in France dispensed with silver tableware and replaced it with the expensive new metal aluminium. About the same time the Chinese were searching for diamonds on their river banks. They wanted them as chips for cutting jade and they pounded any larger stone they found into sharp little pieces.

Regardless of relative values, the point is that throughout history, jewellery has been a store of wealth and a means of exhibiting wealth. Wealth can be expressed as monetary value, such as with the gold ingot pendants of the 1980s or the 'mine is bigger than yours' rivalry of the ubiquitous solitaire diamond ring. But the fine workmanship and artistic excellence, subtler indications of wealth, have also been integral to jewellery since the earliest times. Good taste, after all, is as much expected of the nobility as wealth; indeed, it often outlives it by several generations. But this association of fine jewellery in the past with 'good taste' may be too modern a concept and one that risks missing an important point. Jewellery is a display of power. Only the powerful could command and afford an infrastructure that permitted craftsmanship to thrive. Whether that command came through money or menace is irrelevant. The accomplished jeweller is as much a frivolous luxury in society as the jewellery he produces.

Nevertheless, too great a focus on the jewellery worn by royalty and the upper social strata, can distort our understanding. For the jewellery historian, a minute fragment might provide invaluable historical information, the grandest treasures add little to our pool of knowledge. Things don't have to be grand to be evocative, even for the casual observer. What stirs our hearts more – Tutankhamen's gold funerary mask (fig.100), or a ring found in the burial of a teenage girl in Rome dating from the second century AD? The ring was still too big for the girl's finger and so the hoop had been bound with wool to make it fit.

We even have to be careful about old jewellery being described as 'evocative'. Again, we are pinning new, and somtimes personal emotions, to old jewellery. For example, the mourning ring in memory of Admiral Lord Nelson in fig.24 would have meant a great deal to its original owner – just a teenager when he served under Nelson at the Battle of Trafalgar. Today, the Nelson connection makes the ring interesting and valuable, but how many modern observers would not be moved

just a little bit more when they learn that in maturity the recipient died, frozen to death; a famous explorer seeking the northwest passage? There is nothing wrong with layering old jewellery with new thoughts and emotions, just as long as they are recognised for what they are. Indeed, anything that makes us think about the jewellery is useful. Consider the jewellery from Ur in what in now Iraq (figs.87 to 93). What did its young wearers think as these magnificent ornaments were placed on their bodies; just before they drank the poison and accompanied their sovereign into the next world? We shudder at the thoughts that might pass through our heads at such a time, but what would have passed through theirs? Those girls were just as much a symbol of the deceased's wealth and power as the jewellery that adorned them. But, was their availability in the afterworld a luxury or a necessity?

Applying modern thought to old jewellery brings us to a more obvious paradox. Can we admire something from the past, using modern aesthetic criteria, without inherently misunderstanding it? The more we have to turn to our twenty-first century repertoire of comparisons and concepts, the more we divorce ourselves from the context in which the jewellery was produced and used. It is almost impossible to judge art from the past within its own cultural context, without drawing on modern experience and taste. Inspiration, for example, is a convenient modern artistic term leavened by some hint of spiritual intervention, but is the word 'inspiration' a meaningful concept in any sort of ancient artistic context? Was a gold myrtle design on a Greek gold wreath inspired by a myrtle, or dictated by whatever the myrtle then symbolised?

So, jewellery provides us with a window onto human life stretching back into the remotest past. Often this is a unique window because many of the traditional jewellery materials, gold and gemstones in particular, are little changed by the passage of time. The kilos of gold concealed in Tutankhamen's tomb around 1340 BC still glinted when Howard Carter shone his torch on them some thirty five centuries later. Heinrich Schliemann's wife was photographed wearing the extraordinary gold headdress he had excavated at Bronze Age Troy (fig.94). In comparison, the great cities of the past are rubble, the chariots of their rulers rusted away, and the silks carried from China to adorn the Byzantine aristocracy are but fragile wisps.

What follows attempts to plot something of the course of jewellery history over 5000 years. Inevitably, only a selection of topics are covered and these too briefly and of necessity often with sweeping generalisations, and with selfish biases. Indeed, this book probably raises more questions than it answers. But, in a sense, that is the idea.

JackOgden

June 2006

Fig. 108: Detail of a gold diadem with the protective vulture and Uraeus (cobra).
Set with glass, obsidian, malachite, chalcedony and lapis lazuli. From the tomb of
Tutankhamen, Egyptian, ca 1325 BC. (Egyptian Museum, Cairo)
© Frank Trapper/Corbis

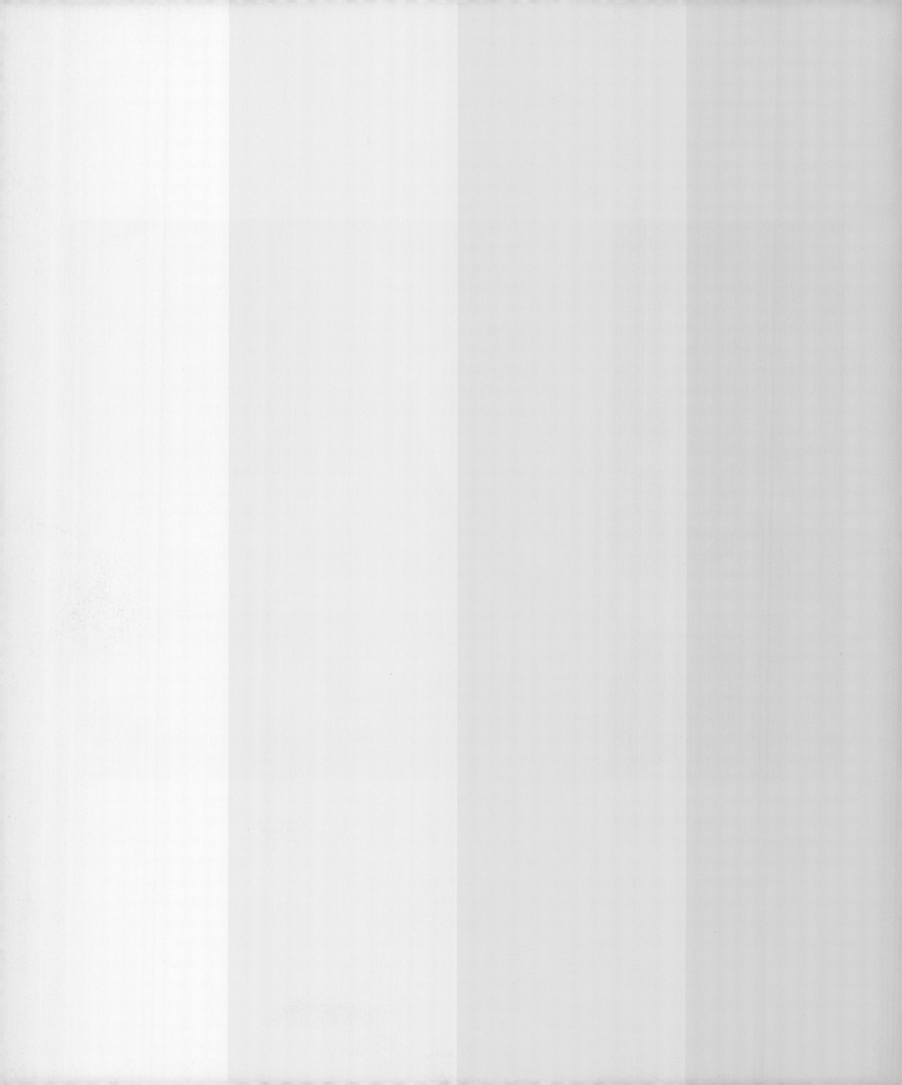

1
Jewellery and its
Beginnings

Fig.1: A woman from Ibiza wears the traditional
emprendada gold jewellery. ca 2003.
© Carmen Redondo / CORBIS

What is jewellery?

We might begin by trying to define our subject matter. What is jewellery? A suitable and sustainable definition is not easy to find. Jewellery is human adornment, certainly, and intentional self adornment may be one of the traits that separates humanity from the other creatures that inhabit the earth. There is little doubt that the woman shown here is wearing jewellery, and lots of it. She's from Ibiza, one of the Spanish Balearic Islands, and is wearing the traditional *emprendada* jewellery that reflects Northern African influences in Ibiza culture. She was photographed as recently as about 2003 in Ibiza.

Jewellery is a complex interaction between aesthetics, symbolism and power. For more than five millennia gold, silver and precious stones have fuelled endless conflicts, prompted conquest, trade and exploration over almost every inch of the globe, engaged some of the greatest crafts people and pandered to every whim of man's vanity and greed.

Jewellery may involve function, whether practical or symbolic, it might simply be self adornment as art, or it could be intrinsic value for the sake of it; or it might be any combination of these. A contemporary jeweller producing an exquisite pendant that deliberately shuns the use of intrinsically valuable materials might well scorn her colleague who makes a diamond solitaire ring of enormous value, but no artistic merit. But both are jewellers. A brass curtain ring used as a wedding ring becomes jewellery in both function and emotion.

We cannot define jewellery as something that is simply frivolous, much jewellery has or had practical function. The obvious examples are the pins and brooches that have for millennia fastened garments, sometimes delightfully expressing their function, as with the Medieval brooch in fig.8. If a gold buckle is jewellery, why not a warrior's gold belt? And if the warrior's belt, why not his horse's gold bridle fittings? A beautiful seventeenth century gold, and diamond button in fig.11 is clearly jewellery, so why not a twentieth century, run-of-the-mill mother of pearl button? Or does mother of pearl have to have been worked by an artist like Lalique before it is jewellery?

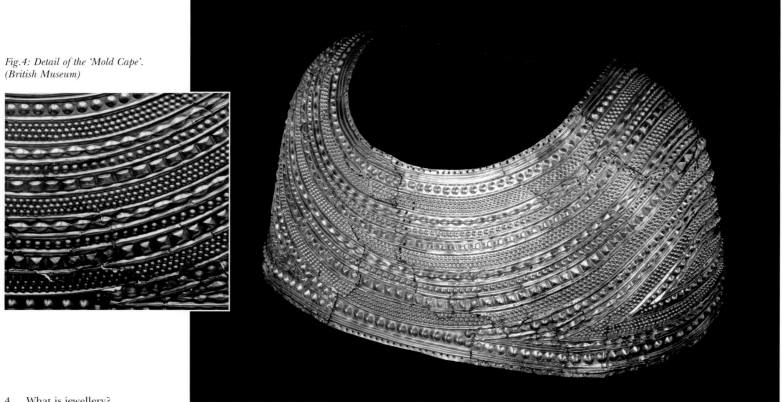

Perhaps we are wrong even to try to seek a definition. Who tries to define furniture; to decide whether its outer boundaries lie in playground swings or village stocks? Who seeks to pin down the concept of clothing or limit its scope on the basis of the textiles used? Most people simply recognise jewellery when they see it. Thus reminding us that essence of jewellery is, after all, visual.

The more we go back into the past, or into less familiar societies, the more we enter the realms where function becomes less fully tangible. A gem would protect you from poison, or keep you on a virtuous path in the face of temptation. Signs of status, or pretensions to status, and a belief in the protective quantities of rare and exotic materials, are probably common features in the wearing of jewellery in the past. Initially they may well have been inseparable. The animal's tooth on the cord about your neck was a warning sign of your fighting prowess to human rivals and other fierce creatures alike. Fighting power was strength and strength was status. Among the earliest surviving examples of jewellery is a necklet of mammoth ivory beads dating back some twenty-three thousand years and found near what is now Moscow in Russia. Few men or beasts would argue with a man who could fell a mammoth, or commanded the men who could – or, of course, few men would mess with the woman to whom such a man laid claim.

A descendent of such 'trophy' jewellery is the necklet shown here (fig.2), which is of tiger's claws set in gold. Such claw jewellery has been worn as amulets against evil in India in recent centuries. This example however was made in India for the European maket and was purchased at the Paris International Exhibition in 1867. For the European wearer, such an object would be an evocative symbol of the exotic east, or a souvenir of residency there. Or tiger claws set in gold might simply be a memento of a tiger hunt, a connection that will raise very different reactions in many observers today.

Where is the dividing line between jewellery and clothing? There are many instances from around the world where it is difficult to say where jewellery stops and clothing or armour begins.

Jewellery and Costume

One early example is the so-called Mold Cape shown here, (figs.3,4) a sheet gold object that was seemingly an upper-body covering. It was discovered in Mold, Flintshire (Clwyd) Wales in 1833 in a crushed state on the remains of a skeleton along with the fragments of a sheet gold diadem and amber beads. The burial dates from around 1900-1600 BC, but the skeletal remains were too decayed to deduce age or sex. However, the size of the object and the lack of any apparent accommodation for a female form suggest that it belonged to an adult male. The row of small perforations along the outer edges show that it was once attached to a leather or textile backing – an indication that it was intended for use not just for burial, although presumably for ceremonial use rather than regular wear. It is possible that the decoration was intended to make the cape resemble a mass of bead necklets. The forms themselves were repetitively made by use of shaped punches from behind, plus some delicate delineation of the forms with a small pointed punch from the front.

Fig.5: Actors Hugh Grant and Elizabeth Hurley.
She is wearing the safety-pin dress designed by Versace.1994
Photo from Rex Features

Function versus frivolity is not a factor in deciding what constitutes jewellery. Several jewellery types have their origin in functional fasteners. The most obvious are brooches and pins. The earliest versions were simple pins. These were made more secure my adding cords or wire attachments and eventually the fully-fledged and often highly decorative brooch developed.

The simplest version of a modern clothing fastener of this type is the safety pin. The recent ones are really little more than slightly more secure versions of a clothing pin type known since antiquity. Even the spring-like coil on a safety pin to provide springiness is exactly matched on examples dating back to before 500 BC. Today safety pins are typically used only for relatively mundane purposes and usually only meet high fashion when an emergency repair is needed. However, there are exceptions, such the Versace dress held together by safety pins worn by Elizabeth Hurley to the 1994 London premiere of *Four Weddings and a Funeral* (fig.5).

Are these safety pins jewellery? If not, why do we define the ancient iron and bronze equivalents as such?

The Tara Brooch, shown here (fig.6) is a particularly fine clothing fastener and a masterpiece of early Christian Irish art made around AD 700. It is decorated with intricate goldwork and silver, copper, glass and amber and nobody would doubt that it is jewellery even though the main structure is made of a copper alloy,

As for its name, 'The Tara Brooch', this is just another example of the nineteenth century archaeological tradition of personalising finds'. In due course we will meet 'Priam's Treasure' and the 'Mask of Agammenon''. In reality, the brooch has no connection with the Hill of Tara, from whence ruled the mythical Kings of Ireland, but was found on a seashore in County Meath, Ireland in 1850. It is said to have been found by two young boys whose mother tried unsuccessfully to sell it to a scrap iron merchant. She then sold it to a watchmaker for eighteen pence and he in turn, after cleaning it, sold it to Waterhouse and Co. a jewellery company in Dublin, for twelve pounds. With an eye to effective marketing, they christened it the Tara Brooch and after exhibiting it widely, and manufacturing copies for sale, sold it to the Royal Irish Academy for two hundred pounds. It is now among the treasures of the National Museum of Ireland in Dublin.

Fig.7 shows one of the gilded silver copies of the Tara Brooch made by Waterhouse of Dublin a year after they acquired it. It is in gilded silver set with diamonds, fresh-water pearls and amethysts. It is a non-functional and highly decorative copy of a functional original.

Several Irish firms produced copies and these varied from some fairly accurate reproductions to what are little more than souvenirs with barely a passing resemblance to the original.

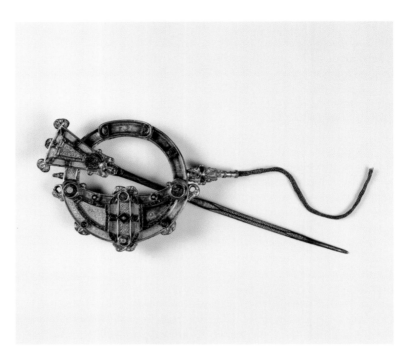

Fig.6: The 'Tara Brooch', copper alloy with gold, silver, copper, glass and amber decoration, Irish, ca AD 700. (National Museum of Ireland, Dublin)
© Courtesy of the National Museum of Ireland, Dublin

Fig.7: Copy of the Tara Brooch by Waterhouse of Dublin, gilded silver. Irish, mid 19th century. (British Museum)
© Copyright the Trustees of The British Museum

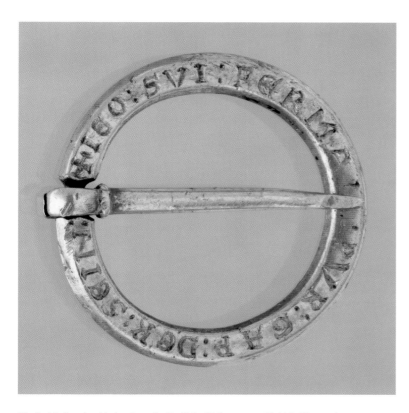

Fig.8: Medieval gold ring brooch. English, 13th century. (British Museum)
© Copyright the Trustees of The British Museum

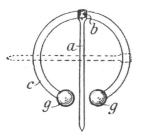

Fig.9: Drawing of brooch design.
British Patent, 1901.

Fig.10: Brooch in copper alloy with blue and white enamel. Romano-British, ca AD 100. (British Museum)
© Copyright the Trustees of The British Museum

This little Medieval gold ring brooch (fig.8) was functional and proudly tells us so. Seldom does an article of jewellery explain its purpose in such charming terms. It was made in the thirteenth century, found in Eastern Britain and is now in the British Museum. Like the previous pieces, and Elizabeth Hurley's safety pins, it served to fasten a garment. The inscription engraved in medieval French says 'I am a brooch to guard the breast that no rascal may put his hand thereon.'

The small size of the brooch – it is just 2 cm (7/8 inch) in diameter – shows that the garment it fastened must have been quite lightweight. The two layers of fabric to be joined, were bunched up, pushed through the ring and the pin inserted through them. Tension would hold the brooch closed in wear, like a buckle

Medieval ring brooches of this type are often engraved and the inscriptions can range from simple names to personal message, such as here. The spelling can be wondrously inventive, which is hardly surprising in the days before the introduction of printing demanded some sort of standardisation. Even so, we hear of one Medieval apprentice engraver loosing his job because although skilled he was illiterate. Some of the inscriptions make little sense to us today and some are conveniently dismissed by jewellery historians as 'magical'. One initially puzzling example is a gold ring brooch that bears the inscription RMOABREGREDETREI. Then came the insight – the letters, taken alternately, spelled the names ROBERDT and MARGEEREI.

The elaborate ring brooch type of clothing fastener survived into recent times in some parts of the world. North African versions, for example, are usually of silver or base metal and decorated with brightly coloured enamels and coral, or, for the cheaper examples, coloured paint and imitation corals.

The earlier types often had a slot to allow use on heavier textiles such as wool. The pin would be pushed through the two layers of the clothing, typically on the shoulders, and then the open ring rotated so tension would hold it closed and secure.

But, despite the two-thousand-year long and well–documented history of the ring-brooch form, a British patent was issued for the concept in 1901. The drawing published with the Patent is shown here (fig.9). This is not a unique occurrence. Over the last century and a half Patents have been issued for a variety of early jewellery types or designs. Another example is a type of chain link commonly used in Roman jewellery that was successfully patented in the mid nineteenth century and then found ubiquitous use in the chains for the flushing lavatories then coming onto fashion.

The need for clothing fasteners varied from place to place, largely depending on climate and the type of clothing worn. In ancient Egypt, for example, clothing fasteners were all but unknown and thus there are no ancient Egyptian brooches and few clothing pins. Then, when the Roman conquered Egypt they brought the fashion for such accessories with them and some, though not many, Roman brooches have been found in Egypt.

But although the need for clothing fasteners varied with local climate, it didn't necessarily vary with social rank. In Roman and later times a huge number of brooches were made in cheaper materials. We might call such ornaments costume jewellery today, and this would be a very apt description, they were indeed functional part of the costumes of the day.

One particular manifestation of the need for functional ornaments is the huge number of ancient brooches and other ornaments made in copper alloys, often enamelled to add colour and sometimes gilded. The enamelled copper alloy brooch shown here (fig.10) dates from around AD 100 and was found in Britain where means of warmly securing garments were as much a necessary then as now. It was cast and then enamelled in blue and white in the depressions. The S-shaped form with stylised animal head terminals is termed dragonesque and derived from the Celtic styles of Pre-Roman Northern Europe.

Buttons and Cuff Links

The button is one of the simplest types of clothing fasteners and has a very long history. Over the centuries the majority have been made from relatively humble materials, such as bone, shell and base metals. However, these modest buttons have also always had their grander versions – including those in gold, silver and set with gems.

Buttons in precious materials are scarce before Renaissance times. The example shown here (fig.11) is in enamelled gold, set with four rubies and a central diamond, and is one of a large number of jewelled buttons contained in the Cheapside Hoard – a huge hoard of early seventeenth century jewellery found in Cheapside, London in 1912. This rich combination of materials and colours on the button is typical for the period. The early seventeenth century was the period when coloured gems and diamonds were reaching Europe from India and the East in ever-increasing numbers – the East India Company was formed in London in 1600.

The distinction between a button and what we today term a cuff link was probably less obvious in the past than it is now. When the types of cuff link we know today first became popular in the seventeenth century they were termed 'sleeve buttons'.

Fig.11: Ruby and diamond button from the Cheapside Hoard.
English, late 16th/early 17th century. (Museum of London)
© Museum of London

During the eighteenth century new materials and new modes of manufacture increased their use and they became common in Victorian times. The two parts could be linked by a chain, but although this type of construction is still common, a whole variety of other methods of attachment and hinging have been invented over the years – particularly in the later part of the nineteenth century when stamping became a common method of shaping.

These two illustrations are based on the drawings from British Patent Applications for 1884 and 1887 and show two new approaches to cuff link assembly. In one the innovation is simply an extra stirrup-shaped link to add flexibility. In the other, there is a steel spring so that the end will held in position after it is inserted through the sleeve.

The celebrated Parisian jeweller Alexis Falize was an early adopter of the Japanese style in jewellery. He exhibited cloisonné enamel jewellery at the 1867 Exposition Universelle in Paris and his customers included Tiffany & Co. of New York. The pair of cloisonné enamelled cuff fasteners showing birds perched on bamboo canes were produced by the Falize firm at about this time. (fig.14)

Falize's enameller was one Antoine Tard and although he worked in an oriental style, his technique differed from the cloisonné enamels of China and Japan. Oriental cloisonné enamels were most typically in copper, sometimes with silver wire cell walls. Falize worked with gold. This is more in keeping with the medieval enamels of Europe, the Byzantine world, Islam and Russia. It is noteworthy that Falize was confidently working in such a technique a generation before medieval Byzantine and Russian enamels were being imitated (and faked) by Russian craftsmen, including at least one of the enamellers working for the Fabergé firm.

Most of the famous jewellery houses produced cuff links – after all, they are one of the few types of jewellery commonly worn by men, a market too lucrative to be ignored. Other jewelled objects for a male clientele included walking stick handles, snuff boxes and cigarette cases. One of the best known makers of such pieces was of course Carl Fabergé in St Petersburg, Russia.

Fig.14: Gold and enamel cuff-links in the Japanese taste by Alexis Falize. French, ca 1870.
© Christie's Images Ltd. 1999

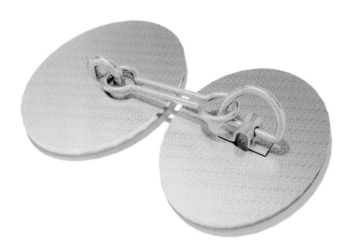

Fig.12: Cufflink construction. Based on British Patent drawing of 1884.
© Jack Ogden

But cuff links were not only for men. These blue chalcedony and enamel cuff links were made by Fabergé in St Petersburg in about 1900 and previously belonged to Marie Bonaparte, princess of Greece and Denmark (1882-1962).

Fig.15: Blue chalcedony cuff-links by Fabergé. Russian, ca 1900.
© Christie's Images Ltd. 1999

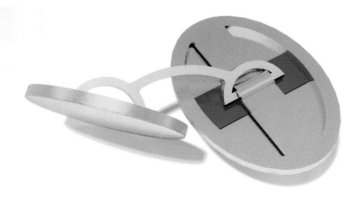

Fig.13: Cufflink construction. Based on British Patent drawing of 1887.
© Jack Ogden

Jewellery as an Amulet

As we have already seen, protection from seen or unseen dangers was an important function of jewellery in the past. The amuletic or talismanic properties of jewellery were far more to the fore than is common today. Small images of the Gods or their symbols would best ensure their protection and particular gems could offer specific safeguards against all manner of ills from diseases to cheating spouses.

(Fig.16) The small gold figure of the Thoth, the scribe of the gods, is from Egypt and dates to about 900 BC. The figure is a sculpture in miniature – it is just 2.4 cm high (slightly under an inch). The god, who has the head of an ibis bird, holds a stylised representation of one of the eyes of the hawk god Horus – the so-called *udjet* eye and one of the commonest amulet forms in ancient Egypt. As is typical for Egyptian gold amulets, this is not cast in one piece but is made up from several separate pieces of gold skilfully soldered together, including the base, the suspension loop and the eye.

Some fine ancient Egyptian amulets in gold survive, but they are vastly outnumbered by those in cheaper materials, especially so-called Egyptian faience, a brightly coloured, fired siliceous material that can be thought of as essentially a crude form of glass. The majority of the faience examples were funerary, but some of the gold ones exhibit signs of wear and must have been worn to protect the owner in life. Indeed, pendant amulets are sometimes shown in wear on private sculptures and other representations.

A question that springs to mind is why all such deity amulets, whether for the dead or living, have flat bases as if they were intended to stand. The addition of the base to our gold Thoth, for example, would have required extra gold and extra work. A likely answer is that these amulets were not intended to represent the deities, but were copies in miniature of the cult statues of the deities that stood in the temples. The cult statues, naturally enough, had bases. This distinction between a deity and a statue of a deity might sound pedantic, but it does raise some important points about how ancient Egyptians viewed their gods.

The insertion of magic spells, devotional texts or charms of some form or another inside amulet pendants is first encountered in Egypt soon after 2000 BC. These pendants typically took the form of vertical sheet gold tubes, sometimes elaborately decorated. In Phoenician times an animal head based on Egyptian deities was often added (fig.99) and then, in the Hellenistic Greek period, amulet cases changed from vertical to horizontal tubes, typically plain. This remained the pattern in Roman and Early Byzantine times and really came into its own in the Medieval and later Islamic world.

Depictions of God or any iconic subjects were forbidden by Moslem law, which greatly limited the types of amulets or talismans that could be worn. A holy text or the equivalent was permitted and such would have originally been contained in the Medieval Islamic silver amulet case shown here. One domed terminal can be removed, but unfortunately there is now nothing left inside.

Fig.16: Gold amulet representing the god Thoth. Egypt, ca 900 BC. (British Museum)
© Copyright the Trustees of The British Museum

Fig.17: Silver amulet case. Iran or Central Asia, ca 11th to 12th century. (The Nasser D. Khalili Collection of Islamic Art)
The Nasser D. Khalili Collection of Islamic Art (JLY 1881)

The wall and ends here have a foliate design with an inscription and painted niello (a black silver sulphide). The style of script points to an eleventh or twelfth century date and the amulet case probably originally came from Iran or Central Asia. It has sometimes been argued that the first ever 'archaeologist' was Constantine the Great's mother Eleni who travelled to the Holy Land to search for the cross on which Christ had been crucified. This was not the earliest quest for holy relics, but it was a high profile one.

The collection of relics became a major feature of the Medieval Period, and one that brought out the worst aspects of religious rivalry, chicanery and pilfering. Some of the finest medieval goldwork was made to contain relics. This beautiful little gold pendant contains a thorn supposedly from the original Crown of Thorns that St Louis had purchased from the Byzantine Emperor Baldwin in the thirteenth century (figs.18,19)

The pendant was made about 1400 and incorporates various other components including fine enamelled representations of the Crucifixion and the Descent from the Cross. The purple stones set on each side have the appearance of amethysts, however amethyst was rare in Medieval times and here the goldsmith has used rock crystal mounted with a purple backing. We don't know if the original owner was aware of this gem deceit, but a modern observer might well wonder whether a jeweller who couldn't be trusted to use a genuine stone could be trusted to incorporate a genuine holy relic. Nevertheless, such basic gem simulation was nothing new. Some of the orangey-red 'carnelians' set in Tutankhamen's jewellery are actually colourless calcite mounted over a red cement,

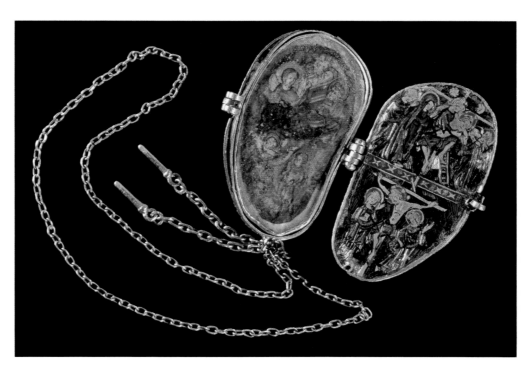

Fig.18 /19: Reliquary of the Holy Thorn. Rock crystal, gold and enamel. French, ca 1330 - 1350. (British Museum)
© Copyright the Trustees of The British Museum

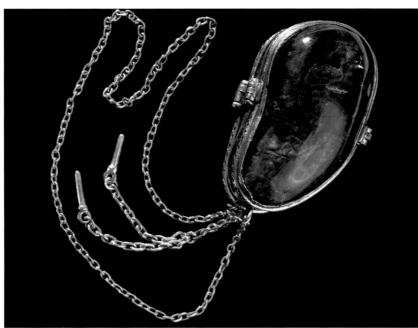

It is said that at ancient Egyptian banquets, an empty coffin was sometimes displayed as a graphic encouragement to 'eat drink and be merry, for tomorrow we may die'. The *Memento Mori* ornaments of the European Renaissance, of which this is a particularly dramatic example, had the somewhat different purpose of reminding people that gluttony and other earthly sins would be paid for when the final judgement came.

This enamelled gold, coffin shaped pendant (the one in fig.20) was made in the middle of the sixteenth century. The English inscription (not visible here) reminds us that the Resurrection will sanctify us all and, of course, provides clear evidence that the pendant is of English origin – although the report that it was found in the grounds of Tor Abbey in Devon, south west England cannot now be verified.

The lid of the coffin can be removed to reveal a scarily realistic skeleton that is fine example of the use of enamel 'painted' over gold, that is a common feature of Renaissance jewellery. The white enamelled skeleton is well contrasted against the black enamelled interior. The intertwined foliate and strap ornament on the lid is also in black enamel, fired in recesses in the gold.

In general the Renaissance was a heyday of fine enamelled decoration, both in the round, as on the skeleton, and for recessed ornament. The very nature of the present object largely limits the colours to black and white, although the jeweller had slightly freer range on the scrolls around the attachment loop, but on some Renaissance pieces there is a far more varied and brilliant enamel palette. As a seventeenth century 'recipe book' for enamels tells us, 'Enamelling on gold and other metals is a fair and pleasing thing, and in it's self not only laborious, but necessary, since we see metals adorned with Enamels of many colours make a fair and noble shew, enticing beyond measure the eyes of the beholders.'

Modern equivalents of ancient amulets include gold crucifixes, Stars of David and emblems relating to various individual Saints.

Jewellery as a Badge

Jewellery showing support for, or allegiance to mortals, rather than soliciting help from deities or saints is also well known through history, though less common. Examples range for jewelled emblems showing political or religious allegiance to the current craze for wristbands or lapel pins showing support for a particular charity or other cause.

The gold brooch here in the form of the number 45 bears the word 'liberty' engraved across the top. This relates to the eighteenth century British politician and radical John Wilkes. He was a supporter of liberty for the American colonies, and an outspoken critic of the English King George III.

In 1762 Wilkes began to publish a radical weekly paper 'The North Briton' and issue number 45 of April 1763 attacked the King's speech to parliament leading to charges of libel and sedition, arrests and all manner of obstructions to his political life. His stand on liberty and free speech received considerable public backing and his supporters chanted 'Wilkes, Liberty and Number 45'. The Number 45 referred not simply back to issue number 45 of The North Briton, but to verse 45 of Palm 119: "And I will walk at liberty: for I seek thy precepts. I will speak of thy testimonies also before kings, and will not be ashamed."

Wilkes had a squint and was outstandingly ugly, but had a great wit. After he had been expelled from the notorious Hellfire Club, and exposed its activities, the Earl of Sandwich told John Wilkes that he would die either of the pox or on the gallows. Wilkes' famous retort was 'That depends, my lord, whether I embrace your mistress or your principles.'

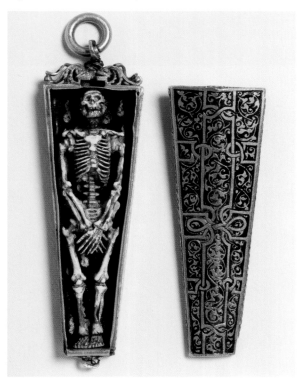

Fig.20: The Tor Abbey Jewel. Gold enamelled in black and white. English, ca 1540-50. (Victoria and Albert Museum, London)
© V&A Images / Victoria and Albert Museum

Fig.21: Gold '45' brooch that demonstrated support for John Wilkes. English, 18th century. (British Museum)
© Copyright the Trustees of The British Museum

Rings

The finger ring is a class of jewellery that can have various functional purposes. Rings can serve as signets to seal documents and as indications of status or rank within society. The latter also includes wedding and betrothal rings. Naturally, with human nature being what it is, a practical function for a ring did not necessarily bar it from being decorative or valuable or both. Indeed, both Jewish and Moslem scholars debated at length the extent to which the functional use of a signet ring might sidestep bans on the use of gold jewellery.

The signet ring is not of as great age as might be supposed, even though seals themselves in one form or other were in use since very early times. Gold signet rings really came into use around the middle of the second millennium BC, and thereafter became commoner – and eventually could bear the names of officials, not just kings. The ring shown here is from Egypt, dates to around 600 BC and belonged to the 'Chief Steward of the God's adorer Sheshonq.' The shape and massive form of this ring is typical for the period, as are the square-cut depressions of the hieroglyphs which can be compared to those carved in stone on the most magnificent of ancient Egyptian monuments.

Through history, signet rings have indicated rank. The prophet Jeremiah even referred to the signet ring on God's right hand. In modern British high society, a signet ring will often be the only jewellery other than cuff links worn by a man, and the design is quite frequently an engraved crest linked, not always entirely justifiably, to his family's past.

Clay and other sealings have survived in great numbers from antiquity, including some made with Egyptian rings of the type seen here. However, not all old rings with engraved designs were used as seals. Some were simply decorative or amuletic. In antiquity a betrothal ring combined the function of our engagement and wedding ring. The practice for a man to present his intended with a special ring is hardly encountered before Roman times when Pliny, for example, in the first century AD mentions an *anulus pronubus* sent as a gift to a woman at the time of betrothal.

Mentions of marriage rings as such only became more common after the third century AD and from this period we begin to find surviving examples. These typically depict clasped hands, sometimes clearly discernible as one male, one female, and in the Eastern end of the Roman Empire they often had the Greek inscription *omonoia* which meant 'harmony'. The ring shown here (fig.23) was found at the opposite end of the empire, at a Roman fort in Britain, at Richborough in Kent. It dates to the fourth century AD. The openwork form with wire spirals and the sheet gold bezel, is typical for the period.

Betrothal rings are typically associated with the third finger and the Roman writer Aulus Gellius gives us an origin for this. "The reason for this practice is, that upon cutting into and opening human bodies, a custom in Egypt which the Greeks call anatomy or dissection, it was found that a very fine nerve proceeded from that finger alone of which we have spoken, and made its way to the human heart; that it therefore seemed quite reasonable that this finger in particular should be honoured with such an ornament, since it seems to be joined, as it were united, with that supreme organ, the heart." The heart at that time was, of course, seen as the seat of all emotions – a view that survives in the symbolism of the modern Valentine's card.

Fig.22: Gold signet ring bearing the title and name of a royal official. Egyptian, ca 600 BC. (British Museum)
© Copyright the Trustees of The British Museum

Fig.23: Gold betrothal ring. Romano-British, 4th century AD. (British Museum)
© Copyright the Trustees of The British Museum

Jewellery specially made to be worn by the living to commemorate the dead is an old but seemingly not ancient practice. I am not aware of instances from before the late Medieval Period and it only became commoner a century or so later. In the early seventeenth century, for example, Shakespeare's will provided for his wife and daughter to receive rings inscribed "Love My Memory".

As befitted their purpose, such rings bore such suitable inscriptions and were often decorated with black enamel. In the later eighteenth century they borrowed much from Classical Greek funerary depictions with urns and weeping figures. Mourning rings continued to be made later through the nineteenth century and a British career guide written in 1842 noted that there were at that time thirty-four specialist makers of mourning rings in London.

The black enamelled gold ring shown here (fig.24) is one of a series made to commemorate Vice-Admiral Horatio Nelson who died at the Battle of Trafalgar in 1805. The bezel has the letters 'N' and 'B' below two coronets encircled by the inscription 'Gloriously Fell on 21st Oct 1805'. Around the hoop are the words 'In the Action with the Combin'd Fleets of France and Spain'. This particular ring was made for John Franklin who had joined the British navy at the age of 15 and a few years later served as a signal midshipman on the 'Bellerophon' at the battle of Trafalgar. He gained fame as an Arctic explorer seeking to prove the existence of a sea passage through the North American Arctic, dying in the attempt,

Jewellery has probably been given as a token of affection since the earliest times, ever since a hunter first hung a claw pendant about his mate's neck to help protect her from real and unseen dangers. However clear references to jewellery as love gifts only come from far later as, for example, when the ever mischievous Roman poet Ovid wrote about the gift of a ring as a love token. He says to the ring `I wish you a warm welcome ... fit her as snugly as she fits me.'

Jewellery that has an inscription that expresses love or desire is probably a Medieval innovation, as with the ring brooches mentioned above. We can hardly count the bland Roman betrothal wish for 'harmony' on rings as the epitome of romantic turns of phrase.

The heyday of wedding rings with romantic inscriptions was in the late sixteenth and seventeenth centuries with the fashion for what are termed posy rings. There was a large repertoire of inscriptions, and whole books devoted to providing them. The sentiments range from various assumptions of God's blessing to all manner of promises of fidelity. The late sixteenth century gold ring illustrated here has the no-nonsense Latin inscription *amor vinsit omniae* – 'Love conquers all'.

Fig.24: Mourning ring for Vice-Admiral Horatio Nelson. Enamel on gold. English, circa 1805. (National Maritime Museum, London)
© *National Maritime Museum, London*

Fig.25: Gold posy ring. English, late 16th century. (British Museum)
© *Copyright the Trustees of The British Museum*

There are areas where jewellery overlaps with arms and armour, and, of course, are plenty of military regalia that are jewellery. But some jewellery actually served a practical function in warfare or hunting. Some of the earliest examples of stones worn on the wrist were plaques worn by archers to protect their wrist from the bow string. Examples of these wrist guards date back to the Stone Age.

A later equivalent that really breaks down the barriers between ornament and function in jewellery is the archer's ring. Such rings were worn on the thumb and were used to draw back a bow string. Surviving examples range from stone and base metals ones to highly ornate versions in precious materials such as jade. The form appears in China several centuries before Christ and some of the most decorative examples that survive come from Mogul India. However, the gold example here (figs.26,27) was made for a Venetian in the fourteenth century.

This ring was a comprehensive traveller's kit. The ring might have been used in firing a bow, for hunting or in warfare, but it also incorporates a seal so that it could be used in communication and commercial dealings. Around the hoop is a magical text to protect travellers from robbers and other misfortunes and the inside of the ring has a further emblem and inscription. Such an object reminds us that in the thirteenth and fourteenth centuries the Venetians were major player in the trade around the Eastern Mediterranean and some of them, such as Marco Polo, plied the overland trade routes as far east as China. Many of the gemstones reaching Syria and Egypt from India were traded by Venetians into Europe.

The seal engraved on this ring links it with the Donati family. The ring was found in what is now southern Greece, where there was much Venetian activity, but it may well be that in the end it failed to protect its original wearer.

Fig.26/27: Gold archer's ring. Venetian, 14th century.
(British Museum)

Earings

Earrings are noteworthy because they are the only common class of jewellery that by nature requires mutilation of the body. This was not lost upon the ancients, and many writers mirrored the Roman Tertullian in complaining about the `tortures of innocent infancy, learning to suffer with its earliest breath, in order that from those scars of the body ,born for the steel, should hang I know not what precious grains'.

Remarkably, earrings were not universal at all periods of our history. The Sumerian royal princesses in what is now Iraq wore them (fig.87), their contemporaries in Egypt did not. Earrings went in and out of favour through succeeding centuries. Wear by men was even more erratic. The Romans thought earring wear by men was a sign of slavery, a view mirrored in the Islamic world until the seventeenth century Mogul ruler Jahangir expressed his thanks to an Islamic saint for his return to health by piercing his ears and hanging pearls from them. The act was intended to show that he was as but a slave to the saint, but it was a fashion that was rapidly and enthusiastically copied in his lavish court.

The size of the holes through the ear varies from the small hole of today's ear piercing guns through the knife slits most common in antiquity to some huge holes through lobes. We see Egyptian ear studs, and the holes in mummified ears to accommodate them, several centimetres in diameter.

There are equivalent studs and distended lobes among some modern wearers of 'alternative' jewellery. In practice, and with practice, there is almost no limit to how much the lobe can be stretched, and thus to the size of ornament that can be placed through it. And here we must take the term ornament in its widest sense – objects recorded as being worn through holes in ear lobes around the world include live snakes.

It might seem strange to praise jewellery made of cast iron as an example of consummate skill, but considerable ability was needed to cast intricate almost lace-like forms in iron. These earrings (fig.28) are examples of the cast iron jewellery produced in Berlin that first appeared during the Napoleonic wars. The Prussians badly needed finance for the war effort, and so patriotic citizens handed in their gold jewellery and received ornaments in iron in return. The practical need lessened with time, but iron jewellery remained something of a fashionable symbol of nationalism, and these earrings were probably actually made in about 1850 – they were exhibited in the 1851 Great Exhibition.

The problems with iron earrings, however, was that iron could not be cast thinly or strongly enough to form serviceable hooks to pass through the ears and, besides, a base metal like iron was hardly suitable for passing through a sensitive ear lobe. So, in what might seem a inversion of the expected, the earrings are of iron, the attachments to hold them to the ear are of gold.

Fig.28: Berlin ironwork Earrings.
Probably made by Devaranne of Berlin. Prussian, ca 1850.
(Victoria and Albert Museum, London)
© V&A Images / Victoria and AlbertMuseum

A small engraved gem showing the Roman goddess of Fortuna with an inscription that equates with 'safe voyage' is the only clue we have to what the Roman Cresconius family might have been doing in Carthage in what is now Tunisia around the year AD 400. We do not know why they had need to conceal their important silver and jewellery on the hill there, later known as the Hill of St Louis. But, we know they never retrieved it. The treasure, now in the British Museum, included silver spoons and dishes and jewellery including the gold, emerald, sapphire and pearl earrings shown here. The treasure also included a necklace that matched the earrings.

The simple, rounded, hoops that form the hooks that pass through the ears are elegantly suited to the purpose, a clean, no-nonsense simplicity that is matched in the necklet – it is long enough to pass over the head and thus neither needed, nor was supplied with, a clasp.

These earrings are a good example of one significant class of jewellery of this period. Gemstones, and transparent ones at that, were the focus. There is not a gold component on these earrings superfluous to the basic task of securely holding the valuable and finely matched range of gems. No frills or embellishments. Only the attachment loop for the earring on the left-hand side in the photograph remains in place. That on the right-hand side has broken off in very recent times and the pendant simply threaded over the hoop. This is a reminder that even gold is not entirely safe from corrosion with time and that solder seams are often the parts most prone to fracture.

The sapphires are the pale blue ones typical of Sri Lanka (Ceylon) which became popular in later Roman and early Byzantine times. The pearls are large, they are beautifully graduated along the matching necklace, and there are emeralds within the rectangular settings. There is little evidence for gemstone values at this period, but fine gems were pricy and these earrings with their matching necklace would have been the Roman equivalent of the diamond parure of a nineteenth century duchess.

Fig.29: Gold earrings set with emeralds and bearing pearls and sapphires. Roman, ca AD 400. (British Museum)Gold earrings set with emeralds and bearing pearls and sapphires. Roman, ca AD 400. (British Museum)
© Copyright the Trustees of The British Museum

*Fig.30: Necklace, bracelet and earrings in gold and diamonds by Bulgari.
Italian, ca 1950. (British Museum)*
© Copyright the Trustees of The British Museum

Suites

The matching sets of jewellery that became such a feature of the nineteenth century are often assumed to be of Classical origin. However, with a few exceptions, such harmonious sets are a more of a Classical revival – or fake classical – phenomenon than an ancient one.

Sets that were essentially matched assemblages of fine diamonds, pearls or coloured gems have always underlined the sheer rarity and value of the jewellery. Sets of jewellery in which the gems were of secondary importance have always been in danger of looking rather unimaginative and hackneyed.

Sets of gold jewellery, however, did provide a neat uniformity perfectly in tune with the more conservative well-to-do jeweller wearer of the 1950s and 1960s. And, conveniently, the introduction of new casting technology made it easier for the manufacturers of the period to create whole ranges from identical components. The diamond and gold earrings here, and the matching bracelets and necklace, represent the higher end of the fashion. These were made by Bulgari in Rome in the later 1950s. The small fan-shaped scroll motifs are typical of the period.

Earrings have been a common subject for contemporary designers – though they still seldom break loose from the tradition of the matched pair. Those shown here (fig.31) are by one of the most celebrated jeweller designers of the second half of the twentieth century, Gerda Flöckinger, whose flowing, fused surfaces can provide an almost Art Nouveau sensuousness and sense of freedom. These earrings were made in the mid 1970s, shortly after she had been the first contemporary designer to have been given her own exhibition at the Victoria and Albert Museum, London.

The 1970s was a heady period for British jewellery design. While Gerda Flöckinger used the movement and often unpredictability of molten metal, Wendy Ramshaw produced precisely machined jewellery that almost resemble engineering parts. There was no overriding style for the period, it ranged from meticulous precision to almost anarchic free-form. But, earrings however formed and whatever the inspiration, still needed to be worn. Practicality constrained the designers to a finite repertoire of earring attachment methods and so set something of a challenge to, and a limit on, their freedom to innovate.

Not all jewellery wearers are prepared to sacrifice comfort for style, and so the search for a means of wearing earrings without requiring the lobes to be pierced gained momentum in the second half of the nineteenth century in parallel with the rapidly growing market for gold jewellery. Various mechanisms and approaches were tried. One of the more successful being the 'U' shaped screw earring attachment that was first patented in the nineteenth century and is still is use, almost unchanged, today.

Spring clips to hold earrings in place on unpierced ears were also being proposed in the later nineteenth century. The drawing shown here (fig.32) is from an American Patent of 1883 and show clips padded with rubber to help hold the earrings to the ear.

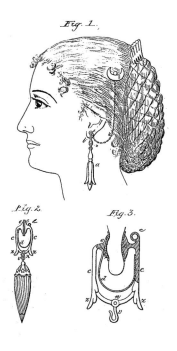

Fig.32: Earring attachment for non-pierced ears, as shown in a patent application. British, 1883.

Fig.31: Silver earrings designed by Gerda Flöckinger. English, ca 1975. (Victoria and Albert Museum, London) © V&A Images / Victoria and AlbertMuseum

The Materials
of Jewellery

One property of 'real' jewellery through most of history has been the use of precious materials in its construction. However, defining preciousness is almost as difficult as defining jewellery. Different materials have had different relative values at different period. Five hundred years ago some natives of South America used platinum to make fish hooks. At least they used it for something – even within the last century, some gold miners have thrown away the annoying little grains of platinum metals that were 'contaminating' their gold.

It comes down to supply and demand – if the demand for something exceeds its supply it will be valued. Of course, the upshot to this is that other people seek to extend supply, an aspect of human nature that has manifested itself in gilded base metals and imitation gems.

The choice of jewellery materials used throughout history reflects usability as well as rarity and availability. The perquisites of a modern gemstone – it should be rare, beautiful and durable – have remained pretty constant through time, but the less tangible properties of 'symbolism' have also been very important through most of history.

Ideally, of course, jewellery intended for wear should be strong enough to withstand use, but the harder the materials, the greater difficulties is shaping. For example, diamonds were justly celebrated for their hardness and the protective qualities this implied, but only found more widespread jewellery use after the development of diamond cutting, and from the Renaissance onwards.

Platinum was known as the devil of metals as late as the eighteenth century, before viable means were discovered to utilise it. Gold, on the other hand was durable – it didn't rust or corrode – and it was soft enough to be easily worked. But although gold could hammered into thin sheet with stone hammers, and then pushed into three dimensional shapes with bone and wood tools, cutting it or piercing it really required metal. This explains why gold jewellery is all but unknown before copper alloy implements could be produced. Even simple copper tools required relatively sophisticated metallurgical skills.

Gemstones have been another important component of jewellery through history. The early Christian writer Clement of Alexandria told his readers that only foolish people would `rush after transparent stones', but neither he nor others who have urged similar caution over the ages were heeded. In fact, the history of jewellery is very much one of people rushing after gems. A history of the jewellery trade is also a history of world trade. Through the centuries, the search for new sources of gems, gold and other valuables were a primary impetus for exploration.

Perhaps the greatest events in European gem history were the almost contemporaneous discoveries of the sea route to India and the New World. Globalisation had begun. The selection of gems show here are from the early seventeenth century Cheapside Hoard that dates from the time when the East India Company was beginning to build up the trade from India and the Orient (see figs.11 and 222 to 226).

Side by side with jewellery in 'precious materials' there has also almost always been jewellery in cheaper substitutes. Gilded copper has imitated gold, glass beads have imitated gemstones. Human nature has meant that the less well-off members of society and those of lesser rank have always sought to copy the possessions that characterise those they envy. But less valuable materials are not always simply 'imitations' of something more costly. Materials that are not conventionally thought of as precious can be used in their own right.

The distinctions are not always obvious to us when we consider the past – was a Stone Age shell necklet 'valuable' in some way or simply pretty? Is this even a meaningful question?

Fig.33: A selection of the gemstones found with the Cheapside Hoard, England, ca 1600 - 1630. (The Museum of London)
© Museum of London

Gold

Here is a fragment of hard quartzite rock containing some veins of gold. Rock like this has been on earth a lot longer than the humans who have fought over it, died trying to find it and died labouring to extract the gold from it. Luckily, nature itself, given time, breaks down the rock through the action of erosion and so for much of human history gold was more conveniently obtained as shiny nuggets and dust from stream beds. The sparkling gold would have always attracted attention, so it is perhaps surprising that we don't find gold in human habitation or burial sites earlier than we do. In practice there is almost no surviving gold jewellery from before about 4000 BC.

Nuggets could be picked by hand, but small gold particles required a more efficient means of recovery. The simplest was to scoop up a basin full of river sand and water and then swill this around until the water and relatively light sand had been sluiced out over the sides, to leave behind any gold. Gold is much heavier than sand. This separation process is termed gold panning. Less labour intensive methods of recovery included washing the river sands down sloping tables with suitable ridges or grooves to trap the gold. Sheep's fleeces are naturally greasy and if placed on a gold washing table will efficiently trap gold particles. The use of sheep's fleeces in this way was probably the origin of the story of Jason and the Golden Fleece.

The reason that gold is found in ready to use metallic form is because it is highly resistant to chemical attack. It doesn't dissolve away in ground or river water. This same chemical resistance means that a gold object can lie in an ancient burial for many thousands of years and still greet its final excavator in almost pristine state. This incorruptibility also accounts for some of gold's symbolic use in the past – and also accounts for its almost universal use for storing wealth – for this life and the next. Gold was employed to cover bodies to aid their preservation and longevity in the afterlife. After all, the sun itself was golden. The properties that made gold ideal for covering the face of a dead Pharaoh, also make it perfect for modern electronic contacts.

Fig.34: Gold veins in quartzite. Australia.
© Jack Ogden

Fig.35: Grinding stones for separating gold from rock.
Eastern Desert of Egypt, ca 300 - 100 BC.
© Jack Ogden

With time, the availability of better tools, gold began to be retrieved from the original host rocks, most commonly hard quartzite, as just seen in fig.34, a sample from Australia. These rocks had to be broken up by hammering and then ground to allow the gold particles to be separated out, by washing. The grinding stones shown here are among those still to be found in large numbers at the gold mines in Egypt's Eastern Desert. They date to a century or two before the Roman period. It was back-breaking work, so no wonder that mining was carried out by criminals and prisoner's of war. Under Roman law, being sent to the mines was an equivalent punishment to being thrown to the wild animals in the arena.

A Greek writer had described the division of labour at the Egyptian gold mines. The strongest males, those between puberty and about thirty, used iron hammers to break up the rock, digging deeper and deeper into the earth. Younger boys carried the rock out through the winding tunnels to the open air where men over the age of thirty pounded these rocks into small pieces. Women and the oldest men then ground this into powder, using large grinding stones such as these. This powder was then washed down sloping wooden tables to sluice away the rock particles to leave the grains of gold that could be dabbed off with sponges.

In fig.36 this ancient Egyptian wall painting shows Nubians carrying gold. Nubia, lay to the south of Egypt, in what is now southern Egypt and part of the Sudan. This area was a major source of gold in antiquity. Some gold had probably reached Egypt from very early times – some as tribute as shown here – but by around 2000 the Nubian mines were being directly exploited by the Egyptians. In this representation from about 1400 BC, some of the gold is in the form of nuggets in baskets, the rest has been cast into gold rods bent into rings. Large nuggets were easy enough to record, transport, and keep secure, but the same was not true for smaller nuggets and gold dust, It was thus sensible to melt the gold into bars or ingots. Nevertheless, the size of the rings and nuggets shown here suggests that the artist is guilty of a little artistic licence.

Ingots are quite well known from pharaonic Egypt. 6.5 kilos of gold bars were found in a treasure at at Tôd in Egypt dating from around 1900 BC. This also included a considerable amount of silver objects and ingots, and rough and uncut lapis lazuli. Twenty three gold bars were found in the so called `crock of gold' at the pharaoh Akhenaten's city of Amarna, but these were melted down in the 1930s to help fund further excavation,.

Gold, whether chipped from hard rocks or gathered from stream beds, could be used pretty much as is. It is seldom found pure, but typically contained some silver and a bit of copper. However by about 500 BC gold began to be refined – that is treated to remove the silver and other impurities to leave essentially pure gold. This refining could be carried out at the mines and, indeed, was the next described step in the Greek description of gold mining at the Egyptian mines just mentioned. The basic process was probably known to the ancient Egyptians a thousand years earlier, but there is little evidence that it was used anywhere on a day to day basis much before the introduction of coinage around 500 BC. After all, coinage required standardised gold purities.

The coin shown (fig.37) is the earliest type of gold coin known from Egypt. It dates to about 350 BC and bears hieroglyphs that say 'good gold' - a testimony to its high purity.

The gold ingot shown (fig.38) is one of a number of ingots, perhaps eighteen, said to have been found at Abuqîr in Egypt at the beginning of the twentieth century. These date from the fourth century AD and were probably on their way from a refiner to a Roman mint. The ingots are stamped and counter struck with the names of various officials. One bar bears a single stamp in Latin `Refined by Benignus', others, like this one, are counter-stamped with another official's stamp. These ingots have a standardised weight of around 342 to 345 g., just over a Roman pound, but similar ingots from elsewhere in the Roman Empire have less regular weights. Analysis of one such Roman ingot indicated a purity in excess of 99% gold.

Fig.36: Wall painting showing Nubians carrying gold. Tomb of Sebekhotep, Egypt, ca 1400-1390 BC. (British Museum)

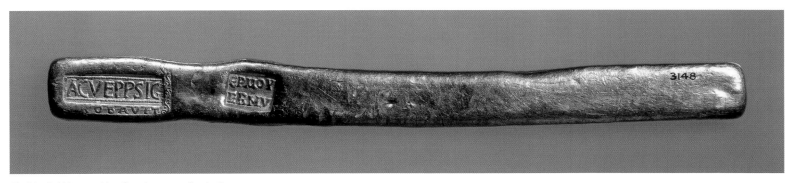

The pre-eminence of gold in terms of both monetary worth and incorruptibility (unusual bed-fellows in most human contexts) meant that many optimistic people attempted to create gold out of other materials. The transmutation of lead or mercury into gold kept these alchemists busy for millennia – even into quite recent times. The engraving shown here has been attributed to Philippe Galle and reproduces Pieter Bruegel's Alchemist that was painted in about 1555.

We should not be too harsh on these people, except the out and out charlatans. In many cases they were probably basing their beliefs on 'secret writings' that ultimately derived from garbled and misunderstood copies of ancient texts describing perfectly respectable processes such as gold plating and refining using mercury. Besides, their experiments did lead to numerous genuine discoveries about the nature and properties of substances.

Modern science is not all that old. In the 1870's the then manager of the 'Assay Office in Liverpool', England, a specialist in gold and its treatment and assay, was quite prepared to state in writing that he was not convinced that gold was itself a single element. He suggested that in due course chemistry would find that gold was made from a combination of "a few elements of which all things will found to be composed."

Fig.39: An engraving, possibly by Philippe Galle, after Pieter Bruegel's The Alchemist, ca 1555. (Bibliothèque Royal de Belgique)
Bibliothèque Royal de Belgique

The high survival rating of gold was demonstrated to divers of the South West Maritime Archaeological group in 1995 when they found the remains of a wreck off the Devon, England coast. There was barely a trace left of the timbers, but there was a large hoard of gold. The treasure now known as the Salcombe Bay Treasure, part of which is shown here (fig.40), included more than four thousand Moroccan gold coins of the sixteenth and seventeenth century, as well as gold ingots and cut and bent jewellery fragments. The presence of clay pipes and even a copper alloy merchants seal reveal links with Europeans, but whether the ship was a legitimate merchant one, or one of the Barbary pirate ships that plagued the south British shores at this time will probably never be known. The latest coin in the treasure was struck in AD 1631.

The fragmentary nature of the god in the hoard, even some of the coins appear to have been cut, certainly suggest that the gold was being collected together and was to be melted down. Looting gold and cutting it up ready for re-use, would have been second nature to a ship's company, merchant or pirate. However, it seems unlikely that smaller ships would have had the facilities to melt down significant quantities of gold. The temperatures necessary would have required furnaces with efficient bellows. If there were blacksmithing facilities on the boat, they could have melted gold, but even then, the blacksmith's forge might well have been in more demand for its primary purposes, and

melting loot might well have awaited peace, or time on shore.

Gold is a yellow metal, but, as noted above, occurs in nature alloyed with varying amounts of silver and also often a little copper. The quantities and varying proportions of silver and copper affect various properties of the gold, including its colour. If silver content rises, then its colour becomes paler, through a greenish yellow to greyish silver colour. Copper, if present in more than a few percent, can impart a reddish hue.

To a great extent, gold was used as it was found in antiquity, and thus the purity and colour can vary considerably. However, different colours of gold could be chosen for decorative effect and sometimes copper was deliberately added to produce a rosy hue. The decorative use of coloured gold has found most use through history for inlay work in other materials. Fine examples include the magnificent inlaid daggers of Mycenaen Greece that date back to around 1200 BC, as shown here. The inlaid designs in this class of dagger range from lion hunts to slain warriors, and the materials used include yellow and sometimes red gold and a pale gold-silver alloy that has the appearance of silver. The gold components are carefully inlaid in black bands that are themselves inlaid along the sides of the blade. In at least some cases, these black bands are a type of blackened copper that is more familiar to us in Japanese shakudo work, but which actually has a long history in the Old World.

Fig.40: Part of the Salcombe Treasure and associated finds, ca 1631.
(British Museum)
© Copyright the Trustees of The British Museum

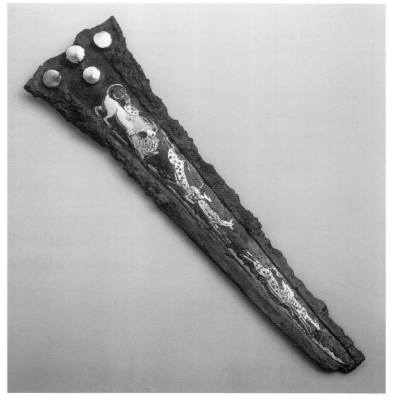

Fig.41: Copper alloy dagger blade with a lion hunting.
inlaid in gold and electrum. Mycenae, Greece, 16th century BC.
(National Museum, Athens)
Archaeological Receipts Fund

The introduction of gold refining around 500 BC in the Eastern Mediterranean seems to have coincided with a preference for pure looking gold, not interesting good colours. Indeed, poorer qualities of gold were from then on frequently surface treated to make them appear purer.

The decorative effects possible by using different coloured gold as we saw in the Mycenaean dagger was largely ignored from the first millennium BC onwards and it was really only in Europe in the second half of the eighteenth century that goldsmiths began to experiment with coloured gold again. This was, after all, not only the industrial revolution, but also the chemical revolution when men began to investigate the properties of metals more scientifically. The colours used on this gold box include normal yellow gold, reddish gold produced by adding copper and a paler gold alloyed with silver.

This fine box dates from the latter part of the eighteenth century and was made in Switzerland. Remarkably, the design in the centre panel includes a hot air balloon and a telescope. The first manned hot-air balloon flight was in November 1783, useful dating evidence for this box.

Gold is yellow. Indeed one of gold's more interesting properties is that it isn't white – most metals are. However, when gold is alloyed with sufficient silver it takes on a whitish shade that, as we have seen, has been used for decorative purposes since antiquity – most typically when a contrast is needed with yellow gold. Such alloys of gold with silver were known as 'white gold' in antiquity and even in the late nineteenth century when they were sometimes used for setting diamonds.

The 'white gold' of more recent jewellery, however, is an alloy of gold with other white metals such as palladium (a member of the platinum family of metals), zinc, manganese and, before allergy problems became apparent, nickel. These white gold alloys became popular in jewellery around the time of the First World War and into the 1920's when the highly fashionable platinum was almost unobtainable. This scarcity was the result of the military need for platinum as a stable material for such things as radio and bomb-timing electrical contacts. Then followed the Russian Revolution which cut off supplies of platinum from Russia, then the main world supplier.

Fig.42: Multi-coloured gold snuff box. Swiss, late 18th century.
(Victoria and Albert Museum, London)
© V&A Images / Victoria and Albert Museum

The little white gold and diamond deer brooch shown here (fig,43) dates from around 1925 and was probably made in Vienna. It is an early example of white gold jewellery.

White gold remains a popular material for jewellery, particularly diamond-set jewellery, but it is worth remarking that white gold is seldom truly white and modern white gold jewellery is usually electroplated with rhodium – a bright white metal that is another member of the platinum family of metals. Since the actual underlying white gold is never intended to be seen, the cynic might well ask why a cheaper white metal would not serve just as well as a 'bleached' gold alloy. Rhodium plating was only developed in the 1930s and was not been used on earlier pieces such as the deer brooch.

The Carat and Hallmarking

The term carat we use today to describe gold purities derives from the Greek word *Keration* which was a small weight unit employed from about the beginning of the Christian era onwards.

Around AD 300 the Greek *Keration* was defined as 1/24 of main Byzantine gold coin then in circulation, the *solidus*, an example of which is shown here. From about this period gold purities began to be described in terms of how many *keratia* of gold there were in every 24 of a gold alloy. This was the origin of our carat system (karat system in America) which is still based on parts gold per 24. Pure gold is 24 carat and thus 18 carat gold is 18 parts pure gold per 24, that is 75% gold

The Greek *Keration* weight quite probably derived from the name of a plant that produced a seed of regular enough weight to be used to weigh gold. There have been numerous contenders suggested over the years for the species of this original seed. The use of seeds as uniform weights has been common throughout history, and is not just a 'primitive' practice. The 'grain' that has formed the basis of weights units for British jewellery materials into modern times - four to a carat, 480 to an ounce Troy – was defined as recently as the 1870s as "the weight of a grain of wheat taken out of the middle of the ear and thoroughly dried."

The use of the carat weight for gold had reached Southern Europe from the Islamic world along with the growing trade contacts by the thirteenth century and within a century or so was used officially describe the fineness of gold in more northerly Europe.. Even then, gold jewellery did not have to be stamped, it merely had to be of no worse than the defined standard, the so-called 'Touch of Paris or 80% gold. Jewellers were liable to checks and severe punishment if their gold was found sub-standard.

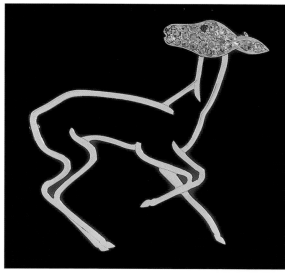

Fig.43: White gold deer brooch with diamonds and black onyx. Probably by Karl Fialla, Vienna, ca 1925. (British Museum)
© Copyright the Trustees of The British Museum

Fig.44/45: Gold solidus coin of the Emperor Constantine. Byzantine, 4th century AD. (British Museum)
© Copyright the Trustees of The British Museum

The requirement that silver be tested and stamped in England dates back to a statute of Edward 1 in 1300. However, the introduction of hallmarking for gold was a later innovation. In 1478 the 18 carat standard (75% gold) was introduced and this remained for almost a century – until 1575, when the standard was raised to 22 carat. 18 carat was reintroduced in the eighteenth century, in 1798, and gold jewellery and other articles could then be made in 18 carat or 22.

This reintroduction of 18 carat was largely the result of lobbying by watchmakers, who wanted to better compete with their European competitors, and because 18 carat was preferable for certain manufacturing and decorative techniques that had by then come into use – such as engine turning. On the other hand, higher carat gold was still preferable for enamelling.

Then in 1854 the new standards of 9, 12 and 15 carat were introduced Britain. In the 1930s the 12 and 15 carat standards were abolished and 14 introduced. Thus, gold jewellery sold in Britain today might be of 9, 14, 18 or 22 carat. The hallmarks shown here (fig.46) are samples of stamps used at the London Assay Office (LAO) in 1985.

Confusingly, except in America where the gold *carat* is spelled *karat*, the *carat* is also used to weigh gemstones and pearls. Its use in this way is also of considerable age and by the early twentieth century almost every country had its own definition of the weight of the carat. Things were then standardised, the carat became the metric carat defined as being one fifth (0.2) of a gram. The carat was one of the 'traditional' and specialised units of measurement that were permitted to retained for use in trade throughout the various twentieth century standardisation and metrification processes – an honour it shares with the 'pint' so beloved of British beer drinkers.

Recent lobbying to retain British Hallmarking in the face of a pan-European approach has often stressed the long 'tradition' of British hallmarking. This may be true with larger silverware,

but legislation introduced in Britain in 1739 had actually largely exempted gold and silver jewellery from marking. This state of affairs lasted in Britain until as recently as 1975 when the hallmarking of jewellery became compulsory (excluding some exemptions on the basis of low weight and such like).

The 1739 exemptions included "Jewellers Work wherein any jewels or other stones are set (other than mourning rings, jointed night-earrings of Gold, or Gold springs of lockets); rings, Collets for rings, or other jewels; Chains, Necklace beads, Lockets …" This means that Georgian and Victorian jewellery is rarely hallmarked and, indeed, can be of a very wide range of purities. Down to 7.5 and even 6 carat (25% gold) was not unusual in later Victorian times.

Mourning rings, however, specifically required hallmarking. The black enamelled ring shown here was made in York and bears the date letter for 1831. The ring had to be hallmarked prior to enamelling, to avoid damage to the latter.

Hallmarked gold jewellery in 18 or 22 carat gold and weighing more than 10 dwts (15.6 grams) were subject to Duty and were stamped with the Duty Mark – the king's head, as seen here, or the Queen's head in Victorian times. 9, 12 and 15 carat gold objects were not subject to Duty – hence they do not bear the Duty Mark. There was also no Duty payable – and hence no Duty Mark – on exempted gold jewellery voluntarily sent for Hallmarking. Wedding rings ceased to be exempted from compulsory Hallmarking in 1855. They had to be made of 18 or 22 carat gold and were subject to duty regardless of their weight.

The Duty payable on Victorian gold jewellery that required Hallmarking was a 17 shillings per Troy ounce, equivalent to 12.5% duty on a 22 gold carat wedding ring. 12.5% is hardly excessive compared to the later purchase tax on jewellery and penalties were severe for not Hallmarking objects that required it. Those who faked Hallmarks could be transported.

Fig.46: Specimen of the London Assay Office hallmarks for gold for the year 1985. Courtesy of the London Assay Office

Fig.47: Mourning ring for James Selby Pennington, gold and enamel, British, 1824-25 (Victoria and Albert Museum, London)
© V&A Images / Victoria and Albert Museum

In the earliest times gold was generally used as it was found, and silver as it came out of the refining process. The regularity of the purity of the gold and silver jewellery and other objects of Hellenistic Greek and Roman times might suggest a deliberate attempt to keep to standards, but there is no certain evidence that the state then attempted to define gold or silver purities other than that of coinage and the ingots from which this was made.

The earliest official stamps we find on silverware are on some objects of the fourth and fifth centuries AD. Only a handful of such marked pieces are known, all in silver, and the stamps are all similar – they show the goddess Tyche. Such stamps probably represent the guarantee of silver content.

By about AD 500, however, we begin to find stamps on some silverware that include the name or monogram of the current Emperor. This suggests that they may have been applied under governmental authority and perhaps, like later European hallmarks, confirmed that appropriate taxes or duties had been paid.

Official Byzantine silver stamps of this type occur until about AD 650 – a date that coincides with the rise of Islam and the beginning of a general dearth of silver ware and gold objects all around the Eastern Mediterranean and into Europe. Whether similar marks continued to be used after this period, but the objects themselves don't survive, is uncertain. However, it is worth noting that the reappearance of precious metal objects in general that occurred in Europe after the eleventh century coincided with the earliest westerly European legislation we have regarding precious metal purities and marking.

The example of a Byzantine silver plate shown here is of special interest because the plate was found in the Anglo Saxon burial at Sutton Hoo. Its reverse bears official control stamps. So, this is a 'hallmarked' piece of silver buried on English soil some 700 years before the marking of silver was first established in the country under the statute of Edward 1.

Fig.48: Silver plate bearing on its reverse Byzantine control marks but found in the Saxon burial at Sutton Hoo, England. Byzantine, 6th to mid-7th century AD. (British Museum) © Copyright the Trustees of The British Museum

As with gold, silver coins have an important source of raw material for the jeweller. The silver bracelet shown here is an example of the silver jewellery produced by Navajo silversmiths of the South Western United States. Much was made using American or Mexican silver dollars.

Native American jewellery is of considerable antiquity, and early examples include shell, feathers, turquoise and other materials worked into beads and into the form of animal and other motifs. The Navajo silversmithing skills are not of great antiquity, since they are generally considered only to have been gained from Europeans during internment in the 1850s and only seriously pursued a decade or so later when they began to follow a settled, reservation life. This bracelet, set with three large turquoise, has two rows of twisted silver wires flanking two narrower bars, each with stamped designs. It was produced about 1900.

Navajo designs derive from a variety of traditional Native American and more recent European sources. The main focus is on the silver, but gemstones, especially turquoise and shell are characteristic. The American South West is a major source of turquoise.

In many societies in the past silver has been linked to the moon, thus balancing gold which was almost universally seen as a symbol of the sun. The sun was identified as male, the moon, with its 28 day cycle, as female.

Silver, unlike gold, very rarely occurs in metallic form. It is found as mineral ores that miners and refiners have to pass through various processes to extract the silver. In practice much of the silver produced in the past was extracted from ores of the metal lead, many of which typically contain a small proportion of silver. The exploitation of lead ores dates back to around 6000 BC in parts of the Old World and silver was being produced by at least 3000 BC. The earliest silver jewellery dates from about this time.

The silver hair pin here is of Roman date, found in London, and shows the goddess Aphrodite (Venus) removing her sandal. Depictions of Aphrodite were a common subject in such pins and numerous Roman silver examples have survived – perhaps the choice of silver for the goddess was significant. These pins are certainly far rarer in gold and it is worth noting that the gold examples that have appeared on the market in recent decades are not infrequently modern castings made in moulds taken from genuine silver ones. Stylistically, of course, the fakes will appear perfect, but their mode of manufacture is usually obvious once they are examined under magnification.

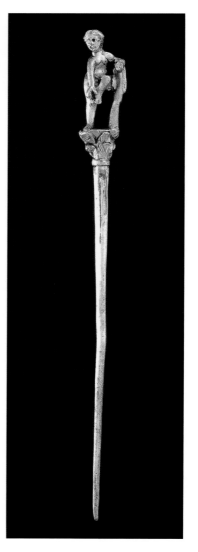

Fig.50: Silver hairpin with a terminal depicting the goddess Venus. Romano-British, 2nd-3rd century AD. (British Museum)

Fig.49: Navajo Indian bracelet in turquoise and silver. Ca 1900. (Museum of Indian Arts and Culture)

Fig.51: The 'Cuerdale Hoard' of Viking silver. Buried ca AD 905 - 910.
(British Museum)
© Copyright the Trustees of The British Museum

Regardless of the possibly symbolic differences between gold and silver, there were basic practical and economic one. When gold was unavailable for what ever reason, silver was the alternative jewellery material of choice. Gold became exceeding rare in Europe after the break-up of the Roman Empire and the vast majority of surviving Viking and even central Asian ornaments dating from around the tenth and eleventh centuries are in silver. Shown here is a part a huge hoard of more than 30 kilos of silver and 7000 coins discovered in 1840 at Cuerdale in the Ribble Valley, Lancashire, Northern England. The deposition of the hoard, dateable by the coinage, occurred around 905-910 AD.

It has been suggested that the hoard might represent a war chest being assembled by Irish Vikings, expelled from Dublin in 902, but raising an army to reinvade. The Ribble Valley was then a main route from the Viking centre of York and perfectly positioned on England's west coast to act as a base for such a campaign.

As is typical with many such Viking hoards, the silver objects in the Cuerdale hoard are almost entirely ingots or scrap – the latter largely derived from Irish Viking jewellery. This hoard is the largest such from Britain, but there are numerous other huge hoards from other areas within the Viking sphere of interest. Such hoards provide clear evidence for the extent of trade and other contacts at the end of the first millennium AD. For example, one large hoard of silver jewellery from this period included just 20 silver coins. However, these originated from Islamic, Sassanian Persian, Anglo-Saxon British, Early Byzantine and Indian mints!

When the Spanish first encountered the Incas in what is now Peru, they noted that gold was associated there with the sun, silver with the moon. Both gold and silver ores occur in the Andes, but silver required more complex production technology and there are fewer surviving silver ornaments than gold. The earliest silver objects from Peru date to the mid-first millennium BC, but most of the surviving pieces date to the last five or six hundred years before the arrival of the Europeans. At all periods such silver was the preserve of the highest social circles.

This silver figurine of an Inca Woman is from Cuzco, a Andean city in southern Peru that according to Inca legend was founded in the twelfth century. It became the centre of the Inca Empire and was plundered by Pizarro in 1533. The red colouration on the face is deliberate. This object belongs to the Peabody Museum of Archaeology and Ethnology at Harvard University, one of the world's oldest museums specialising in Anthropology.

Fig.52: Inca silver figurine of a woman. Cuzco, Peru, ca AD 1430-1532.
(Peabody Museum of Archaeology and Ethnology, Cambridge, Massachusetts)
© Werner Forman/CORBIS

Filigree is the term used to refer to wire work, gold or silver wires applied in decorative patterns to a background or, as here, in openwork. Openwork filigree work provides an attractive and relatively rigid ornament for a minimal amount of metal, but it is very labour intensive. Hence in Europe silver filigree is often associated with 'peasant jewellery'.

The main patterns are made up of pairs of twisted wires which were then flattened – producing a thin strip capable of being bent into tight curves. Using pairs of twisted wires in this way provided a strip with what appears as almost a serrated edge, giving more texture to the piece. This visual effect had been noted by Greek and Etruscan jewellers two thousand years earlier. Later in the nineteenth century a machine was invented in England that provided a serrated edge to a gold or silver strip – thus further mechanising the production of filigree work.

The little 'nests' made of spring-like coils of wire with a single central grain we see interspersed here, are typical of this sort of work. They occur in nineteenth century jewellery, such as the Cannetille work of the 1820s and 1830s (see figs.257 and 258) and also far earlier, for example in some Etruscan gold jewellery. This particular brooch is possibly German and might be as early as the eighteenth century. However, the timelessness of the forms and the technique make it almost impossible to date. A jewellery historian might attempt to narrow the dating by an analysis of the materials, the solder alloys in particular. Solder, of necessity in abundance here, can contain a wide range of additive metals and the nature of these can often be a good dating guide. That said, techniques varied according to time and place, and the working methods of a German village jeweller, perhaps a travelling tinker, would not necessarily correspond to the alloys and approaches used by a major silversmith in a larger manufacturing centre.

Fig.53: Silver filigree brooch. German, 18th century. (Victoria and Albert Museum, London)
© V&A Images / Victoria and Albert Museum

Silver is not just the poor relation of gold, it was chosen in its own right by some jewwllery designers, such as Georg Jensen a Danish silversmith (1866-1935) who has been described as one of the most talented and influential silversmiths of the twentieth century. He trained as a goldsmith, but aspired to be a sculptor. He attained artistic, but not financial success, as the latter and after an equally unrewarding foray into ceramics returned, to metalwork. He opened his own workshop in 1904 and his reputation for fine silver jewellery grew rapidly. His organic, flowing designs show their roots in the Art Nouveau styles of his youth.

In the Post World War I years Jensen opened shops in other European cities, including London, and in New York. He died in 1935, the same year that he was awarded the grand prix at the international exhibitions in Brussels.

The brooch shown here was designed for the Jensen Company in about 1950 by the Danish sculptor Henning Koppel, one of the designers who helped to keep Jensen at the forefront of jewellery design after World War II. The clean lines and abstract form are characteristic of the type of post-war design for which the firm of Jensen, and indeed Scandinavia, is famous.

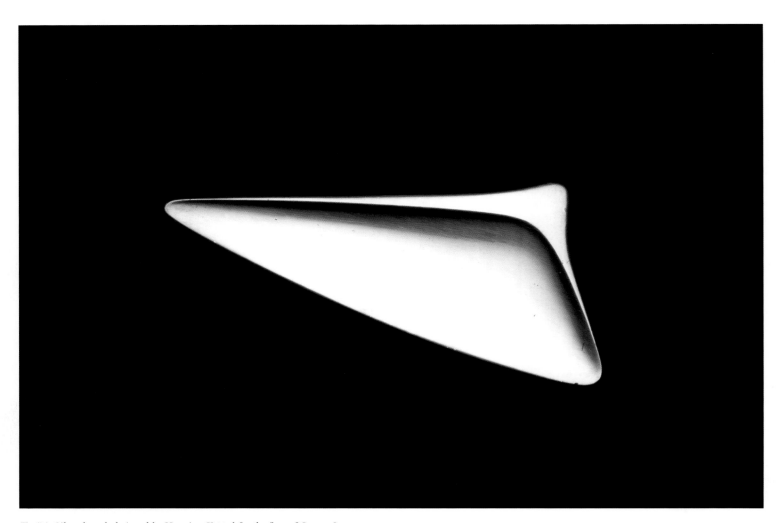

Fig.54: Silver brooch designed by Henning Koppel for the firm of George Jensen.
Danish, ca 1950. (Victoria and Albert Museum, London)
© V&A Images / Victoria and Albert Museum

Guilded Alloys

Gold plating over less expensive metals provided jewellery that looked like gold, but at a fraction of the price. Gilding of one form or another dates back to the early Bronze Age, but demand and improving technology means that the heyday for gilded jewellery was in the Roman and later periods. This large gilded silver brooch was found in the burial of an Anglo Saxon woman at Chessel Down, Isle of Wight. It dates the sixth century AD and is decorated with the abstract, intertwined animal ornament typical of the period.

Here the gilding was carried out by a process we call fire or amalgam gilding. Gold was dissolved in mercury and this mixture then spread over the silver surface. Heat was applied and this drove off the mercury (as highly toxic fumes) to leave a thin layer of gold. The gold surface was then burnished with a smooth metal or stone tool to produce an even, bright, shiny finish. 'Fire gilding' of this type was the commonest gilding technique until the introduction of electroplating in the 1840s.

The gilded surface of the brooch also has niello decoration. Niello is an inlay material made by fusing sulphur with silver, often copper and, later, with lead. The resulting black metal sulphide could be fused into depressions in gold or silver. Niello is thus somewhat akin to enamel in application, but of very different composition.

Both the gilding and the niello required heat in their application and so the jeweller had to carry out the work in the right order. The niello was applied first, since it required a higher temperature, then the gilding was carried out at a lower temperature. On early jewellery of this type, there will often be areas where under a microscope the gilding can be seen to overlap the niello. When ornaments were enamelled as well as nielloed and gilded, care in the order of work was even more critical.

Plating with gold was not the only way to imitate gold. By Roman times a type of copper-zinc alloy very similar to modern brass was in use. When new and polished this resembled gold closely. It was much like the Pinchbeck and other copper-zinc alloys used into recent times to imitate gold. A huge number of such ornaments have survived from Roman and later times, usually cast. Some are even wrongly identified as 'gold' by archaeologists today. The resemblance to gold is particularly marked when such 'brass' ornaments have lain in certain damp environments, such as in the mud along the sides of the river Thames in London.

Fig.55: Gilded silver brooch with niello decoration. Anglo-Saxon, 6th century AD.
(British Museum)
© Copyright the Trustees of The British Museum

Gemstones

The use of attractive or interesting minerals as beads and pendants is as old as jewellery itself and the stones so-used include almost every member of the mineral kingdom. Initially colour and appearance were of paramount importance. The presence of beads of bright blue lapis lazuli and red carnelian in this jewellery from the Royal Tombs at Ur in what is now Iraq dating back to around 2500 BC is a clear indication of the 'value' of these stones (fig.56). The lapis lazuli was carried all the way from the remote mines of Badakhshan in what is now Afghanistan, and at least some of the finer carnelian came from northern India.

Lapis lazuli and carnelian, like the majority of the gem materials used at an early period, are opaque – that is, they are not transparent. They were used for their colour and, particularly in Egyptian jewellery, essentially as blocks of pigment. Also, when set in gold, the stones were almost invariably cut to fit the setting. Setting a gemstone, of course, requires relatively sophisticated goldsmithing procedures and is thus seldom encountered much before about 2500 BC in the Near East and far later in Europe.

The fashion for transparent gemstones really only developed in the Mediterranean world after contacts increased between the Greek and the Persian Empire, culminating in Alexander the Great's conquest of the Persian Empire as far east as the borders of India. Now bright red garnets became popular, along with emeralds from Egypt and, to a lesser extent, other gemstones such as amethysts.

A puzzling aspect of early jewellery can be the absence of certain types of stones in particular areas or at particular times. For example, lapis lazuli, so highly prized by the ancient Egyptians and Sumerians, is almost totally absent in Greek and Roman jewellery. Turquoise is similarly rare in Greek and Roman jewellery, but more remarkably is almost absent in ancient Egyptian jewellery, even though there is ample documentary and archaeological evidence that the ancient Egyptians mined turquoise in Sinai on a significant scale.

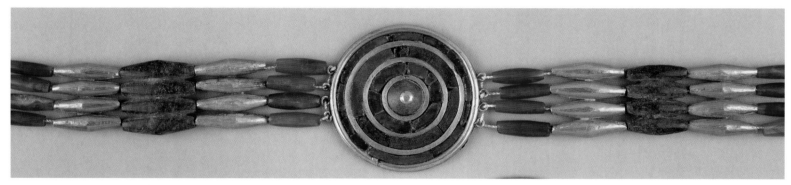

Fig.56: Gold headdress ornament set with carnelian and lapis lazuli.
From Ur, Sumerian, ca 2300 - 2100 BC. (British Museum)
© Copyright the Trustees of The British Museum

Early Diamonds

Today, of course, pride of place among gemstones often goes to the diamond, although there are many who would prefer a fine ruby, emerald or sapphire. Diamond rings are known from Roman times (fig.154) but diamonds really only came in greater prominence from about the fourteenth century AD with the growth in trade with the East. Diamonds then came only from India.

In the 1370s, the English poet William Langland talked of 'diamaundes of derrest pris' set in gold rings. The gold ring shown here, set with a natural, uncut diamond crystal, is of about this date and was found in England. Diamond set gold rings are actually mentioned in England a century earlier, for example one was listed as being in the treasury of Edward I of England, but the one shown here is one of the oldest surviving examples from England.

Fig.57. This ring was found in 2002 in Manley, Cheshire, by a metal detectorist. The inscriptions are in French and read 'Loiaute sans fin'- 'Loyalty without end'. The letters 'V' and 'A' on the ring and the three letters 'E' alternating with five pointed stars are of uncertain and much debated significance. The ring is in almost perfect condition apart from the original enamel of which only traces remain.

There are other similar late fourteenth century diamond rings, such as the one in the Victoria and Albert Museum shown here (fig.58), but the Manley one is the only example with a known English provenance.

Fig.57: Medieval gold ring set with a diamond, found at Manley, Cheshire, 2002. English or French, late 14th century. © Christie's Images Ltd. 2006

Fig.58: Medieval gold ring set with a diamond. European, late 14th century. (Victoria and Albert Museum, London) © V&A Images / Victoria and Albert Museum

Coloured Gemstones

The Roman introduced coloured gemstones to more northerly Europe, but the heyday of European interest in fine gemstones came after about the twelfth century when the trade in gems from the east began to expand. Now Indian diamonds, Persian Gulf and Indian Pearls, Sri Lankan sapphires and Burmese rubies began to reach Europe in increasing numbers. This trade increased greatly when the expansion of European sea trade from the late fifteenth century onwards allowed direct trade with India and the East, and South America.

The brooch shown here (fig.59) is of Medieval origin from northwest Europe and probably dates to within a generation or so either side of about 1400. It is set with red spinels, sapphires and pearls. The spinels were almost certainly from what is now Afghanistan, the sapphires are pale and are probably from Ceylon (Sri Lanka).

In more recent times these pale Ceylon sapphires became less desirable, not the least because of the discovery of a new source of bright blue sapphires in Kashmir following a landslide in 1881. Many gem dealers still consider 'Kashmir sapphires' to be the finest.

This raises the question as to whether it is possible to determine a gem's source. Some gemstones do have characteristics, particularly inclusions, that point to particular types of geological environment and sometimes to individual areas. More recently, highly sensitive analytical processes have been used in an attempt to trace the origins of gemstones.

However, determining provenance is still a matter of experience and the often best a gemmologist can do is provide a well informed opinion.

Most European jewellery of the Renaissance had a somewhat limited repertoire of gemstones. Diamonds, rubies, emeralds and pearls, of course, but sapphires less commonly and other gemstones are even scarcer. However, there are exceptions, such as the English gold pendant of around 1550 shown here (fig.60) that not only has a pale sapphire drop – indeed probably from Ceylon – but also contains a green peridot (top) and an orangey-red variety of garnet termed hessonite. Peridot is found in various parts of the world, but the traditional early source was the Isle of St John in the Red Sea.

The peridot and hessonite garnet are set in open-backed settings, an unusual feature for the period, and have around them inscriptions that include a spell that we believe was intended to ward off fits. According to the Renaissance lapidaries, the peridot could indeed help cure lunacy. This supposed property, which we also find described in Medieval times, is one bit of 'lore' about gems for which we might have a logical origin. Pliny, the Roman natural historian, described peridot with customary care, including the fact that it was softer than most gemstones. Indeed, it could be 'touched by the file'. It has been suggested that the Latin *linem* in Pliny's original, meaning a file, was misread by a Medieval scribe as *lunam*, the moon. As the word 'lunatic' tells us, being touched by the moon was indeed madness.

Fig.59: Gold brooch set with spinels, sapphires and pearls. Northwest Europe, late 14th or early 15th century AD. (British Museum)
© Copyright the Trustees of The British Museum

Fig.60: Gold prophylactic pendant, set with a garnet and peridot, and a sapphire bead. English, 1540-60. (Victoria and Albert Museum, London)
V&A Images / Victoria and Albert Museum

Jade

The term jade actually covers two types of material – jadeite and nephrite. Jadeite, mainly from Burma (Myanmar), has been employed in China for several centuries, but fine jadeite, in a variety of colours was also used in ancient central America.

The Mayan civilisation, situated in the regions between what is now southern Mexico and northern Honduras, has left us magnificent architecture and evidence for a high level of mathematical and astronomical accomplishments, but little in the way of metalwork. However, the Mayan and other Mesoamerican cultures have provided use with some very fine carved jade objects. And some of extreme size - in 1968 a carved jade head weighing nine pounds (4.1 kg) was found at the Mayan site of Altun Ha in Belize. The jadeite plaque here (fig.61), with two figures, is said to have been found in Mexico and is of Mayan origin. It was carved around AD 600 – 800 and was probably worn as a pendant. The larger figure, shown seated cross legged on an elaborate throne, wears jewellery including ear ornaments and a complex headdress. The motif emanating from his mouth represents speech – an ancient version of a cartoon speech bubble.

In recent years the source of the jade used by the Mayans and their predecessors the Olmecs has been discovered in Guatemala and a local industry re-established.

Emerald

In fig.62 this clip brooch was made by Cartier, London, in 1935. However, the emerald set in it is carved with a floral motif and is almost certainly of earlier Indian origin. The clip brooch was a characteristic form of Art Deco jewellery and the shape and the clip mechanism on the back – here with two prongs – gave it great versatility.

That the emerald was carved in India does not necessarily mean that the stone was mined there. The gemstone trade has long been globalised. As an example, just a generation after Columbus first landed in the New World, rumours of this new source of emeralds had reached the Indian court and within no more than a century, South American emeralds brought to Europe by Portuguese merchants were being traded into Burma by Venetians.

The question as to whether any South American emeralds had reached India and the Orient across the Pacific prior to the European discovery of South America is raised from time to time, but remains unproven. However, in the 1713 edition of the accounts by the French traveller Jean Baptiste Tavernier, we find his tantalising reference to a trade in emeralds from South America through the Philippines 'before the West Indies were discovered.'

There are actually a bewildering range of possible sources for emeralds. In antiquity many probably came from the mines in Egypt, but there is some analytical evidence that some originated in what is now Pakistan. Later further sources were discovered in Europe and India, and then the magnificent emeralds of Colombia came to European attention around 1500 and were directly exploited by Europeans by the 1550s. The finest Colombian emeralds are usually considered the best and these have characteristics that will usually still allow their identification.

Since then there have been numerous more discoveries of emerald sources, including Brazil (mined since 1910) and in particular in various parts of Africa during the course of the twentieth century – including South Africa, Zimbabwe and Zambia. Most recently emeralds have been found in Canada, China and Madagascar.

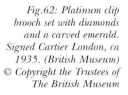

Fig.62: Platinum clip brooch set with diamonds and a carved emerald. Signed Cartier London, ca 1935. (British Museum) © Copyright the Trustees of The British Museum

Fig. 61: Carved jadeite plaque of a Maya ruler. Central America, ca AD 600 - 800. (British Museum)V&A Images / Victoria and Albert Museum
© Copyright the Trustees of The British Museum

Ruby

The magnificent ruby and diamond suite of necklace and earrings was made by Cartier, London, in 1954. The central part can be removed to be worn as a clip.

The finest rubies are usually agreed to be the 'pigeon blood' rubies of Burma (Myanmar) a source that was certainly known in Medieval times. The colour and quality of the rubies suggest that they are of Burmese origin, but it would take careful laboratory study to determine this. A Burmese origin for the rubies in the pair of gold anklets (fig.64) is probable, however, because the anklets themselves are from Burma and date from the first half of the nineteenth century. They must have been worn by a woman of high, if not royal, status.

Other ruby sources today include East Africa and India. There are also poor quality rubies found in Madagascar and other regions, some of which are treated by heating and glass impregnation to greatly improve their appearance. Buyers must either know enough to recognise the signs, or demand laboratory reports.

New Discoveries

In addition to discovering new sources of known gemstones, there are also occasional discoveries of gemstones that are recognised as previously unknown species. For example, alexandrite was first discovered in the Ural Mountains, Russia in the early 1830s and in 1868 a beautiful green stone, also from Russia, was identified as a new variety of green garnet. This gem was later named demantoid because of its diamond-like lustre.

In the middle of the nineteenth century Australia was beginning to reveal its wealth of gold and even diamonds, then in the late 1880s black opals were discovered at Lightening Ridge, New South Wales. The first parcel of black opals are said to have been put in the market in 1903 and sold for next to nothing, but prices soon rose and the beautiful gem attracted some of the great names among the jewellers of the period.

The amazing boat pendant shown here was designed by Louis Comfort Tiffany for Tiffany & Co in about 1915-1920. It is set with two large black opals as well as demantoid garnets and sapphires.

Other recent gemstone discoveries include tanzanite, This stone (fig.66) was first discovered in the shadow of Mount Kilimanjaro in Tanzania in 1967 and named and introduced to the world by Tiffany & Co, of New York. Tanzanite is a beautiful blue gemstone that exhibits pleochroism – that is, its colour ranges from bright sapphire blue to more of a purplish blue depending on the angle at which it is viewed.

Tanzanite is rare – the mines may be worked out within a generation – but it needs to be treated with care as it lacks the hardness of the traditional coloured gemstones such as sapphire, ruby and emerald.

The magnificent colour of tanzanite is not evident when the gems are mined, but is induced by heating – a process that has been used since antiquity to enhance the colour of many gemstones. Carnelian beads were heated to brighten their red colour in the early Bronze Age and the pale rubies of Sri Lanka were being heated to improve their colour at least as early as the sixteenth century. However, there is considerable discussion today as to when and how jewellery-buying customers should be told that the colour or clarity they see represents an improvement over what nature had intended.

Fig.65: Pendant in the form of a ship in gold, silver, opal, tourmaline, small diamonds and enamel. Designed by C.R. Ashbee and made by the Guild of Handicraft. British, ca 1903. (Victoria and Albert Museum, London) V&A Images / Victoria and Albert Museum

Fig.66: A pear-shaped tanzanite.
© Tanzanite Foundation

Pearls

The so-called organic gem materials are those that are produced by the animal and vegetable kingdom. Well known examples of organic gem materials include pearls, amber (a form of fossilised pine resin), jet (a coal-like form of fossil wood) and coral (the skeleton of the coral polyp).

Pearl-set jewellery is almost unknown before about 300 BC, but then became highly popular. One of the earliest surviving ancient examples of pearl-set jewellery – and one of the largest known natural pearls – is that forming the head of a gold pin from Paphos, Cyprus shown here (fig.67). This dates to around 300 BC and is now in the British Museum, London.

This large pearl, now partly decomposed, must have been about 2 cm in diameter originally – a huge size even by recent standards. Pliny tells us that the two largest pearls ever recorded were on earrings which belonged to Cleopatra. She is said to have dissolved one of these in vinegar and drank it in order to impress the Roman by establishing a record price for a banquet

The market for natural pearls suffered with the introduction of cultured pearls in the 1920, but today there is a strong market for fine quality natural pearls and their rarity has pushed their prices ever higher. This pair of diamond and natural pearl earrings made by Van Cleef and Arpels in Paris around 1950 fetched just over half a million Swiss francs when sold at auction in Geneva in 2000.

Fig.67: A gold pin set with a large pearl and a smaller fresh-water pearl. Cyprus, ca 300 BC. (British Museum)
© Copyright the Trustees of The British Museum

Fig.68: Earrings in diamond and pearl.
Van Cleef & Arpels, Paris, ca 1950.
© Christie's Images Ltd. 2000

Fig.69: Platinum sash clip in cultured pearl, diamond, emerald and sapphire. By Mikimoto, Japan, 1937. Mikimoto Pearl Island

Pearls grow inside oysters and some other mollusks when an irritant enters inside the shell. Popular legend has it that pearls are typically formed around a grain of sand, but in practice the intruder is often a parasitic worm.

The idea that an oyster might be artificially encouraged to produce a pearls if some foreign substance was introduced into it is an old one and might even date back to antiquity. In any case the Chinese were putting small figures of Buddha into oysters to coat them with a thin pearl layer centuries ago and Europeans were experimenting in pearl cultivation by the eighteenth century when Carl Linnaeus of Sweden had some success. Charles Dickens, no less, described a necklace of two rows of such induced pearls in the 1850s, explaining that "There is a species of pearl mussel in which the Chinese produce artificial pearls by introducing small shot and sand between the mantle of the animal and its shell."

However, the commercial reality of culturing pearls is very much a twentieth century phenomenon and the havoc caused to the 'real pearl' market when cultured pearls were first introduced in any number in the early 1920s by Kokichi Mikimoto in Japan is etched on the jewellery industry's collective mind.

The elongated sash clip, of 15 carat gold set with cultured pearls, was made by Mikimoto in around 1923. The larger pearls in this piece have flat backs and are thus not quite spherical. Set, as opposed to strung, cultured pearls allowed the use of the less-than-perfectly shaped cultured pearls. The grander cultured pearl, diamond, sapphire and emerald sash clip, also by Mikimoto was exhibited at the World Exposition in Paris in 1937.

Today cultured pearls are produced in a variety of mollusks in various parts of the world, and in fresh water as well as the sea. Most are bleached, many are dyed, and some are plastic coated, but not all jewellers are entirely open when disclosing nature, origin and whether colour is natural or not.

Fig.70: Gold sash clip mounted with cultured pearls. By Mikimoto, Japan, 1919 Mikimoto Pearl Island

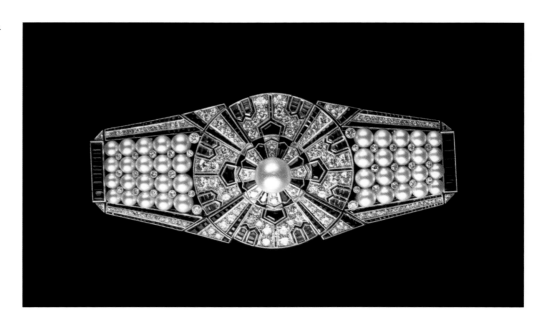

One of the more extraordinary jewellery fashions in recent centuries – and one of the most labour intensive – was seed pearl jewellery (fig.71). The minute pearls, were threaded into thin strands and bound with fine silk or horsehair onto pierced, mother of pearl backings.

This seed pearl jewellery was in particularly in fashion for a few decades in the middle of the nineteenth century. Despite its complexity, it was relatively inexpensive, but it still was sold by high-end jewellers in Europe and America – Tiffany exhibited a particularly fine example at the New York International Exposition in 1855.

The pearls with the smaller diameter perforations - 'Chinese pearls' - were strung on horsehair, those with larger perforations – 'Madras pearls' - on silk. Horsehair plucked from a live horse was deemed preferable since it was less brittle. The work was carried out in Europe, including Britain, and in the United States.

The great problem comes when such seed-pearl jewellery requires repair. Few jewellers are prepared to take on such intricate and usually uneconomic work.

Coral

The little gold-mounted coral pendant (fig.72) dates from the seventeenth century and was produced in Italy. On one side, it depicts Jesus between Mary and Joseph, with the holy dove above, and on the other the Annunciation.

Coral is the skeletal framework of a polyp that lives in certain seas. The better qualities have been highly valued through history and one of the main sources of the finest is the Mediterranean off the coast of Italy. Coral was thus easily available in the Romans' own back yard. However the number of surviving pieces of ancient Roman jewellery set with coral can almost be counted on the fingers of one hand.

The Roman traders made the long and dangerous trip to India to obtain precious gemstones including sapphires and even diamonds and one of the things they took with them to barter for these valuable goods was Mediterranean coral. A millennium later the Venetian traveller and merchant Marco Polo described the same trade pattern – coral was carried to the Orient, other gems were brought back.

Even in the eighteenth century, the East India Company exported coral beads and rough coral to Fort St. George (later Madras) in India, and brought back to London 'Pearls, Diamonds, Diamond Boart or other Precious Stones or Jewels'. Boart was industrial quality diamond, used in particular in diamond polishing.

As the Roman writer Pliny had pointed out, one of the more ironic aspects of the demand for jewellery materials is that absence seems to make the heart grow fonder. People just do not seem to value things if they are too readily obtainable.

There was a considerable vogue for coral in the mid-nineteenth century when Italian craftsmen provided a wide range of coral cameos and other ornaments for the increasing number of wealthy tourists visiting the country. It was thus popular in Victorian jewellery, particularly in jewellery in the archaeological taste that drew inspiration from Classical art styles.

The strong orangey-red colour of coral also suited the strong colour contrasts of Art Deco jewellery where we often see it combined with black onyx, diamonds and pearls. The diamond, coral and seed-pearl tassel pendant shown here (fig.73) dates from about 1925 and is by Cartier of Paris.

Today climate changes and pollution are threatening many coral reefs and the international trade in coral is strictly regulated - as it is with ivory and some of the other organic materials used in jewellery.

Fig.71: Mother-of-pearl and seed pearl necklace. English, circa 1820. (Victoria and Albert Museum, London) © V&A Images/Victoria and Albert Museum

Fig.72: Gold and carved coral pendant. Italian, 17th century.
(British Museum)
© Copyright the Trustees of The British Museum

Fig.73: Tassel pendant in onyx, coral and seed pearls.
Signed Cartier Paris, ca 1925.
© Christie's Images Ltd. 2004

Amber

The amber ring with the raised head of a woman is Roman and dates back to the first or second century AD. It is carved from a single piece of amber.

Amber is resin from a species of pine that has hardened over the passing millennia and which often contains trapped insects and sometimes even larger creatures. There are various types of amber from different parts of the world, but a major source throughout history has been around the Baltic Sea.

Amber is among the few gem materials found in prehistoric European goldwork. It was traded south to Mediterranean countries at an early period and we find amber beads and pendants in Mycenaean Greek burials from about the seventeenth century BC onwards. It also turns up in Northern Italian and Greek Iron Age jewellery. Strangely it seems not to have been used to any great extent into Egypt or the Near East.

The ancients noted the fact that amber sometimes contained insects and that it was softer and lighter than most gems. Some even speculated that it might be fossilised lynx urine. The Greeks also observed that when rubbed on the hair, amber attracted small particles, indeed their name for amber – electron – provided our word electricity.

Amber doesn't survive long burial (or even some museum storerooms) too well and ancient amber beads and small carvings now often present the appearance of granular brown sugar.

Fig.74: A ring with the raised head of a woman
carved in a single piece of amber, Roman,
1st century AD.
© Elio Ciol/CORBIS

Jet

Another organic gem material is jet, a form of fossilised wood. It is often thought of as a characteristically Victorian jewellery material when its black colour and ready availability in Britain made it suitable for wear after her husband, Prince Albert's, death in 1861 (fig.274).

However jet also found far earlier use, and the source of jet at Whitby in North Yorkshire that became famous in the nineteenth century almost certainly also supplied the jet used for this collar which was found in North Yorkshire and dates to the Bronze Age. There are also jet ornaments of Roman date found in Britain.

Whitby is not the only jet source, it is also found in Spain and found much local use there. Spanish jet was even imported into Britain in Victorian times as a cheaper competitor to Whitby jet, but it was less durable. A source in Turkey probably supplied some jet in antiquity and the name jet may derive from Gagas, the Greek name for a town in modern day Turkey from which came Lithos Gagates or 'Stone of Gagas' – our jet. There is not much evidence for Greek use, but eastern Roman jet jewellery includes fine examples, sometimes combining gold and jet – such as jet bangles with gold hinges.

Enamel

Ground glass can be applied onto metal surfaces and then heated to melt and fuse it in place. This is termed enamel. The areas to be enamelled can be defined by engraved hollows, filigree wire borders and other boundaries and the nature of these varied through history, and also depended on purpose.

Enamel, of course is not a gemstone, but it added colour and so it is most convenient to consider it here.

There are examples of rudimentary enamelling on gold from around 1500 BC, and sporadic examples over the following centuries. However, the enamelling of gold did not become common until about 500 BC when, perhaps, the use of gold refining resulted in gold with more predictable melting properties. Prior to this, the gold used for jewellery varied in composition enormously and in many cases the gold jewellery, or the solders used to assemble it, would have been liable to melt at the temperatures necessary to fuse the enamel.

New enamel compositions introduced in the Medieval period lowered enamel melting temperatures and allowed the development of ever more sophisticated enamelling processes. By about the 10th century AD we find a form of enamel where the design is delineated by narrow sheet-gold strips forming cells. This type of enamel work is termed cloisonné work and a very fine tenth century example is shown here (fig.76). This pendant was made in the form of a cross and is hinged so that it might contain a relic - perhaps a piece of the true cross. The enamelled front panel, which would have depicted Christ, is now missing, but the back depicts the Virgin Mary between Saints Basil and Gregory. The missing enamel panel was simply set into a sheet gold setting, much as a gemstone would have been set. This assembly approach for enamels was characteristic of this period right across the European, Byzantine and Islamic worlds. The interwoven gold wires on the large, hinged suspension loop are also characteristic of Byzantine jewellery of this period (fig.184).

Cloisonné enamel work of this type was built up in several separate firings and then when the enamel filled the cells, the surface was polished down by rubbing on a flat abrasive stone. The process is described in detail by the twelfth-century writer of a workshop manual for a goldsmith who called himself Theophlius, but was quite probably the goldsmith Roger of Helmershausen. He explained the whole technique, all the way to ensuring the best shine on the enamel by rubbing it with ear wax.

Fig.75: Jet elements from a necklace.
North Yorkshire, Britain, Bronze Age.
(British Museum)
© Copyright the Trustees of The British Museum

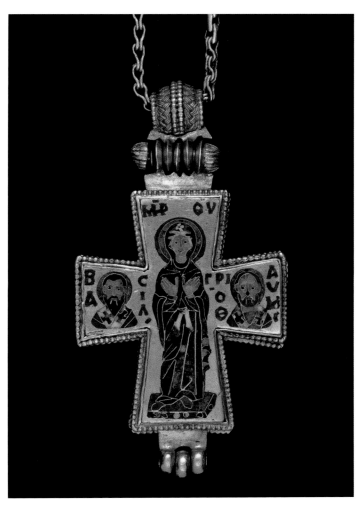

Fig.76: Gold reliquary cross with cloisonné enamel.
Byzantine, 10th century AD. (British Museum)
© Copyright the Trustees of The British Museum

Fig.77: Reverse side of the Gold reliquary cross in fig.76.
Byzantine, 10th century AD. (British Museum)
© Copyright the Trustees of The British Museum

A new form of enamelling was introduced in Medieval times that consisted of applying enamel as a coating over a shaped sheet gold surface. The technique was made possible by various technical innovations that had reduced the temperature at which enamel melted and made its coefficient of expansion much closer to that of gold – so it didn't crack and fall off as the work cooled down after firing. The enamel layer was typically bright, opaque white. This white enamel layer could then be painted with a wide palette of coloured enamels to create all manner of images and patterns.

Renaissance and seventeenth century jewellery is often embellished with simple painted enamels, but the medium found its fullest expression in highly sophisticated painted enamel miniatures. The piece shown here is a locket by the seventeenth century French master goldsmith Henri Toutin (1614 - c. 1683). It depicts a military scene on the front, a naval one on the reverse. Henri's father Jean is credited with the realisation that painting with enamels in this way was possible

and that the different enamel colours did not have to be enclosed by cell-work or wires. However, simpler painted enamels predate Toutin senior.

Enamel is most typically applied onto the surface of metal, but sometimes, as in fig.79, it is used to give a transparent, stained glass-like effect. The technique perfectly suits the wings of this dragonfly by Boucheron, made at the end of the nineteenth century.

Open work enamel of this type became an impressive part of the Art Nouveau jewellery repertoire with designers such as Lalique making masterful use of it. Enamelling within an openwork filigree frame is actually a technique of great age. The earliest examples include a two thousand year old gold pendant from what is now the Sudan. However, this type of enamel was never common in early times because the early enamel compositions were too liable to crack on cooling after firing. Besides, early enamels lacked transparency.

Fig.78: Painted enamel locket by Henry Toutin. French, 1636.
(British Museum)
© Copyright the Trustees of The British Museum

Fig.79: Dragonfly brooch with blue and green openwork enamelled wings with rose-cut diamond borders, set 'en tremblant' on the diamond body. Boucheron, Paris, ca 1890. © Christie's Images Ltd. 2004

The Earliest Jewellery

Today the town of Varna is a Bulgarian sea-side resort which provides little obvious indication that it is also the site of the earliest gold jewellery we have in any quantity. Varna lies on the West Coast of the Black Sea and was clearly a prosperous trading centre, already linking eastern Europe, the Balkans, Turkey and the Russia Steppes as early as the Late Chalcolithic period. Many of the early settlements in the area now lie several metres below the water line, but the cemetery is higher and was accidentally discovered in 1972 when a trench was being dug for electrical cables. Almost 300 graves, one shown here (fig.80), have been found containing not only gold and copper objects, plus flint tools and pottery vessels, but clay models of boats and carts reflecting the importance of transport. The jewellery has been dated to between about 3200 and 3000 BC.

The quantity of gold jewellery found in the burials was remarkable for the period – some six kilograms in total. Some of the gold objects can be paralleled elsewhere, but many of the forms are so far unique. The variation in the wealth of the tombs certainly indicate a hierarchy and the use of gold as a discriminator of rank.

So far archaeologists have not found any gold jewellery, or even nuggets, in human habitation that date to before man was making the first steps towards copper metallurgy. It is true that gold is soft and could be hammered into thin sheet with stone hammers, and then pushed into three dimensional shapes with bone and wood tools, but cutting it or piercing it required at least rudimentary copper tools. Securely joining separate gold components also meant at least basic understanding of alloying metals, in order to create solders.

Gold, of course, was not the earliest jewellery material. The working of metals was unknown in the Stone Age and jewellery was largely limited to small objects that could be threaded on, or tied to, cords, hair or other fibrous materials. Softer materials could be drilled with flint points or simply abraded until they were worn though. The earliest surviving jewellery thus consists of various types of beads including shells, teeth and the softer stones, even wood and dried berries. The use of shells for beads has been common over the passing millennia and right across the inhabited world. A 10,000-year old cemetery at Mount Carmel, near modern day Haifa, included the body of an adult who wore a seven-row necklet of dentalia shell beads.

Fig. 80: Grave of a man of importance, with gold jewellery in situ.
Varna, Bulgaria, ca 3200 - 3000 BC. (Varna Museum of Archaeology)
Photo courtesy Varna Museum of Archaeology

The wolverine depicted on the pendant in fig.81, pierced with a spear, may or may not have appeared on the menu, but its shaggy, warm coat, carefully depicted here as incised lines, was enough to make it a desirable prey. This pendant is made from a sliver of antler pierced for suspension and engraved with a flint point. It is from Les Eyzies Cave in the Dordogne, northern France, and dates back to about 12,500 BC.

A relatively small, agile and fierce animal of this type would not have been easy to corner, and kill with a simple spear. Maybe the wearer of this pendant hoped it would assure successful hunts, or perhaps it was made to celebrate a specific kill.

The two polished stone pendants in fig.82 come from Northern France and date to the Upper Palaeolithic Period, around 12,500 BC. They were drilled for suspension, probably with a small flint point, and would have hung from a leather cord or suchlike. The use of pebbles to produce simple jewellery is an indication that appearance was already a significant factor in at least some jewellery wear. Whether pierced pebbles such as these had some special significance to the original wearer is unknown to us, but they certainly do not have the readily apparent status associations that we would associate with trophy and apatropaic objects such as teeth or claws.

The Neolithic period is marked by the change from hunting and gathering to a more sedentary life-style related to the pursuit of agriculture. The fine turquoise-like colour of these stones beads and pendant from Morbihan in southern Brittany, France (fig.83), would have appealed as much to their original wearer in Early Neolithic France as they do to us today. Mineralogically speaking, the stone is a form of variscite, often termed 'Callais' by archaeologists.

Variscite is a relatively soft stone by modern gem standards, but perforating these ornaments would still have been a major achievement some 6000 years ago when they were made. They were drilled from both sides, probably with a very small flint drill, the perforations are relatively narrow.

Almost all the stones and other materials used for beads before about 500 BC could be worked with nothing any harder than sand as an abrasive. Green variscite is found in Brittany, but the beads might also have been imported from the south, perhaps Portugal, where green variscite is also recorded.

Fig. 81: Antler pendant incised with a hunted wolverine. France,
Upper Palaeolithic Period, ca 12,500 BC. (British Museum)
© Copyright the Trustees of The British Museum

Fig. 82: Stone pendants. France, Upper Palaeolithic Period, ca 12,500 BC.
(British Museum)
© Copyright the Trustees of The British Museum

Fig. 83: Beads of blue variscite.
Brittany, France.
Early Neolithic Period ca 4000 BC.
© Copyright the Trustees of The British Museum

Much of the Gold jewellery from Varna (see fig.84) is made by simply hammering and cutting sheet gold. These charming two horned animals, perhaps a cow and a calf, bear simple dotted outlines. The gold may be of local origin – there are various known gold sources in Bulgaria – but the extreme purity of the gold is noteworthy. Certainly there was copper mining at this period, since the miners have left clear signs of their smelting, but gold mining from placer mines would leave no trace.

Another treasure from Bulgaria was found at Hotnitsa and included disk pendants plus forty-four gold rings made of simple spirals of gold wire and thin rod – of varying diameters and weights. This treasure was found in ruins of habitation and might well have been a votive hoard in a shrine of some sort, or simply some type of early amassing of gold for trade or trading. Melting gold and hammering it into simple wire spirals has been an efficient way to keep, record and transport gold – small nuggets and dust were too easy to loose or otherwise waylay.

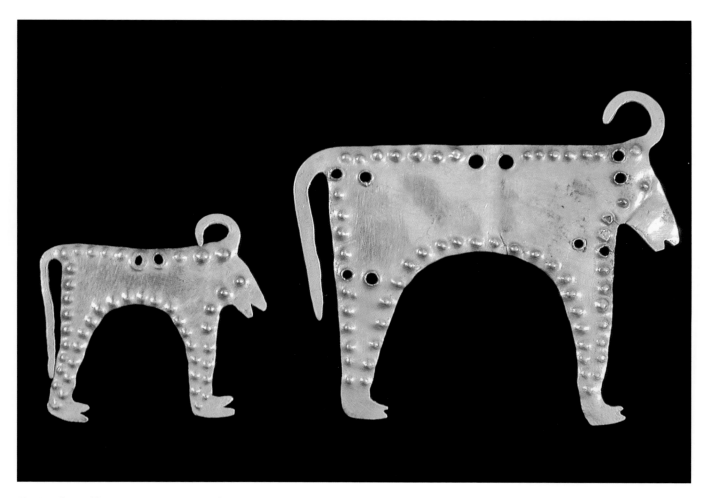

Fig. 84: Sheet gold ornaments representing cattle. Varna, Bulgaria,
ca 3200 - 3000 BC. (Varna Museum of Archaeology)
Photo courtesy Varna Museum of Archaeology

Gold objects that can de dated to before the third millennium are uncommon in the Eastern Mediterranean. Exceptions include a group of eight gold ring-like objects found in a cave burial at Nahal Qanah, Israel (fig.85). This find, which included some sceptres in a copper-arsenic alloy, date, like the Varna objects, to the Chalcolithic Period. This means, literally, 'copper-stone' and is applied to the period when flint tools and weapons were beginning to be replaced by those of copper.

These rings weigh about one kilogram in total and were produced by melting gold dust or nuggets into simple moulds, then hammering to final shape. The hammer marks are clearly seen. Their original function is uncertain and they were quite possibly ingots rather than ornaments. They may simply have been ingots for trading.

Even today it is often hard to decide whether an imitation stone is intended as a deception or simply as an convenient alternative when supply or finance limits access to the genuine stone.

The necklace illustrated here comes from Arpachiya in what is now Iraq and dates to around 5000 BC. Most of the finely shaped black beads on this necklace are obsidian, a form of natural volcanic glass used in the past for both ornaments and tools – it can be chipped to sharp flakes like flint. These beads alternate with simple sliced cowrie shell beads. However, one of the smallest dark beads at one end of the necklace is not obsidian at all, but just dried, molded clay. It is not even fired. We might assume this interloper was a replacement, added at the time of burial, but even so, it represents one of the earliest deliberate imitation gemstones.

There is also another subtle fraud, not visible in the photograph. The obsidian beads are only finished on one side, the backs are left in their chipped state.

The cowry shells retain traces of some sort of red pigment in their interiors and the traces of bitumen around their outer surfaces might also have been deliberate colour. So, the necklet must have been far more colourful, even garish, originally.

Fig. 86: Necklace of cowrie-shells, obsidian and clay. Arpachiya, Iraq, ca 5000 BC. (British Museum)
© Copyright the Trustees of The British Museum

Fig. 85: Gold hoops of uncertain purpose. Nahal Qanah Cave, Israel, Chalcolithic period, late 4th millennium BC. (Israel Museum)
© The Israel Museum, Jerusalem

Western Asia

As Stone Age hunting and gathering was superseded by more permanent settlements, agriculture, and then the growth of city states, rulership became a matter of organisational skills as much as fighting and hunting abilities. Those in control had others to fight, hunt, trade and manufacture for them and could best demonstrate their rank by what became the traditional accoutrements of the rich and powerful – including magnificent buildings, the best transport, fine clothing and ornaments skilfully wrought from rare materials. To support the privileged life style of the lucky few, vastly outnumbered by the less fortunate, it was of benefit to have a religious establishment that confirmed this hold on power as the gods' wish. The more powerful the ruler, the more powerful his gods and the more they deserved his thanks, so temples also became patrons of the jeweller and goldsmith's art.

This establishment of 'civilisation' is essentially synonymous with the establishment of cities – stable, settled societies with an efficient leadership. The city that can feed its inhabitants, police the surrounding region and fend off attacks by neighbours, also provides the stable environment and clientele, temple or royal, to provide work and security for craftsmen. And it has the wealth and power to seek precious and other raw materials by warfare, trade or direct exploitation.

UR

There are various contenders for the title of earliest city in the Old World – and new excavations are constantly modifying our views – but one region stands out in the history of the rise of city states - Sumeria. This is now southern Iraq and the south of what the Greeks called *Mesopotamia* – 'between the two rivers' – the fertile lands of the lower Tigris and Euphrates river.

Since the seventeenth century European travellers had noted Tell al-Muqayyar, a huge oval mound more than a kilometre long that rose 20 metres above the surrounding flood plain some three hundred kilometres south of what is now Baghdad. This was the site of the ancient city of Ur, the supposed birthplace of Abraham. The area came under British control during World War I and was excavated between 1922 and 1934 by a joint British Museum and University of Pennsylvania expedition led by the young British archaeologist Leonard Woolley. He discovered some 1850 Bronze Age burials, probably less than half of the original number there, excavating and publishing them with a care that puts some more recent archaeologists to shame. The burials ranged from simple private graves to royal tombs. The latter contained not only astonishing jewellery, but also clear evidence that some 4500 years ago the wealthy owners' retainers had taken poison and their oxen had been slaughtered in order to accompany them to the after world.

The heady combination of treasure and human sacrifice naturally appealed to the public imagination, but even setting this aside, the discoveries at Ur are among the most exciting archaeological finds ever. Sir Leonard Woolley, knighted because of his work, himself wrote "The excavation of the Royal Cemetery brought to light a civilisation of whose existence science had until then been ignorant."

The most spectacular of the Ur jewellery dates to the so called Early Dynastic III period, between about 2600 and 2400 BC. This is not the earliest jewellery from the region, but it is the earliest jewellery from the Sumerian cities in the south and it is by far the most important assemblage of Early Bronze Age jewellery to have survived.

The jewellery shown here on a modern wood bust was found on the remains of a woman in the so-called Great Death Pit at Ur. She was one of the sixty eight women who 'lay for the most part in well-ordered rows across the pit' and who had died to accompany a royal deceased to the after world.

The most distinctive of Ur ornaments are the elaborate head-dresses consisting, as here, of gold ribbons, wreaths of sheet gold leaves, lapis and gold triangular 'dog collar' choker necklet, gold and lapis pendants and beads, and a type of floral hair pin that Woolley called a 'Spanish comb' since it reminded him of the similar ornaments worn in nineteenth century Europe. This group of head ornaments is by no means the most elaborate. The richest burial from Ur was that of Queen Puabi. The 'Spanish comb' shown here, like many such, has three gold flower heads (the silver 'stalk' is a modern reconstruction of the corroded original). Queen Puabi's comb had seven flower heads, some others from Ur have five.

Our unknown woman also wore large double lunate earrings, another characteristic Early Dynastic III Ur type.

Fig. 87: Sumerian gold, silver, lapis lazuli and cornelian jewellery are originally worn. From Ur, Sumerian, ca 2300 - 2100 BC.
(British Museum)

Sumeria may have been blessed with fertile land, but it had little in the way of precious metals or gemstones. Gold was imported from Anatolian Turkey and Afghanistan, Silver from Anatolia and perhaps Central Asia. Grain was traded in return.

The stones used here in jewellery from Ur are predominantly bright blue lapis lazuli traded from the mines in far away Afghanistan, and orange-red carnelian, perhaps from India or Arabia. The contrasting colours of these two stone types against the gold provide a simple elegance that compliments the geometric form of most of the jewellery components – the graduated biconical lapis beads, the more attenuated carnelians and the circles and triangles of the gold.

The relative absence of recognisable symbolic or animal forms among the Ur jewellery is noteworthy. Representational jewellery forms are not entirely missing (see fig.89), particularly among the richer burials, but they are far rarer than, for example, in early Egypt. Perhaps there is a link with writing. The Egyptians wrote with a huge repertoire of animal and other hieroglyphic symbols, the Sumerians in the stark and abstract wedge-shaped cuneiform script.

Among the jewellery found buried with Queen Puabi was a remarkable diadem, a detail of which is shown here (fig.89). The diadem is composed of more than a thousand small lapis lazuli beads, originally sewn onto a leather band, with four pairs of animal figures – stags, bearded bulls (as here), antelope and

sheep – with fruit, ears of wheat and other forms. Woolley used the terms 'charming' and 'exquisitely modelled' to describe this object, the most magnificent of the queen's jewellery.

The most striking aspect is the natural animal and vegetable forms, rare among the Ur jewellery, and one can only assume that the object in some way embodied fertility and reproduction. Even so, the animals are not presented in Noah's Ark-like breeding pairs, and may all be intended as male. Fertility significance would be apt for a royal burial since royalty had an all important religious as well as secular function. The ruler of Ur was chosen by, and acted on behalf of, the city's principle deity the moon god Nanna. The King's duty was to build and maintain Nanna's temple in befitting manner and presumably in the expectation that Nanna would ensure good harvests, healthy flocks and herds, and abundant game in return – the very things depicted with such realism on this ornament.

The gold figures are made of very thin gold foil over a supporting core of bitumen. Despite the relatively simple tools then at their disposal, the Ur goldsmiths had ample skills in forming and decorating even quite massive sheet gold and silver, as numerous bowls and beakers also demonstrate. Here the thin gauge of the gold might be due to the need to minimise weight and reduce distortion to the leather and bead backing as much as the constraints of simple tools in working complex three-dimensional forms on such a small scale, the animal figures are about four centimetres high.

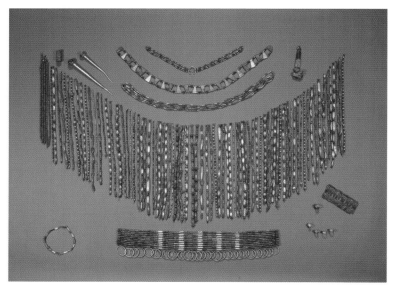

Fig. 88: Lapis lazuli and cornelian beads. From Ur, Sumerian, ca 2300 - 2100 BC. (University of Pennsylvania Museum of Archaeology and Anthropology) University of Pennsylvania Museum of Archaeology and Anthropology (152106)

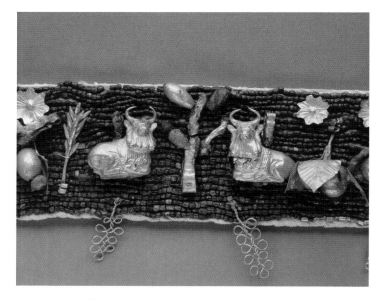

Fig. 89: Gold and lapis lazuli diadem of Queen Puabi. From Ur, Sumerian, ca 2100 BC. (University of Pennsylvania Museum of Archaeology and Anthropology) University of Pennsylvania Museum of Archaeology and Anthropology (152101)

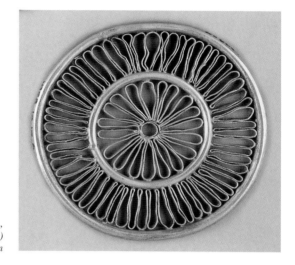

Although the women's burials at Ur contained the greatest wealth of most lavish jewellery, men were also buried with a range of personal ornaments, albeit simpler. Most typical of male ornament was this type of ornament composed of two or three elongated beads flanked by length of chain. From its position in burials it was clearly worn around the head just above the ears and Woolley suggested it might have held a fabric head covering in place. However, no traces of such headwear were found and the original function of the ornament remains unclear.

The chains are early examples of the loop-in-loop chain that was the standard chain form for the next three thousand years. Interestingly, gold chain necklets were not found at Ur, nor, seemingly, were chains found in female burials, although some elongated gold beads might be intended to imitate length of gold chain.

The three long beads on these head ornaments are usually of sheet gold flanked by lapis lazuli with little carnelian beads between them. More rarely, as here, the long beads are carnelian and the smaller ones lapis.

The sheer abundance of the Ur jewellery tends to distract us from appreciating the individual details. Even relatively minor pieces warrant a second look. Casting was extremely rare for gold jewellery and only slightly more common for silver. The gold jewellery from Ur is almost entirely made from cutting, shaping and soldering sheet gold and wire.

This early example of the openwork rosette design in jewellery (fig.91) is noteworthy because of the resourceful and perhaps unexpected way in which it was formed. Rosettes of this general shape can be found at many later dates, but here, as in several other examples from Ur, the jeweller has formed the petals and even the inner circle from a single gold strip. It starts in the centre in two coils to form the 'hub', and then continues to form each of the 'petals' in turn. This approach to forming the petals did not reduce the amount of the soldering required, but it would have helped to ensure all the petals stayed in place until they were soldered within the outer, heavier gold wire frame.

The rosette and flower head form is common in the Ur jewellery. We find it as necklet or head ornament components, such as the present example, surmounting the tips of 'Spanish Comb' headdress ornaments, as in fig.87, and incised onto sheet gold. On some jewellery rosettes are clearly intended to represent flowers, but here the design is more stylised and the significance unclear.

The majority of the gold used for jewellery such as this piece was used just as it was mined and imported, that is with a very variable, natural silver content. When there is more than about 25 percent or so silver present the gold will have a pale silvery yellow colour and is often termed 'electrum.'

The ornament shown here in fig.92 is a pendant found in the grave of a very young child at Ur, one of the few richly furnished children's graves. The burial contained several pieces of jewellery including a gold, lapis lazuli and carnelian head ornament and three gold earrings that were in place on the young skull. This simple pendant however is of a timeless design that echoes down through the millennia. We can find similar ornaments in early Iron Age Greece, in Pre-Colombian America or in more recent works from the Philippines – and in modern jewellery-making evening classes worldwide. We do not know the significance of the double spiral, but other similar pendants are known from Ur, as well as from Bronze Age sites further afield.

The pendant was made by hammering wire from either a small cast ingot or a strip cut from sheet gold and then simply bending and coiling it into a double spiral with an integral suspension loop. A sophisticated touch, however, is the way in which the two flat coils have been consolidated with solder. This would keep the wires in place during wear and is a simple but handy expedient that we will also find in some later wire-coil jewellery.

It might be suggested that such a practical reinforcement shows that the pendant was originally intended for wear, not just burial. However, we should be wary of assuming that a distinction was made this early between the practicalities needed for life and the afterlife. If the deceased nobility in those days needed real servants and real weapons in the afterlife, they certainly needed functional jewellery.

In about 2360 BC the king Sargon from the city of Akkad further to the North, conquered Ur. This conquest ushered in a whole new historical and artistic period – what we term the Sargonid Period. The jewellery buried with the dead changed in style significantly as can be seen with the pieces shown here (fig.93). Lapis, carnelian and gold beads remained popular, but out went the elaborate women's headdresses with their 'Spanish Combs', gold ribbons, foliate wreaths and such like. Now all that was worn on the head was a simple thin sheet gold diadem, much as we find in much later burials, even from the Classical world. The large lunate earrings also disappear, to be replaced by somewhat similarly shaped, but far smaller lunate earrings i.e. the one shown here. These occur in gold, silver and copper, the latter sometimes clad in thin gold foil. The simple chain and bead head bands worn by men also seem to have passed out of favour.

We do not know what lay behind these changes. There was no less love for precious metals and gems. If the surviving texts are a true indication, the Sargonid period actually saw an increase in the use of jewellery, and perhaps greater secular use, and the search for sources of raw materials was stepped up.

Fig. 92: Gold spiral pendant. From Ur, Sumerian, circa 2100 BC.
(University of Pennsylvania Museum of Archaeology and Anthropology)
University of Pennsylvania Museum of Archaeology and Anthropology (152169)

Fig. 93: Jewellery from Ur, lapis lazuli, cornelian, and gold, Sumerian, circa 2100 BC. (British Museum)
© Copyright the Trustees of The British Museum

Troy

Troy, an ancient site on the Aegean coast of Turkey, has provided us with some spectacular jewellery dating to around 2000 BC that can be compared to that from Ur and other Western Asiatic sites, but which also shows connections with goldwork from what is now Eastern Europe.

In the 1860's the German businessman and amateur archaeologist Heinrich Schliemann set out to discover the ancient city of Troy, as described in Homer's Iliad. He found the ancient city, now Hisarlik on the Asian coast of the Dardanelles strait, Turkey, and found amazing treasures, but the levels he excavated predated the site of Homer's great city by about a millennium. Even so, one of the groups of jewellery Schliemann found there is still often called 'Priam's treasure'. The quantity of gold was amazing.

Treasure A from Troy, some 2.5 kilos of gold, contained a vast array of truly wondrous goldwork that stunned the public and scholarly world when it was finally displayed. Remember this was still more than half a century before the discovery of the Royal Tombs at Ur or the tomb of the Tutankhamen. There were gold and silver vessels, numerous earrings, studs, beads, neck rings and so on. Among the most spectacular objects are two gold diadems. The one shown here, being modelled by Schliemann's wife Sophia, consists of more than 4000 small leaf-shaped gold motifs affixed to ninety chains creating a shimmering waterfall – or perhaps evoking the shady fronds of a willow tree. On the ends of the longer chains to each side are sheet gold pendants in the form of stylized idols.

The diadem shows signs of use and at least one pendant reveals signs of repair in antiquity. This clearly indicates that the head-dress was worn and was not simply a funerary ornament. The combination of leaf-like motifs and stylized idols suspended on chains is matched in several of the grander earrings from the same Treasure.

The later story of the Troy treasures reflects late nineteenth archaeology and a century of world history little less turbulent than in Homer's day. Schliemann, by less than ethical means, spirited his finds out of Turkey and into Greece and eventually presented them to Berlin where they were displayed in their full glory in the Berlin Museum. For safety in the Second World War they were removed to a hiding place in a mine complex, and then in the chaotic final days of the war they disappeared and for fifty years feared lost. They had actually been removed to Moscow by the Russians and remained there safe but out of sight in the Pushkin State Museum. In the mid 1990's, with the fall of the Iron Curtain, Schliemann's Troy treasures were once again revealed to scholarly and public eyes. The story is not over. At the time of writing, the final home of the Troy treasures is still to be decided – several countries now claim legal ownership.

The date of the Troy jewellery is still debated. A date of around 2000 BC, maybe a century or two later, suits much of it, but the treasures range in date over a period of time and some of the earliest Troy jewellery might even date back to before 2500 BC.

Fig.94: Sophie Schliemann wearing the great gold diadem from Troy. Photo ca 1875.

Early Granulation

The geographical position of Troy in what is now Western Turkey suggest likely contacts with the Aegean and Eastern Europe. Indeed, the Greek legends of the Trojan Wars that inspired Schliemann to discover the ancient city are ample evidence for such interaction. There are also some tangible indications of links in the objects found at Troy – including a twisted gold torc (neck ring) in Troy Treasure A that might be more European than Anatolian.

Of course, modern political borders and politics, tend to compartmentalise our view of antiquity. The pair of earrings shown here (fig.95) are directly comparable to examples from Troy, we might even suspect a single workshop, but they come not from Troy but from what is now the Greek Island of Lemnos.

The upper part of these earrings are essentially formed from a broad U-shape with a high arching hoop to pass through the ear. From the upper part of each earring hang four pendants of chains with small leaf-shaped gold attachments and terminating in sheet gold 'idol' pendants, reminiscent of those on the magnificent diadem from Troy.

The upper parts are made in side-by-side gold wires with granulated decoration. Granulation is a decorative effect produced using lines or patterns of small gold spheres and the examples shown here, and the equivalents from Troy are among the worlds earliest examples. Over the last century and a half this ancient technique has held a position of some mystique, in no small part because the nineteenth century goldsmiths, such as Alessandro Castellani, eager to reproduce ancient jewellery forms, were unable to replicate it effectively. In practice, the production of the small gold spheres is simple enough, albeit time consuming. Small particles of gold, whether little bits of wire or sheet or small gold grains from a river bed, will melt and roll up into a minute ball when heated. This is an effect of surface tension, not a goldsmith's skill. The complexity lay in positioning the minute grains, keeping them so positioned while soldering them in place, and minimising the quantity of solder so as not to flood the little spheres. There were various granulation processes used in antiquity at different times and places, but in essence the processes were the same as those used to join other gold components such as wires and thin sheet.

From Lemnos, from the same context as the earrings also come attenuated, barrel-shaped hematite gold weights, which are a Sumerian characteristic. This is hardly surprising, the Island of Lemnos, though part of modern Greece is far closer to Modern Turkey than it is to mainland Greece and almost visible from Troy itself. This underlines the importance of largely disregarding modern political borders when we consider ancient cultures.

Fig. 95: Pair of Gold earrings of 'Trojan' type. Greek island of Lemnos, ca 2300 - 2100 BC. Archaeological Receipts Fund

Most of the characteristic ancient gold working technologies, fine gold wires, chain manufacture, delicate soldering and granulation work, and so forth, had been well established in the Near East by about 2000 BC and for the next three millennia the advances lay more in the perfection, dissemination and application of these techniques than the development of new ones.

These two earrings come from the site of Tell el-'Ajjul in Gaza, Palestine. They date from about the beginning of the sixteenth century BC and the clusters of granules on one of them relate to other jewellery of this period from Syria and Iraq, and even one find from Mycenae in Greece.

As noted above there are various ways in which granulation work can be achieved. The production of the small individual gold sphere is not particularly complex, merely time consuming. The difficulty lies in soldering the minute grains to their backing in such as way that the solder does not flood the grains. If the grains were stuck in place with a mixture of organic glue and a finely divided copper compound (such as the copper ore and gem material we know as malachite, ground to powder) heat would first burn the glue to carbon and then, in the presence of the carbon, the copper compound would be reduced to pure copper. This copper alloyed with the surrounding gold and quite literally produced a simple solder within the joint area.

It works, and study of existing ancient gold suggests that it was used in many, but not all cases. The problem for the jewellery historian is to understand how some Bronze Age jeweller figured it all out. The answer is probably quite simple. There is evidence to suggest that in antiquity gold was alloyed with copper by mixing gold with ground copper ores such as malachite, rather than by adding metallic copper. If so, this practice could easily have led to the observation that the malachite helped to fuse the gold.

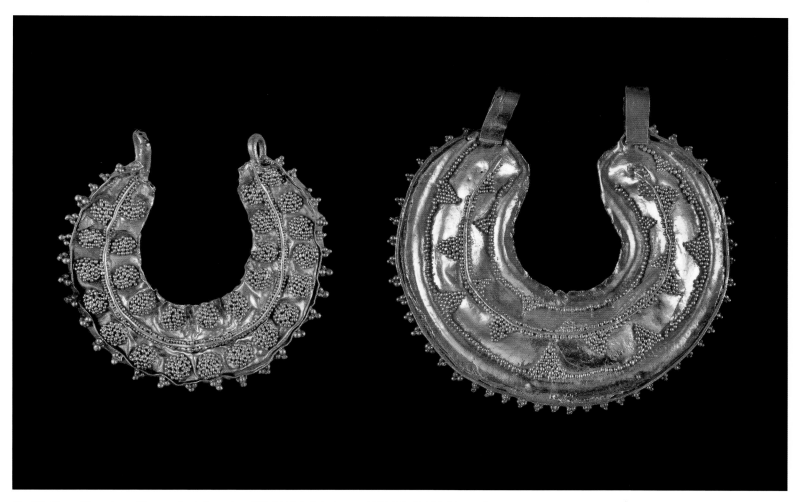

Fig. 96: Two gold earrings with granulated decoration. Tell el-'Ajjul, Palestine, ca 1600 BC. (British Museum)
© Copyright the Trustees of The British Museum

Scythian Gold

The recumbent stag shown here is a good example of the elegant and compact form typical of Scythian art. It is formed in sheet gold and dates from the late seventh to early sixth century BC.

The Scythians were nomadic horsemen who lived on the Northern shores of the Black Sea in a region that more or less corresponds to the modern Ukraine. We know little about their early religious beliefs, but they clearly invested much in the afterlife. They were buried in impressive burial mounds and with all the necessities of their existence, from their all-important horses, sometimes, to magnificent gold jewellery and other valuable possessions. The Greek historian Herodotus tells us about some of their customs – their warriors drank the blood of the first man they killed, they used cups made from human skulls and so forth. Whether or not Herodotus is painting a rather biased view, the overall impression is of a barbarism that contrasts strangely with the exquisite goldwork that has survived.

Perhaps swayed by Herodotus, archaeologists long assumed that multiple human burials within a mound were those of wives or servants killed to accompany their master or mistress to the afterworld, much like their Sumerian equivalents two millennia earlier. However, recent reassessment suggests that in at least some cases, the secondary bodies were relatives or other associates of the dead who died at a later date and buried in the same mound – much as a family might have been buried in a family vault in more recent times.

The origin of the Scythians is still debated. It was undoubtedly further east and on the basis of their art and other cultural links, was seemingly in the region of the Altai Mountains in Southern Siberia. This makes sense so far as the goldwork and jewellery are concerned. The sheer weight and quantity of gold is as striking as its artistic mastery and implies that the Scythians has access to abundant gold. The Altai Mountains would be just such a potential source. The gold of this region was legendary and, according to various ancient writers, the gold mines were guarded by griffins or, in some accounts, ants. Fierce creatures guarding treasure is not unusual in folklore – in one widespread later legend snakes guarded gemstones – but the presence of ants in this role is unexpected. It has been suggested that the activities of burrowing ants brought gold to the surface and thus announced its presence.

The Scythians are evident on the northern Black Sea in the seventh century BC and they were dealing with Greek traders at this same period. The art styles also reinforce indications of contacts between the Scythians and Anatolian, Persian and other ancient Near Eastern cultures.

The Scythian demand for exquisite goldwork drew Greek goldsmiths to the northern Black Sea region, where they produced objects for their new clientele, sometimes conventional Greek forms, sometimes more flamboyant than their home market had demanded, and sometimes distinctly adapted to Scythian taste. At the same time Scythian metalworkers, and perhaps those from other cultures drawn to the region, learned from the Greeks resulting in a range of hybrid forms.

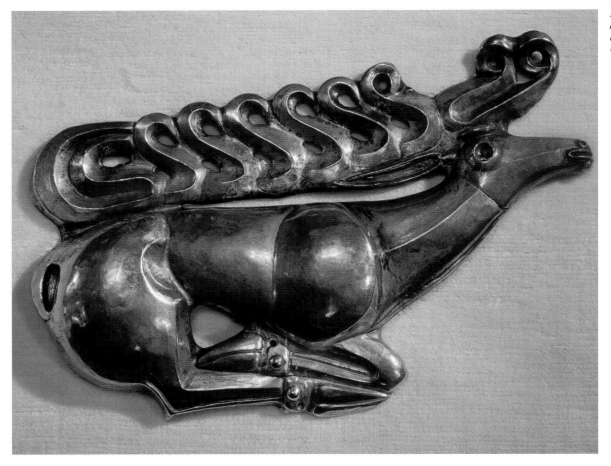

Fig. 97: Gold ornament in the form of a stag. Scythian, Ukraine, late 7th-early 6th century BC.
© Gianni Dagli Orti/CORBIS

The Oxus Treasure

The story of the recovery of the so-called Oxus Treasure reads like a Boys Own adventure. In brief, the vast gold treasure was retrieved by an English Captain – F. C. Burton – in 1880 when he came to the rescue of merchants in Afghanistan who were attacked by brigands in the Oxus region of between present Afghanistan and the Caspian Sea. Most of the hoard finally came into the hands of the British Museum. Because of its recent history it cannot be ascertained whether it was one find originally, plunder from a ransacked burial ground, or objects amassed by tomb robbers over a period of time. Most of the objects are probably of about the same date – fifth to fourth century BC – and many are in a fragmentary state having been deliberately cut up for division or recycling. However, it is not always clear if this chopping up was done in antiquity or in the nineteenth century. A fuller study in due course will hopefully answer some of the questions, but for the time being we can note that a cursory examination suggests that some of the cuts might well be ancient, thus suggesting that the hoard could represent ancient plunder or even a goldsmith's hoard.

The two large armlets from the treasure are shown here. The terminals take the form of elaborate winged griffins. The incurved back of the hoops is a characteristic feature of many Persian armlets of the period. Some practical purpose might be supposed, and the most likely explanation is that it was to prevent the armlet from turning around when worn on the upper arm. The original inlays are now all missing, but originally the armlets were set with a variety of stones including carnelian and lapis lazuli. Many of the inlays were still present in one of these armlets before it was packed away for safety during the Second World War.

Phoenician Gold

We encountered a Medieval Islamic 'amulet case' above (fig.17) and mentioned the Phoenician animal headed variety. Here is an example (fig.99). This has the head of a lioness, surmounted by a sun disk and the uraeus, the cobra symbol of Egyptian rulership. The tongue-shaped motifs around the sun disk and around the middle band retain some badly decomposed enamel.

The Phoenicians were the great sea traders of the first millennium BC with major bases on the Levantine Coast and at Carthage, North Africa. This amulet comes from a burial in Tharros, Sardinia. Their art style is clearly derived from Egyptian and the deity shown here on the terminal is almost certainly intended to be the Egyptian lioness goddess Bastet. The presence of a mane on a lioness might seem strange, but it wasn't just a Phoenician error. Monumental Egyptian sculpture of the goddess can also show Bastet with a mane. A magnificent pair of gold armlets from the Ukraine, dating from the fourth century BC and now in the Hermitage museum, St Petersburg, also terminate in lionesses with what we might best term 'gender confusion.' Rather than simply assume some sort of naive lack of observation on the part of the ancients, we might ponder as to whether there was some special significance.

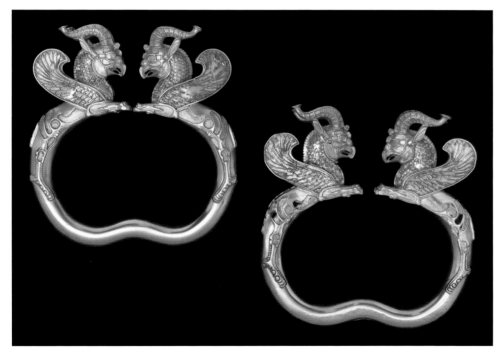

Fig. 98: Pair of gold armlets from the 'Oxus Treasure'. Central Asia, ca 5th-4th century BC. (British Museum)
© Copyright the Trustees of The British Museum

Fig. 99:
Gold amulet case with lion-head terminal. Phoenician, from Tharros, Sardinia, circa 7th-6th century BC. (British Museum)
© Copyright the Trustees of The British Museum

Egypt

The words 'Ancient Egypt' and 'treasure' are often associated. This might largely originate in the discovery of the tomb of the boy King Tutankhamen in 1922 and the extraordinary treasures it contained – such as the well known gold mask shown here - but it is not a recent phenomenon. Egypt had gold. The gold mines within Egypt, or in the kingdoms to the south, led one Mesopotamian ruler to say with envy three and a half thousand years ago that gold was a common as dust in Egypt. Two millennia later the Medieval Islamic conquerors of the country looted so much gold from the old tombs that they devoted whole books to explaining how to find it.

In addition to gold mines, Egypt had other geological and geographic features that influenced its history, art and jewellery. The country might have been less arid in early days than it is now, but it was a land where agriculture and thus habitation was mainly limited to the banks of the river Nile that ran from South to North. The Nile thus provided the main conduit for travel and transportation, and neatly divided the country into two symmetrical halves. To the East, where the sun rose, there was the Eastern Dessert where gold, the metal of the sun, was mined and, ultimately the Red Sea. To the West, where the sun set, was essentially a vast nothingness, apart from a few habitable oases. To see geographical characteristics as the root cause of Egypt's view of life and death and its highly symmetrical art is to oversimplify, but one terrain did help to define culture.

Egypt's fertile river banks had been inhabited since very early days, but there is little surviving jewellery prior to the beads of stones and natural materials such as coral and shell we find in use by about 4000 BC. Remarkably, the stone beads of this early period include lapis lazuli that had been traded all the way from what is now Afghanistan.

By about 3500 BC the meagre supplies of eastern lapis lazuli and turquoise were supplemented by quartz with a blue or green glass-like glaze layer and, related to this, a wholly man-made material we call faience, which was a kind of crude glass.

The earliest gold jewellery we have from Egypt is from burials and dates to about 3200 BC. It is typically formed from simple pieces of bent and shaped gold foil, in many cases unsuitable for day-to-day wear.

To the Egyptian the afterlife was a continuation of the present one – assuming the deceased's heart revealed truth when judged after death. The deceased thus required both the necessities and luxuries that he or she had owned, or aspired to, in life. And the luxuries were often also necessities.

Magnificent jewels depicting deities and ritual served a serious practical purpose by suitably honouring the gods and thus best ensuring the deceased of a long and happy sojourn in the afterworld.

The vast majority of Ancient Egyptian jewellery that survives – whether of humble faience or highly elaborate gold – has been found in burials. Some was used in life before being destined to join its owner in the afterlife, but much was deliberately made for burial.

Naturally, the jewellery and other possessions buried with the deceased were a huge temptation to their survivors. Tomb robbers looted some tombs almost before the mud sealings on the doors had dried. Not only do we have surviving reports of the trials (and disagreeable interrogations) of some tomb robbers, we actually have the remains of one – buried when a tomb roof collapsed and only found when more recent excavators rediscovered the tomb. The coffin lid had been half dragged off.

Fig. 100: Gold funerary mask of the pharaoh Tutankhamen. Egypt, ca. 1325 BC. (Egyptian Museum, Cairo) © CORBIS

The beads forming this ornament (fig.101)) come from a site called Abydos in Egypt and belong to the Naqada I culture, around 3200 BC. This was actually a diadem worn around the head and seemingly held a veil of some sort in place. We know this because it was found in situ in the burial of a woman.

The simple little gold beads are among the earliest gold objects from Egypt. The red beads are garnet, a stone that is well attested in burials of this period, but which is rare later on. We must assume a local garnet source. The blue beads are of turquoise, and this reminds us that the famous turquoise mines of Sinai were relatively close at hand. However, turquoise use presents us with one of the great problems of Egyptian gem history. The Sinai mines were close to hand and there is ample documentary evidence that they were exploited on a significant scale later in Egypt's history. But what happened to all the turquoise? Turquoise is very rare in Egyptian jewellery. One possible suggestion is that turquoise was used as a colouring agent for glass or other glaze materials, but more analysis is needed to double check this.

We know little about how jewellery was viewed by ordinary wearers in the earliest times because such information was seldom recorded. One popular ancient Egyptian story sheds some light here. The earliest surviving version of this tale is in the so-called the Westcar Papyrus, housed in the Berlin Museum, which dates to around 1500 BC. However, it concerns the far earlier King Khufu, the builder of the largest pyramid at Giza. This pharaoh was being entertained by scantily clad girls rowing a boat around an ornamental lake. The fish-shaped pendant made of malachite worn by one of these young women fell into the water and despite a promise by the king himself to replace it, she was inconsolable until a magician parted the waters and returned her ornament to her. This story reveals to us that even more than four thousand years ago an individual piece of jewellery could have enormous sentimental value of some sort for its original owner – enough to counter even the king's offer of a replacement.

Ancient Egyptian children wore fish pendants as a protection against drowning. The gold fish pendant shown here post-dates the king Khufu by several centuries, and the inset stone is green feldspar rather than green malachite, but perhaps the choice of the green colour for a fish pendant was significant.

Fig. 101: Gold, garnet and turquoise diadem. Egyptian, ca 3200 BC. (British Museum)
© *Copyright the Trustees of The British Museum*

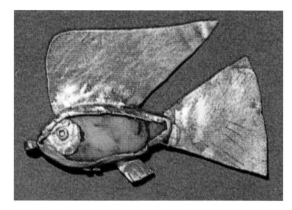

Fig. 102: Gold pendant in the form of a fish set with green feldspar (amazonite). Egyptian Middle Kingdom, ca 1900-1800 BC. (British Museum)
© *Copyright the Trustees of The British Museum*

So-called Egyptian faience was a characteristic ancient Egyptian material, though by no means limited to Egypt. Faience was a fused mixture of sand, an alkali and a colouring agent. It was most typically of a greenish-blue turquoise colour, though many shades were produced later. It was used for a myriad of little amulets, vessels, figurines and a wide range of other objects.

Faience was easy and inexpensive to make, sand, after all was abundant in Egypt, but fragile, which made it a jewellery material eminently suitable for deposit with the dead rather than for use in life. Little faience beads, often small spaghetti-like tubes, are found in their thousands in Egyptian burials, sometimes forming complete nets covering the body.

The faience collar shown here (fig.103) dates from 2020 BC. This is a faience version of a characteristic ancient Egyptian ornament type – the so-called broad collar. Broad collars in gold were in use by in Fourth Dynasty of Egypt – that is by around 2550 BC, the time when the great pyramids at Giza were being constructed.

We encountered early granulation in Western Asiatic jewellery from around 2000 BC. Granulation work also first appeared in Egypt at about this same period – the time of the Middle Kingdom, around 1900 - 1800 BC. Indeed, some of the objects with granulation work of this period found in Egypt may be imports, but certain classes of object – such as these so-called amulet cases (fig.104) – were probably local products.

Amulet cases of this type were originally intended to contain some sort of amulet, whether a text or a special bead or such like. Here the upper cap is removable.

The granulation work on this example is amongst the most

regular known from Middle Kingdom Egypt. The use of double lines of grains, something we find from all periods of granulation work, made it easier to produce regular patterns. Grains arranged in lines single file, tended to clump together during laying out or soldering, double lines were more stable.

The magnificent gold pectoral (fig.105) bears the name of the Egyptian king Sesostris III, who ruled around 1800 BC. It is a perfect example of the cloisonné ('cell-based') inlay work characteristic of ancient Egyptian jewellery. The coloured gemstones, here carnelian, lapis lazuli and turquoise, are used much like blocks of pigment. These are not the transparent, glittering gems of the modern world, but bold, opaque stones that reinforce the iconic nature of the jewel as well as endowing it with their own supposed powers.

Another characteristic of ancient Egyptian jewellery – and one that is in stark contrast to most of that from Ur and Troy – is its representational form. The jewellery is sculpture in miniature: a whole pantheon of small deities, intricately shaped symbols and inscriptions. Indeed, a complete piece of Egyptian jewellery can often be read like an inscription – every component spelling out some wish for the owner or linking the piece to the attributes of the gods. This is particularly noticeable in the more two-dimension forms such as the large pendant shown here. Each of the symbols is a hieroglyph that together spell out the Sesostris' name, titles , attributes and good-luck wishes directed towards him.

There was a strict canon of proportions in ancient Egyptian art that transcended scale or purpose – the hawk god is shown on this pendant in the same proportions and pose as he would have been carved into stone on the towering entrance gate to a temple.

Fig. 103: Broad collar composed of glazed composition ('faience') beads and pendants. Egyptian, 11th Dynasty ca 2020 BC. (British Museum)
© Copyright the Trustees of The British Museum

Fig.104: Gold cylindrical amulet-case pendant with granulated decoration. Egyptian Middle Kingdom, ca 1850-1800 BC. (British Museum)
© Copyright the Trustees of The British Museum

Fig.105: Gold pectoral inlaid with lapis lazuli, turquoise and carnelian and spelling out the name and titles of the pharaoh Sesostris II. Egyptian Middle Kingdom, ca . 1880 BC. (Egyptian Museum, Cairo)
Photo courtesy of The Egyptian Museum

In the mid-nineteenth century tomb robbers were continuing and excavation begun, but then left, by the French archaeologist Auguste Mariette when they discovered the coffin of Queen Ahhotpe. This queen was already known as an important figure in Egyptian history. After the collapse of the Middle Kingdom in the seventeenth century BC, Egypt had been invaded and then ruled by foreigners known as the Hyksos. Seqenenre, king of Thebes, started a revolt against these interlopers and died on the battlefield. His sons Kamose and Ahmose continued the fight and after Kamose's death, Ahmose eventually threw the Hyksos out of Egypt. Ahhotpe was their mother.

Many fine treasures from Ahhotpe's coffin were eventually retrieved, including this necklace with three large and stylised fly pendants. Gold flies were a military order in ancient Egypt – a symbol of persistence, and an apt one as any visitor to Egypt today would agree. The gold flies are also apt jewellery to illustrate this turbulent period in Egyptian history. The victorious Ahmose was the founder of the Eighteenth Dynasty of Egypt in about 1550 BC, the first dynasty of the New Kingdom that was to see such pharaohs as Tutankhamen and Rameses the Great.

The chain on this necklet is a version of the loop-in-loop chain technique that first appeared at Ur some seven hundred years earlier, and it closes with a simple hook and eye attachment. The flies are made in sheet gold and have openwork bodies that presumably originally held inserts in some other material.

Fig.106: Gold necklet with three fly pendants from the burial of Queen Ahhotep I. Egyptian, ca 1530 BC. (Egyptian Museum, Cairo)
© Sandro Vannini/CORBIS

Fig.107: Gold collar in the form of a vulture inlaid with carnelian and blue glass. From the tomb of Tutankhamen, Egyptian, ca 1325 BC. (Egyptian Museum, Cairo) © Frank Trapper/Corbis

Tutankhamen

The discovery of the tomb of Tutankhamen by Howard Carter and Lord Carnavon in 1922 is one of the most famous events in world archaeology. Few discoveries have matched the sheer excitement and wonder as that of this almost undisturbed tomb in the Valley of Kings on the west bank of the Nile near the modern city of Luxor (known as Thebes in Greek times).

Tutankhamen died when young, probably in his late teens, in about 1340 BC. Recent examination has suggested that he died from gangrene following a leg wound – not the murder by a would-be rival that was hitherto proposed. In any case Tutankhamen was a relatively insignificant king who historically owed his fame to being ruler at the time the capital of Egypt was re-established at Thebes and the religion brought back to a reassuring polytheism after his predecessor Akhenaton's flirtation with monotheism. It was probably Tutankhamen's very insignificance that preserved his tomb almost intact. It was lost and forgotten and, small and tucked away as it was, it was not ransacked by tomb robbers over the passing centuries.

The magnificent jewellery and goldwork buried with Tutankhamen is familiar to most from books and exhibitions. Some objects, such as the inlaid gold funerary mask (fig.100) have achieved iconic status.

The object shown in fig.107 is an elaborate collar in the form of the vulture goddess Nekhbet. The smaller component is the counter balance that was worn hanging down the back – though here its small size means that is was probably more traditional than practical. Nekhbet was a vulture goddess who become patron of Upper Egypt and one of the protectors of the Pharaoh, the other was the uraeus cobra. The vulture head and the uraeus can both be seen on the forehead of Tutankhamen on his gold mask (fig.100), on the diadem (fig.108) and on the pendant (fig.109).

The collar is a fine example of the dense inlay work in coloured stones that so characterises ancient Egyptian jewellery.

The vulture head and the uraeus cobra are seen again here on this spectacular inlaid diadem, also from Tutankhamen's tomb. It is inlaid with various coloured stones and in glass and faience. The vulture head with its eyes inlaid in obsidian is very finely modelled. The undulating tail of the uraeus cobra arches over the head.

Fig.108: Detail of a gold diadem with the protective vulture and Uraeus (cobra).
Set with glass, obsidian, malachite, chalcedony and lapis lazuli.
From the tomb of Tutankhamen, Egyptian, ca 1325 BC. (Egyptian Museum, Cairo)
© Frank Trapper/Corbis

We saw the eye of the hawk god Horus being carried by the little gold figure of the god Thoth in fig.16. Here the same eye forms a magnificent pendant. It is inlaid in lapis lazuli (dark blue), pale blue glass, what is probably red glass, and a pale bluish stone that might be a rare example of the use of turquoise. The beads on the three strand necklet are in green, red and blue faience, a material that we encountered above (fig.103)

Much of Tutankhamen's jewellery is set with coloured glass rather than natural stones. But glass was a new and exciting material then, so maybe it was deliberately chosen.

What is less commonly realised is that Tutankhamen's jewellery, which includes much of the finest ancient Egyptian gold jewellery discovered to date, provides us with some tantalising insights into the rushed funerary arrangements that must have accompanied the young king's untimely death. Some pieces were clearly not made for Tutankhamen, but were adapted from ornaments made for, and perhaps buried with, some other person. Just who this other person was remains uncertain. They were undoubtedly royal, but although we can speculate, their identity will probably remain unknown until a fuller study of the jewellery is carried out.

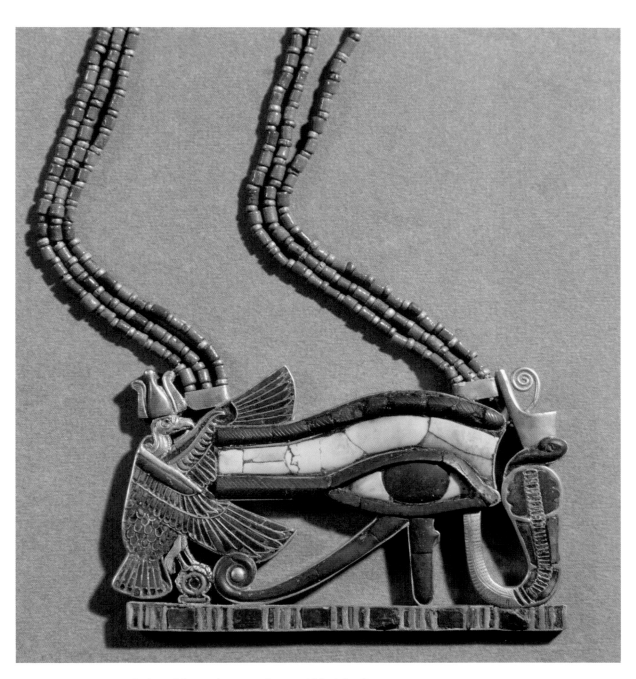

Fig.109: Gold pendant in the form of the eye of Horus (Udjat) set with lapis lazuli,
stone and glass. The bead necklace is in glazed composition (faience).
From the Tomb of Tutankhamen, Egyptian, co 1325 BC.
© Werner Forman/CORBIS

We met an Egyptian faience collar earlier in fig.103, an example dating to around 2000 BC. This one in fig.110 some six and a half centuries later, shows the enormous advances made in the production of faience in bright colours and of uniform quality.

This necklace comes from the site of Tel el Amarna, the capital of Egypt's 'heretic' king Akhenaten, who ruled in the mid fourteenth century BC. Excavations are Amarna have revealed considerable signs of faience manufacture, including little baked clay moulds for the production of components just like these.

The individual components here take the form of yellow mandrake fruit (upper row), green leaves of the date palm (middle row) and subtle yellow, white and mauve-blue lotus petals (bottom row). The terminals take the form of lotus flowers, a common terminal on collars of this type. The terminals have the separate colours inlaid, a technique that closely allies the technique with later enamel work. This raises the question as to why the Egyptians did not enamel on gold – by this period they had ample experience in both fine gold working and glass and glaze production. The answer might be a rather mundane practical one. The Egyptians at this period do not seem to have paid much heed to the purity of gold alloys and made no obvious attempts to refine them. This meant that the melting temperatures of the gold jewellery components were too low to permit enamelling, for the solder, if not the gold itself, would melt at about the same temperature as the enamel.

The Later Periods

Thanks to the Greek historians, who recorded something of the ancient Egyptians own view of their past, Egyptologists subdivide almost two and a half millennia of Egypt's history into 30 Dynasties. These dynasties, of varying lengths and with varyingly verified kings names and dates, are also grouped into longer periods. The three 'grandest' periods are the so-called Old Kingdom, the time of the building of the great pyramids; the Middle Kingdom, with great kings like Sesostris whose pendant was described above (fig.105); and the New Kingdom, with such justly famous kings as Rameses the Great and the most fortuitously famous one – Tutankhamen. The interludes between and following these periods are referred to as the First, Second

and Third Intermediate Periods and in older Egyptological view were essentially periods of supposed governmental fragmentation or political chaos or, put simply, were devoid of interesting history or remains.

However, archaeology is an unpredictable science, and the 'uninteresting' Third Intermediate was transformed into one of the most chronologically intriguing and archaeologically rich periods with the discover of the royal burials of this period at Tanis, far to the North in Egypt in the Nile Delta in the 1930s. These burials included a vast array of magnificent jewellery – and even gold death masks – some of exquisite workmanship and design. Of the kings buried here was Psusennes I who reigned in about 1040-993 B.C. The gold necklace in fig.111 is from his tomb. It has been chosen because it is in gold alone – its lacks the polychrome stone inlays that characterises so much Egyptian gold. The trapezoidal plaque at the base bears a hieroglyphic inscription with the name of the king.

In ancient Egypt the falcon represented the sun. The falcon god Horus was one of the major deities and his eye alone was a powerful amulet – we saw it carried by a diminutive god Thoth earlier and forming one of Tutankhamen's striking pendants and (figs.16 and 109). Representations of the falcon, as here with wings outstretched, were probably predominantly if not entirely funerary ornaments that were placed on the mummy at the time of burial. The falcon's head, though formed in sheet gold, is on the underside of the ornament and the viewer is just confronted by the back. This might be thought strange, but the falcon was hovering over and watching over the mummy, it had to face downwards.

It is not easy to date this object. It might be as early as the sixth century BC, when the Persians invaded Egypt, or a few centuries later, even after Alexander the Great's conquest of the country in 332 BC. It is true that following Alexander conquest of Egypt, the Egyptian jewellery became almost totally Hellenised, but the traditional Egyptian jewellery forms, such as this falcon, did linger on in temples and in funerary contexts.

The feathers on this falcon are delineated in narrow gold strips forming cells that are inlaid in glass. The glass was cut to fit the settings, not fused in place as enamel.

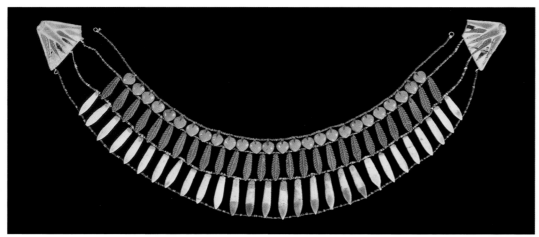

Fig.110: Broad collar in glazed composition ('faience'). From Amarna, Egypt, ca. 1350 BC. (British Museum)
© Copyright the Trustees of The British Museum

Fig.111: Gold collar with a pendant bearing the titles of the pharaoh Psusennes I. Tanis, Egypt gold, ca 1000 BC. (Egyptian Museum, Cairo)
© Sandro Vannini/CORBIS

Fig.112: Gold amulet in the form of a falcon inlaid in coloured glass. Egypt, ca 600 - 200 BC. (British Museum)
© Copyright the Trustees of The British Museum

2
The Rise of
European Jewellery

Fig.113: Gold pectoral showing a deity or ruler grasping two waterfowl, with snakes and stylised lotus flowers. Found on the Island of Aegina, Greece, ca 1700-1500 BC. (British Museum)
© Copyright the Trustees of The British Museum

2

Greece

H aving just encountered the Greeks under Alexander the Great in Egypt, it is time to backtrack and look at the development of jewellery within Greek lands themselves. Our view of the history of Greek jewellery is often so drawn by the spectacular treasures from Mycenae and the ornaments of Classical and Hellenistic times, that we can forget that the Greek jewellery can be traced back many centuries earlier and, indeed, has provided a few sparse examples of some of the earliest gold jewellery from anywhere in the ancient Old World.

Once into the second millennium BC, the Greek jewellery-making spotlight moves to Crete where the Minoan culture produced some remarkable goldwork, including some highly sophisticated granulation that can best be compared to jewellery from Syrian and Mesopotamian finds. The finest Minoan goldwork dates to the seventeenth to sixteenth centuries BC. Examples include the amazing hornet or bee pendant from Mallia, Crete (fig.115), and the various gold pieces making up the so-called Aegina treasure which includes the large pendant shown opposite.

The Aegina Treasure is a group of jewellery, now in the British Museum London. It is remarkable both for the gold objects contained within the hoard and its recent history. The hoard, said to be from the Greek Island of Aegina, was offered to the British Museum in 1891 and purchased the following year. There was no clear information about the circumstances of the find, but there was the rumour that the gold came from a Mycenaean tomb or tombs on Aegina. The seller's connection with a sponge-dealing company led to the more recent suggestion that the treasure was actually from Crete and had been smuggled by sponge divers to Aegina. Certainly the gold appears more Minoan Cretan than Mycenaean, but there is really little evidence to substantiate this ingenious theory.

The Aegina Treasure epitomises many of the difficulties encountered in archaeology in general and jewellery history in particular. Circumstances of discovery are often, at best, circumstantial and seldom is there clear evidence for provenance or chronology. In the case of the Aegina treasure it is unlikely that we will ever know the truth for certain, and so, like many other objects in museums, we must make of it what we can, based on its own merits and the parallels we can find for its form and construction.

The pendant shown here show a male figure who grasps a large bird, perhaps a goose, in each hand while flanked by lotus flowers. Possibly, he is standing in a boat, a suggestion made tenable by the somewhat similar depictions in Egyptian wall paintings. As this suggests, there is something Egyptianlike about the design, but the lack of inlaid stones would be unexpected in Egyptian jewellery and the back of the figure is simply a flat sheet of gold. The reverse of Egyptian figural jewellery characteristically mirrors the design on the front. This type of symmetrical figural composition is, however, matched in Cretan jewellery, such as the famous bee or hornet pendant from near Mallia, Crete (fig.115). Perhaps the best we can say is that the Aegina pendant is Egyptianising, but not Egyptian, and has its closest parallels in Minoan Cretan goldwork dating to somewhere between about 1700 and 1500 BC.

Shown here (fig.114) is one pair of earrings from two very similar pairs that, like the pendant, formed part of the so-called Aegina Treasure. They are described as earrings, although it is by no means certainly their original purpose. The chain pendants and little birds look wonderful when splayed out like a dead butterfly for modern photography or display, but it is hard to see how these ornaments could be worn in life without the pendants hanging in a tangled clump.

The ornaments each appear to depict a dog flanked by monkeys and they have a fringe of chain pendants terminating in small birds, probably intended as owls. The pendants also incorporate small carnelian beads.

The basic penannular form and double-sided nature of these earrings recall Mycenaean examples, but the dogs can be most closely matched with a gold pendant recently excavated by Austrian archaeologists at Tell el-Daba, ancient Avaris, in the Egyptian Delta. This has confronted winged griffins with falcon

heads. Tell el-Daba is also well known for its amazing Minoan style wall paintings. Symmetrically paired dogs are also seen in slightly later Mycenaean Greek gold jewellery, but their significance is unknown.

The gold hornet, or bee – people still debate the identity – pendant from Malia, Crete, is one of the great masterpieces of Bronze Age gold jewellery (fig.115). It dates to around the seventeenth century BC. The precision of the central granulated 'nest' is remarkable and must surely be related to the domes of granules we encounter in gold jewellery of this period from Western Asia. The notched borders on the wings match the decorative strips on some of the gold jewellery from Troy.

As with many 'iconic' ancient gold objects, the last word has by no means been written about this piece. First of all, we must surely suspect that the wings and circular pendant disks were originally inlaid with some coloured substance – perhaps a pigment mixture or even a primitive enamel. These flat, recessed areas hardly seem to have been intended to be plain gold. Then there is the problem of the surmounting skeleton sphere bead. This is remarkably crude compared with the pendant proper and microscopic examination shows that the interior little gold sphere bead is accidentally fused to one side. The suspicion might be that the piece was repaired in antiquity, not a unique occurrence. This suggestion – and this is only my opinion – is supported by the absence of antennae which a goldsmith would surely not have omitted on such finely depicted insects.

This beautiful little Minoan bee pendant in the British Museum warrants comparison with the Mallia hornets. It is also from Crete, dates to around 1700 – 1550 BC and, as with the bees, we might suspect that originally the wings and central circle here were inlaid.

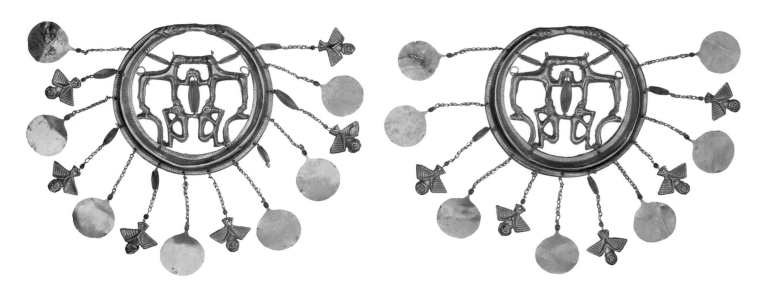

Fig.114: Gold ornaments, probably hoop earrings, with dogs, monkeys and owls.
The stone beads are carnelian. Found on the Island of Aegina, Greece, ca 1700-1500 BC (British Museum)
© Copyright the Trustees of The British Museum

The quality of the workmanship of Minoan gold jewellery such as this bee pendant and Mallia hornets raises the question as to where the original goldsmithing influences came from. Parallels to the goldwork from Troy was noted above, but there are also close links with jewellery of about 1700 BC from Syria and what is now Iraq.

If you look at the little horizontal wires down the 'tail' of the bee you will be able to see faint spiral lines on some of them. These are the result of the early wire making technique that was employed. A little strip of gold was twisted and then rolled between two flat surfaces to compact it into a fairly even round wire. This 'strip-twist' wire first appears soon after 2000 BC and, seemingly, in association with granulation. Early instances of this combination include jewellery from Troy.

Fig.115: Gold pendant in the form of confronted bees or hornets. Mallia, Crete, ca 1700 BC. (Archaeological Museum, Herakleon) Archaeological Receipts Fund

Fig.116: Gold pendant in the form of a bee or hornet. Minoan Crete, ca 1700-1550 BC. (British Museum)
© Copyright the Trustees of The British Museum

The end of the Minoan period coincided with the rise of the Mycenaean civilisation which spread over most of what is now Greece and reached its height around the fourteenth to thirteenth centuries BC. Some highly sophisticated goldwork was produced and large assemblages of Mycenaean goldwork have been found, much excavated by the nineteenth century German archaeologist Heinrich Schliemann who also discovered Troy. There are many objects in thin sheet gold, though with masterful embossed decoration, and also more massive pieces in the round, such as the signet rings on the bezel of which we see many aspects of Mycenaean life, perhaps predominantly religious.

The famous gold mask from Mycenaen Greece dates to around 1500 BC. It is shown here not simply because it is always chosen in books like this, but because it sums up some interesting points about jewellery history.

First of all, it was found by Schliemann, discoverer of Troy and just as the diadem from Troy in fig.94 was from 'Priam's treasure', so this mask became 'Agamemnon's Mask'. This desire to link major finds with major personalities from the past was a feature of nineteenth century archaeology – and of some tabloid archaeology to this day. One reason was that such personalisation of finds made good PR. It helped publicize the finds and it helped the fund excavations. The names, such as Priam and Agamemnon, were well known to an educated nineteenth century population raised on the Classics.

A second aspect of this famous mask is the controversy it has aroused among some more recent scholars. Is it exactly as it came out of the grave? Is the rather Victorian looking 'handlebar' moustache really all original, or was it embellished after discovery to some extent? Certainly it is not the only gold mask from Mycenae that appears to have undergone at least

some re-shaping after excavation. I must stress that this is not the place for me to take sides in any controversy, but simply to point out that old finds should not always been taken for granted – they need critical reconsideration at regular intervals, however great their 'iconic' status.

Such well known 'treasures' can be so familiar to us that we forget to subject them to the same archaeological and art historical scrutiny as humbler finds. If the closed eyes of this and some other Mycenaean masks are as originally intended, what does this tell us about Mycenaean funerary beliefs? Surely, the idea of a gold mask was to preserve the person as he or she looked in this life and keep them brisk and healthy in the next. We cannot imagine Tutankhamen's funerary mask (fig.100) with closed eyes.

This beautifully preserved Mycenaean gold ring of about 1500 BC was found in a chamber tomb at Mycenae in southern Greece – in what is now the northern Peloponnese. It has the characteristic slightly convex, oval bezel typical of its class. The scene shows a man standing before a holy tree or altar and a goat that is presumably intended for sacrifice. The hoop bears three rows of granulation – the outer two with smaller grains than the inner one, a subtle feature seen on other rings of this type.

A remarkable aspect of Mycenaean jewellery is the way in which it was technically ahead of its time. Rings, such as this one, have designs produced partly by punching, to produce the larger depressions, and partly by engraving, in which a sharp metal tool is used to gouge out gold to produce a pattern. This engraving technique, and another zigzag or 'tremulo' type of engraving that is also seen on some Mycenaean rings, have not been identified elsewhere in the Near East in the second millennium BC. This use of engraving might relate to a relatively early adoption of iron tools in the Mycenaean world.

Fig.118: A gold ring with bezel design showing a man before an altar with a sacrificial goat. Mycenae, Greece, ca 15th century BC. (National Museum of Athens) Archaeological Receipts Fund

Fig.117: The so-called Mask of Agamemnon, a gold funerary mask. Mycenae, Greece, ca 1500 BC. (National Museum, Athens) Archaeological Receipts Fund

The large gold hoop earrings are from a woman's burial at Mycenae and date to the sixteenth century BC. They are not obviously representational, although it might be presumptuous to apply the modern term 'abstract' to them. But they are exceptional for their period in design terms. Notice the lozenge-shape patterns of small gold granules. The sizes of the lozenges, and the individual little granules, diminish as the hoops taper towards the back. This deliberate use of graduated granulation is remarkable.

This raises all sorts of interesting questions about the concept of artistic innovation and responsibility with ancient jewellery in general, and origins with respect to these earrings in particular. We can recognise superb craftsmanship, of course, perfectly formed and joined components and the precise way in which a pattern or representation is realised. Also, we can often spot, and admire, individual instances of the maker's ingenuity – how they solved a particular constructional problem, or compensated for some shortfall or error. However, basic patterns are usually pretty run of the mill and any representational part will probably follow the more general artistic canons of the period. For example, if we consider the magnificent jewels from Tutankhamen's tomb illustrated earlier, we can imagine the exact design being formulated by the priests in the temple, following the strict Egyptian artistic traditions. One or more

goldsmiths would then have produced this to the best of their abilities. But with these earrings, there is no obvious canonical design and, surely, only a master goldsmith would have understood the potential to vary the size of grains along with the design. And this was a sophistication a century or so before granulation became common in mainland Greece. Possibly we are looking at an import from Minoan Crete – but what was imported, the earrings, the jeweller or a bride?

In the middle of the fifteenth century BC the Island of Crete was invaded by the Mycenaean Greeks who made Crete a part of the Mycenaean Empire. This beautiful little gold duck pendant – it is about 2.6 cm long (just over an inch) – dates from the fifteenth century BC and was excavated at Knossos in Crete, the city the Mycenaeans established there as their capital.

The duck is shown in a simple, though realistic form, with wings close to its sides and its beak held down against its body. This compactness provided not only a pleasing naturalistic form, but simplified manufacture. The pendant was made in sheet gold, in two halves, and the lines of even granulation run along slight hollows worked in the sheet gold. The lateral perforation across the breast shows that it was worn vertically and the position of the hole means that it must have hung with the head facing uppermost.

Fig.119: Gold earrings with granulated decoration. Mycenae, Greece, 16th century BC. (National Museum, Athens)
Archaeological Receipts Fund

Fig.120: Gold pendant in the form of a duck.
From Knossos, Crete, 15th century BC.
(Archaeological Museum, Herakleon)
Heraklion Archaeological Museum

The island of Cyprus in the Eastern Mediterranean has always been a cross-roads of cultures. Its strategic position within reach of Egypt, the Near East, Turkey and Greece has made it a major centre for maritime trade and something of a political football for the last five thousand years.

The earliest personal ornaments from the Island of Cyprus date back to the third or fourth millennium BC, and include small cruciform stone figures, but gold jewellery is rare until we begin to find stronger links with Egypt and then Crete and the Greek world after about 1500 BC. The relatively late use of gold on Cyprus may reflect the lack of exploited gold mines on the island. There are some gold deposits there, but little evidence for their mining in antiquity. But Cyprus was famous for its copper – indeed our word copper derives from the same source as the name for the island.

The strong Egyptian influence during what would have been the Egyptian New Kingdom, about 1500 – 1100 BC is reflected in the range of Egyptian objects found in Cyprus and the evidence for trade in the other direction – opium as well as copper. Characteristic local jewellery forms include hoop earrings with bull head pendants and sheet gold diadems with embossed decoration (fig.121). Sheet gold diadems are known in Mycenaean Greece and indeed these have similar, though often more precise, domes, S-spirals and other geometric designs, However, repetitive animal forms as shown here are very much a Cypriot characteristic. Here we see the repeated use of an S-spiral and also a seated, winged sphinx-like figure. The spiral impressions were probably made using a tool consisting of coiled wire stuck onto a piece of wood or metal. The presumably inadvertent rotation of the left-most sphinx suggests the use of a patterned punch, because this would be easy to rotate in the hand and the mistake not seen until too late. Such an error would be far less likely if the gold was being pressed over a die of some sort. We describe this little figure as a sphinx, but it bears no direct relationship with the Egyptian creature of the same name. Each end of the diadem has a pair of perforations for attachment.

After the thirteenth century BC, Mycenaean gold jewellery became simpler and with the final decline of the Mycenaean Empire around 1100 BC, gold jewellery became all but unknown in Greece. Greece had entered what is known as the Dark Age, although modern research suggests that this intermediate period may have been shorter and less dark that hitherto assumed. When, culturally speaking, the lights were switched on again around the ninth century BC, we begin to find some goldwork and major production began again in the eight century.

This heavy gold brooch (fig.122) is one of a pair from Greece that date from the eighth century BC. They are part of the collection brought back to Britain by Lord Elgin of 'Elgin Marbles' fame. The flat 'catch plates' are engraved with designs showing a deer on one side and a swastika emblem on the other – the swastika is a very ancient good luck symbol. The deer are in the elegant linear style characteristic of the period, similar forms can be seen on Greek pottery of the period.

Near Eastern influence is usually also assumed for the re-awaking of the Greek jewellery industry, but this is by no means certain. There also seem to be close links with Northern Italy and the Balkans. Modern research also tends to suggest some continuity between the late second millennium Mycenaean goldwork and the jewellery that reappears after the so-called Dark Age. In particular, the design on this brooch and its pair was engraved with a sharp metal tool for the lines and with zig-zag tremolo engraving as an outer border. As noted above, these two techniques are also found side-by-side in earlier Mycenaean Greek gold jewellery but are seemingly unknown in Near East goldwork. These brooches, and others like them, are also made in quite massive solid gold, each brooch wrought in one piece. This use of massive heavy gold is, by and large, more a European than Near Eastern characteristic.

Fig.121: Sheet gold diadem with embossed decoration. Cyprus, ca 14th century BC. (British Museum)
© Copyright the Trustees of The British Museum

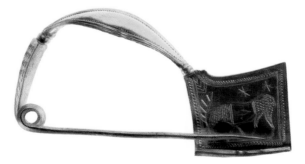

Fig.122: Gold brooch made in one piece, with a large catchplate engraved with a deer. Greek, 8th century BC. (British Museum)
© Copyright the Trustees of The British Museum

There is not a great deal of elaborate jewellery from what is now Greece that can be dated to the seventh century BC. The only major exception is that from the Island of Rhodes. The two commonest types of gold jewellery found on Rhodes are rosette shaped ornaments, probably originally parts of diadems, and large rectangular pendants. An elaborate example of the latter, from Camiros on Rhodes, is illustrated here. The Rhodian rosettes and rectangular pendants characteristically have figural ornament in the round and are decorated with granulation and filigree wirework. The rectangular pendants, like that shown here, often show a mistress of the animals figure, a winged female deity who is flanked by, or grasps, a pair of lions.

Greek gold jewellery had long included the masterful use of fine granulation and other decorative techniques, but this type of representational, figural design in the round has no precedents in Greek jewellery. However, it can be related to Near Eastern forms – reflecting the proximity of the island of Rhodes to southern Asia minor. In addition to pendants showing the Mistress of Animals, there are also examples showing a centaur – a man and horse combination.

These rectangular pendants could be worn, en-masse, probably from shoulder to shoulder. One magnificent set in the British Museum consist of seven such plaques, the two at each end surmounted by rosettes.

Greek gold jewellery from the sixth century BC was all but unknown until the excavation of burials at Sindos, near Thessaloniki in Northern Greece in the early 1980s. The jewellery found here shows a remarkable mastery of goldsmithing. Nevertheless, there are still many elements that hearken back to

Mycenaean Greek work, in terms of the repertoire of forms and techniques.

The Sindos necklet shown here dates from about 560 BC and includes some of the characteristic forms of the period including globular vessels and small cone shaped pendants. These latter, like the later Hellenistic Greek invented pyramid pendants on earrings, may represent corn baskets. The Sindos jewellery has much the same technology as the Rhodian, with fine granulation and twisted wire borders. There are also decorative wires of a type types disseminated around the Mediterranean by the Phoenicians in the seventh century B.C.

Naturalism is not common in jewellery in the round from Sindos, apart from the occasional human mask or the stylized snake heads that form the inevitable terminals to chains and bracelets. However, we often see animal and other figures embossed on thin gold foil – in styles and linear arrangements that compare closely to those painted on ceramics. The Sindos goldwork has close parallels in gold jewellery excavated in what was formerly Yugoslavia, another reminder that modern political boundaries are just that – modern.

There is a lack of polychromy in the Sindos goldwork. There was another century before enamel became common in Greece, and gemstones seem limited to amber beads and the occasional rock crystal pendant. European amber and rock crystal are both known in earlier Iron Age and Mycenaean Greek jewellery, but both all but disappeared from the Greek jewellery repertoire in the fifth century BC when the Greek traders concentrated more and more with the Persian Empire, including by then Egypt, and the northern coasts of the Black Sea.

Fig.123: Gold pectoral depicting the 'Mistress of the Animals'. Rhodes, Greece, 7th century BC.
(British Museum)
© Copyright the Trustees of The British Museum

Fig.124: Gold necklet of granulated beads and pendants. Sindos, Greece, 6th century BC.
(Archaeological Museum, Thessaloniki)
© Archaeological Receipts Fund

Prehistoric Europe

Goldsmithing technology tended to pass through three main evolutionary stages. In the earliest times, with the first few hesitant steps towards metalworking in general, gold ornaments were typically of thin, sometimes extremely thin, hammered gold foil. Shaping and decoration was minimal. Next, came the realisation that gold could be melted and poured into a mould to take on a desired shape. This stage often coincided with some experimentation with alloys, typically adding copper to reduce the temperature needed to melt gold and to improve the detail of the castings. Then, finally, came the development of better metal tools and thus the ability to shape and decorate the gold, and an understanding of soldering. This led to the ability to construct complex three-dimensional forms out of numerous individual components in sheet gold and wire.

The rate at which these goldworking stages were passed through varied from society to society. Thus, in the Ancient Near East, the first two of these stages had almost passed before the time of the great early city-based civilisations, such as those of Sumeria and Egypt. However the simple sheet and casting stages were still the norm in much of South America four thousand years later when the Europeans first arrived.

It is thus not surprising for the jewellery historian to find that the earliest gold jewellery from Europe north of the Alps, which dates to the later years of the third millennium BC, was largely limited to ornaments of hammered sheet gold. The crescent shaped, sheet gold collar we call a lunula is one of the most characteristic of Bronze Age Irish ornaments, it is seldom found elsewhere. The design might ultimately hearken back to bead collars.

The lunula shown here dates from about 2400 – 2000 BC. The designs on these ornaments, as with other Northern European goldwork of this period, were based on simple dots or lines, the latter were sometimes incised or scratched with a fine flint point, as here. This stone-tool incised decoration was a characteristic of much of the earliest goldwork from many parts of the world, including the earliest Egyptian gold seals, but then fell into disuse as hard metal tools superseded flint ones.

The sheer size and weight of some of the European Bronze Age gold ornaments are a sure indication that the makers knew how to melt together large quantities of gold nuggets and dust. Even if a single large gold ingot had been found, it would be too porous and too irregularly shaped to be hammered out into such form. So the goldsmith, whether he started with one or two large ingots, a pouch of gold dust or a handful of scrap, melted it all together to create a single, homogeneous ingot – probably often of rough bar-like form made by pouring the molten gold into grooves in wood or clay. This melting required a furnace, much as would have been used by a smith working copper or copper alloys. There is evidence to suggest that the lunulae were sometimes hammered from very regular gold bars after these had been hammered out from the ingots and then bent into penannular hoops. Study has shown that in at least come cases the thickness of the gold in these collars increases towards the end as the width narrows. This is exactly as expected if they were hammered from rod of regular cross section.

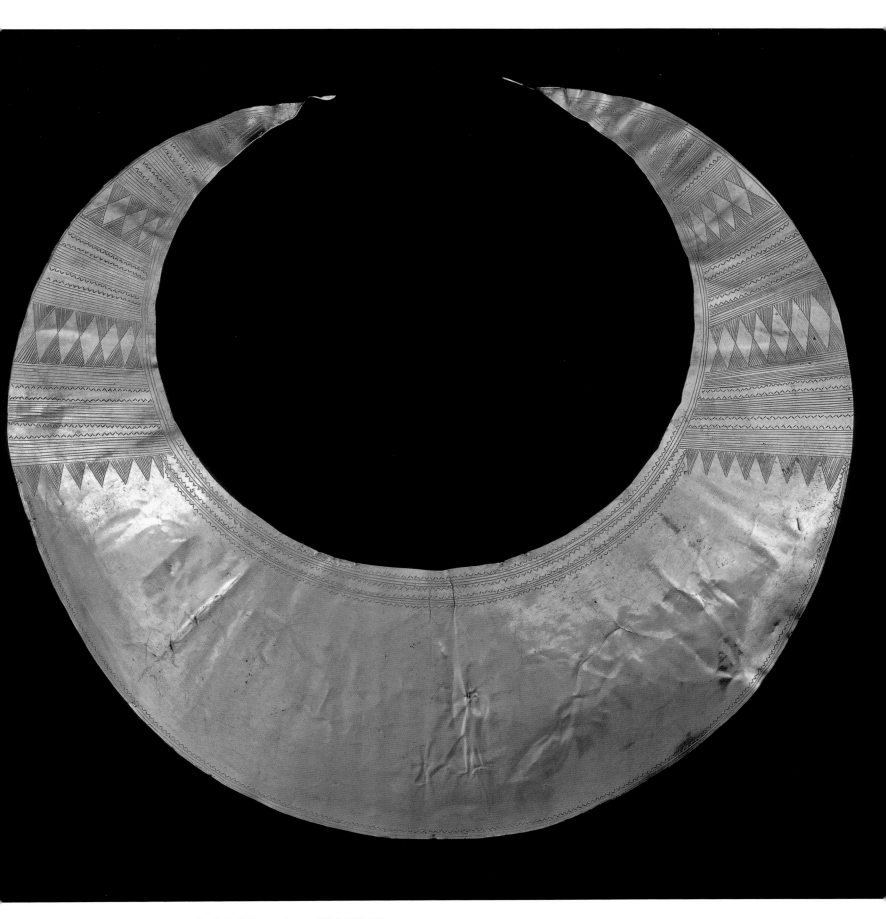

Fig.125: Gold 'lunula' or collar. Ireland, Early Bronze Age, ca 1800-1500 BC.
(British Museum)
© *Copyright the Trustees of The British Museum*

The Mold Cape (fig.126) is a particularly spectacular example of Northern European gold work of the early second millennium BC – contemporary with the jewellery of Middle Kingdom Egypt. Of similar date to the Mold Cape are these two gold armlets from Lockington in Leicestershire, UK. The armlets were found with the fragments of two pottery vessels. The attenuated repetitive shapes embossed along one of these armlets recall those on the Mold Cape – both in their overall production and in the use of finer delineating punching from the front. However, there is also a difference in approach. The Mold Cape was rendered wearable by attaching it to a leather or textile lining, thus keeping the thin and sharp sheet metal edge away from the wearers skin. The armlet on the right here shows a different means by which the goldsmith sought to ensure comfort in wear – the edges of the sheet gold are folded back on themselves to produce a smooth outer edge.

The other armlet has neither holes for the attachment of a liner, nor a turned back edge. However, the outermost corrugation is higher, meaning that the edge pressed down less on the flesh. This may or may not have been intentional. Indeed we do not know to what extent the use of the corrugated form for both armlets, or indeed for other early sheet gold objects including vessels, was a deliberate way in which to maximize strength and rigidity.

The jewellery in fig.127 presented no problem regarding strength or rigidity. The fragmentary pottery vessel was probably originally used for simple domestic purposes such as storing or serving food, but when, for whatever reason, the owner needed to conceal some two kilos of gold ornaments, the pot found a secondary use as a container for this buried treasure. This gold hoard dates back to between about 1100 and 800 BC and was found in the year 2000 at Milton Keynes, north Buckinghamshire, England.

It is a rare British find of gold with a pottery vessel from the Middle to Late Bronze Age and is thus a useful link between everyday and high-status possessions. Such associations also

reflect the greater care and greater skills of modern archaeology, the pot has been described as having had "the consistency of soggy biscuit" when it was found.

The ornaments consist of two massive gold neck rings (torcs), a heavy pair of bracelets and a single bracelet. The torcs both have similar linear chased decoration towards their terminals, but one has the added elaboration of a series of close parallel lines around its length produced by careful use of a narrow chisel tapped with a hammer, not engraving or incising.

The pair of bracelets is of massive gold of near-circular section with flaring ends. The single bracelet is of more oval section, with flattened sides. The sheer massiveness and weight of ornaments such as these raise questions as to their original use. Frequent wear seems unlikely and it is often assumed that there primary purpose might have been as a repository of wealth. This is quite possible; precious metal jewellery has served as portable wealth over much of the world for the last five thousand years.

The group of jewellery was found in what is now Hungary on the banks of the Danube and is generally thought to date to 1200 BC or perhaps a little earlier – although there are also parallels from a few centuries later. The group consists of a pair of brooches, two double spiral pendants and a larger quadruple spiral ornament that might originally have been worn as a pendant of some sort. The goldwork is of the simplest technique – gold cut, hammered and twisted to shape without soldering – but skillfully and thoughtfully realized. For example the two brooches are a mirrored pair, not identical, and the wires of the four spirals of the largest ornament taper gracefully.

Flat coils of hammered gold or copper alloy wire and rod are simple and thus a recurring form in jewellery. They form the basis of several classes of late Bronze Age and Early Iron Age jewellery from Eastern and Central Europe, as here, but they also occur earlier, as with the spirals from Ur (fig.92) and later in almost every corner of the world.

Fig.126: Two gold armlets with corrugated decoration. Lockington, Britain, ca 1800 - 1500 BC. (British Museum)
© Copyright the Trustees of The British Museum

The torc or rigid collar is one of the most characteristic of ancient European ornaments. We have already encountered the sheet gold lunula from Ireland and the massive torcs from Milton Keynes.

One of the most elaborate and intriguing Late Bronze Age examples is this collar from Sintra, near Lisbon in Portugal. It dates to about the seventh century BC. The main body of the collar is formed from three conjoined, tapering rods, but there is a hinged opening section at the back to allow it to be put on and off the neck, and two tulip-shaped projections on each side. The rods themselves have chased linear decoration at the front,

an indication that suitable hard copper alloy tools were now available. Despite the massiveness of the gold, the actual neck size is quite small and it may even have belonged to a child.

An intriguing feature is the opening ribbed at the back. This was adapted from a bracelet of well known type, but which slightly predates the manufacture of the torc. The re-use and recycling of gold has been a common feature of the goldsmith's workshop throughout history, but the direct incorporation of adapted earlier objects or components into later ornaments is rare.

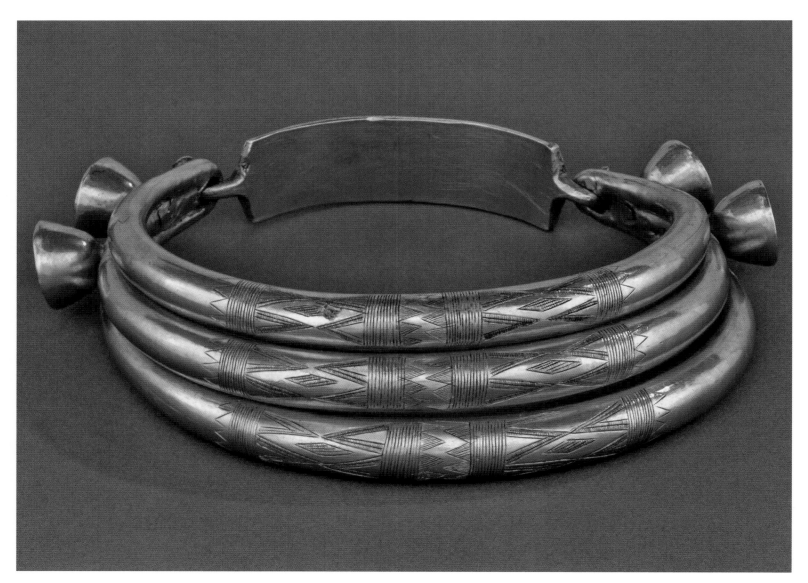

Fig.129: A gold torc incorporating an earlier bracelet as a closure. Sintra, Portugal,
ca 7th century BC. (British Museum)
© Copyright the Trustees of The British Museum

The gold jewellery of North West Europe remained something of a homogeneous tradition right up until the Roman armies advanced in the closing years of the first century BC. Casting had largely taken over from hammering for many of the ornaments, but fine soldering, including granulation and filigree was still almost unknown, as was the decorative use of set gemstones.

The largest known deposit of gold and silver ornaments of late Iron Age date from Northern Europe are the hoards – at least eleven in number – from Snettisham on the Norfolk coast of England. The hoards, dating back to about 70 BC and found over the years since 1948, include a large number of torcs, mostly of twisted rods, and in gold, silver and copper alloy. The reason for their concealment in this place is uncertain, but a small jewellers hoard from the same place dating from a couple of centuries later might indicate a long tradition of metalworking in this area.

Fig.130: Gold torcs from Hoard L as found. Snettisham, Britain, ca 70 BC. (British Museum)

Figs.130 and 131 show one group of gold torcs – so-called Hoard L – as found and one of the torcs in it. The most famous the gold torcs from Snettisham is that from Hoard E (fig.132). It consists of eight twisted gold strands, each itself made from eight wire twisted into a cable. The terminals were added to the ends by a technique termed 'casting-on' which involved applying melted gold over the wire terminals. This was a metalworking process known elsewhere in the ancient world, but which required very careful temperature control and skill.

The multi-part construction of gold jewellery using soldering only became common in Northern Europe in the later Iron Age and was rare before the Roman Period. This means that jewellery and jewellery components that relied on precision forming and soldered assembly such as chains and stone settings, were essentially a very Late Iron Age innovation in Europe. The lack of set stones in prehistoric European goldwork, as in the objects shown here, is particularly noteworthy. Beads were used, of course – they didn't require settings – but the polychrome magnificence of, say ancient Egyptian or Hellenistic Greek gold work is absent.

Fig.131: Large gold torc from Hoard L. Snettisham, Britain, ca 70 BC.
(British Museum)
© Copyright the Trustees of The British Museum

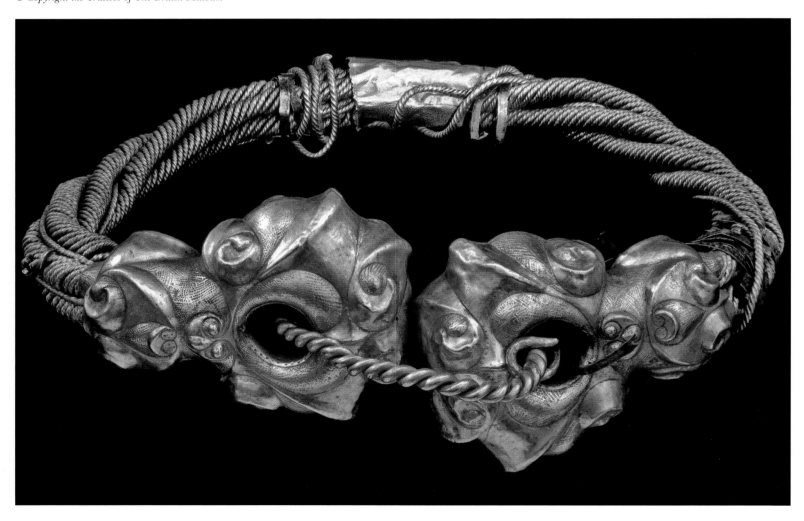

Fig.132: The 'Great Torc'. Snettisham, Britain, ca 70 BC. (British Museum)
© *Copyright the Trustees of The British Museum*

Etruscan

The earliest sophisticated jewellery from Northern Italy dates to about the ninth century BC and belongs to the Villanovan culture. It is thus contemporaneous with the jewellery that appears in Greece after the Dark Ages, and indeed has much in common with it. The jewellery from this and the following century are mainly from burials and are made of gold, copper alloys, some silver and amber. The latter was traded down from the Baltic, across the Alps and into Northern Italy and the Balkans.

The Vilanovans were succeeded by the Etruscans in the seventh century, though in what manner one replaced the other is still unknown. Unfortunately the Etruscans, though clearly literate with their own unique form of writing, have left no literary or historical works. Their main trading partners to the north, across the Alpine passes were, quite literally prehistoric ('before writing') and the contacts they had with the Near East cultures was probably mainly via the Phoenicians who, despite being the ancient Mediterranean sea traders par excellence, have also left no significant documentation.

Generally speaking, throughout some five thousand year history of sophisticated gold jewellery production, intricacy of workmanship has been inversely proportional to the amount of gold that goldsmith had at his disposal. In part, this is due to the constraints of the technology used – fine filigree and granulation work can only be applied to relatively flimsy sheet gold, not to more massive beaten gold surfaces. However, we also have the distinct impression that jewellers or their customers compensated for lack of gold by over-elaborating the decoration. The finest Etruscan jewellery is the ultimate example of this.

The decoration, if not the flimsiness, can be compared with jewellery produced in Greek lands in the seventh and sixth centuries BC. There is the same combination of granulation work with filigree in a variety of plain and decorative wires. This is not to necessarily suggest any direct links between the Greek and the Etruscan goldsmith, the same comment could be made about the decoration of gold jewellery of this same period from throughout the Phoenician world, from Spain to North Africa, and in Asia Minor. The major exception is goldwork from Egypt, which was then under Persian rule and which seem to have been largely isolated from the rest of the increasingly cosmopolitan Mediterranean jewellery network.

Representations of Etruscan jewellery wearers are uncommon. The particularly well-preserved Etruscan terracotta figurine here dates from the seventh or sixth century BC and clearly shows large hoop earrings and a shoulder clasp in wear. The clasp is a simpler version of the type shown in fig.134.

Fig.133: Terracotta figure showing a shoulder clasp in use. Italy, 7th - 6th century BC. (British Museum)
© Copyright the Trustees of The British Museum

Characteristics of seventh century Etruscan jewellery include use of representational forms and, most specifically, the use of intricate granulation. These characteristics strongly suggest that the impetus now came from the Eastern Mediterranean and in particular via the Phoenicians. This change in sources is also reflected in the lessening use of Northern European amber – though this didn't disappear altogether – and a move to extreme intricacy and almost fussiness in what was often extraordinarily thin gold foil.

The magnificent gold attachment plate with elaborately granulated lions, as shown here, dates to around 680-660 BC.

It was found in the Berdardini Tomb at Palestrina in 1876. The terracotta in fig.133 shows a fastener of this type in use to hold the cloak fastened to the shoulder.

Typical motifs of this period include lines or opposing arrangements of sheet gold animals, here lions, but also sometimes sphinxes or ducks. Some such figural forms might hearken back ultimately to Egyptian and Near Eastern origins, but via the Phoenicians. The small animal and human figures in the round on jewellery of this period are typically made in two thin sheet gold halves soldered together, the halves formed by impressing the gold foil over or into copper alloy dies.

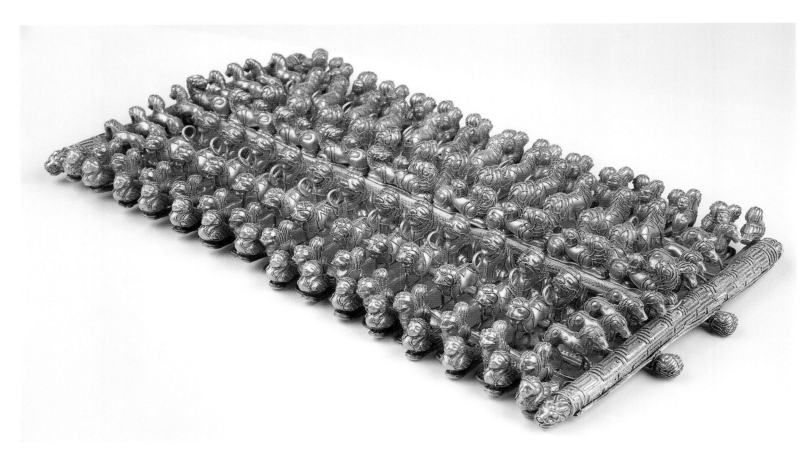

Fig.134: Elaborate gold shoulder clasp with granulated lions, horses and fantastic creatures. Italy, ca 680 - 660 BC. (Villa Giulia, Rome) Photo courtesy of Villa Giulia National Museum

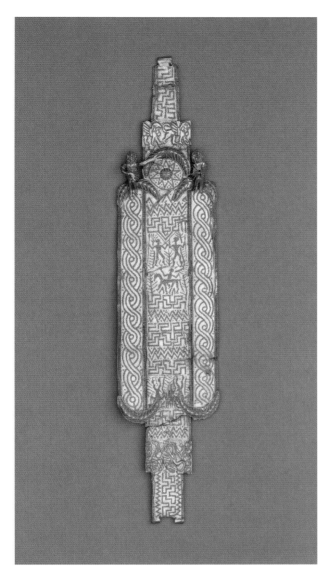
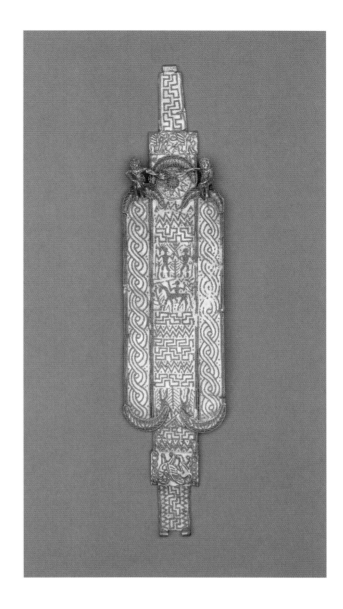

Fig.135/136: Pair of gold bracelets with elaborate granulation work.
Tarquinia, Italy, 7th century BC. (British Museum)
© Copyright the Trustees of The British Museum

The exquisite contrast in Etruscan jewellery between extreme lightness and extraordinarily intricate design is epitomised in this pair of bracelets from Tarquinia. They date from the seventh century BC and their basic form is matched in far simpler Etruscan embossed gold foil examples. The linear designs in miniscule granulation consist of geometric patterns and small figures including horsemen and are fine examples of the finest Etruscan granulation work. It is no wonder that 'Etruscan Granulation' is often considered the epitome of the ancient goldsmith's skills.

A characteristic of much of the earlier Etruscan jewellery, as here, is the lack of colour. Coloured gemstones are seldom found set in the gold until after the fifth century, from which time enamel also became common. Enamel, however, has often totally decomposed and disappeared during its long burial. We can also note that silver jewellery is commoner in Etruscan contexts than it is in Greek jewellery of the same period. This is somewhat strange because there ample supplies of silver within Greece itself.

Shown here is an Etruscan gold disk earring that dates to around 530 - 500 BC. It is said to have been found in Southern Italy, although it is clearly Etruscan work. The decoration is composed of a variety of types of decorative wire and granulation work. The rather monotonous filigree work is in various types of decorative wire and the object is probably a little too early in date to have originally been enamelled. The six little rosettes around the centre dome represent flowers of some type and they have centres made of circles of coiled wire, like tiny springs. These coiled circles are another characteristic that links Etruscan with Phoenician gold jewellery.

The central dome and band around it are of such fine granulation that they almost look like powder. This powder granulation is a hallmark of the finest Etruscan gold jewellery and despite concerted attempts, nineteenth century replicators such as Alessandro Castellani were unable to copy fully . As can be seen here, even the tiniest grains stand independent of their neighbours. The nineteenth century experimenters tried ever more sophisticated ways to divide and minimise the solder they used, but they still could not avoid flooding the tiny spheres. In fact the secret was quite simple. The grains were either fused in place without any solder – the work was simply carefully heated until their surface just began to melt and fused the grains in place – or a chemical mixture containing copper was used that in essence introduced just enough copper into the joint areas to fuse with the gold and join the parts.

There are some exceptionally fine Etruscan gold ornaments that we can date to around 500 BC, such as this magnificent pair of earrings from Cerveteri (fig.138). They are examples of a form of box-like earring called 'a baule' that seems ill-designed to hang well on an ear, and although a popular Etruscan form, it has no close parallels in other cultures.

Despite their intricate design, the earrings shown are each little more than 2 cm wide. Though complex, they, like the previous disk earring, reflect the move to greater simplicity and a more geometric and unimaginative repertoire of forms that characterizes later Etruscan goldwork. Like the disk, these earrings also include fine 'powder granulation' in the background. These earrings were in the Castellani collection and may have been among the tantalizing examples of ancient work that both spurred and frustrated the Castellanis in their attempts at replication.

Fig.137: A gold disk earring with intricate granulation and filigree. Italy, ca 530 - 500 BC. (British Museum)
© Copyright the Trustees of The British Museum

Surviving Etruscan gold jewellery is seemingly always from burials and, luckily for archaeology, the Etruscans set great store by the cult of the dead. Family prestige meant that the deceased required fine jewellery. Considering this, the extreme flimsiness of much ancient Etruscan goldwork might be taken to suggest that it was made for funerary use and never intended to be worn. Possibly some Etruscan jewellery was purely funerary, but Etruscan jewellery often has a practical feature that might indicate when wear was intended. The pins passing through gold hinge fittings, such as those with which the arching hoops on these earrings are attached, were commonly of silver not gold. This was because silver was harder and thus better wearing than gold. This silver has always largely corroded and in recent centuries dealers and collectors have often removed most traces of it by what can most charitably be described as enthusiastic cleaning. Incidentally, this use of silver hinge pins is one of the constructional features of Etruscan gold jewellery that suggests a Phoenician influence.

This is a ring from Chiusi in Northern Italy. The employment of colour in Etruscan jewellery grew from the fifth century onwards with more and more gemstones being used including banded agate, as here and carnelian. By the fourth century, when this ring was made, Etruscan jewellery had mostly lost its unique character and become largely indistinguishable from Classical and Early Hellenistic Greek.

The Etruscans became fine gem engravers and a common stone form was the scarab beetle shape we see here. This shape ultimately came from Egypt, but it came to the Etruscans via the Phoenicians who probably also sparked off the art of gem engraving itself. Here the scarab is in a naturally banded agate. It is also mounted in a way that derived from Egypt via the Phoenicians – as a freely rotating swivel.

The ring is relatively massive, compared to most Etruscan jewellery, and signs of wear can be readily seen, indicating that it was worn in life. It is something of a puzzle as to why these functional and relatively sturdy rings typically have soft gold wires supporting the swiveling gem, while the flimsy Etruscan earrings, as we have seen, usually had sturdy silver hinge wires.

Fig.138: A pair of gold earrings with intricate granulation and filigree. Cerveteri, Italy, ca 500 BC. (Villa Giulia, Rome) Photo courtesy of Villa Giulia National Museum

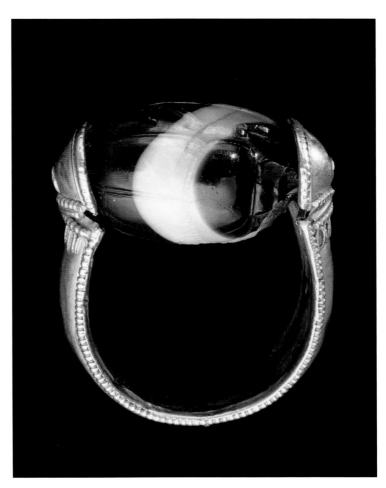

Fig.139: Gold and banded agate ring. Chiusi, Italy, 5th century BC. (British Museum)

The Greek world after 500 BC

During the sixth century BC, the Greek colonies in what is now Turkey began to rebel against Persian rule. The Athenians joined in and the Persians were thoroughly trounced at the battle of Marathon in 490 BC, when they eventually sought revenge on Athens. Marathon has been described as possibly the most important battle in Greek history, and certainly the confidence and pride it afforded the Athenian city state laid the foundation for the rise of the golden Classical age, with its architecture, art, philosophy and mathematics. This was also a period of increasing exploration abroad for the Greeks. Colonisers, including jewellers, appeared in Southern Italy and in the Northern Black Sea, what is now the Ukraine, where there was access to gold and corn. This was the Classical Period, the hey-day of Greek Civilisation. The arts and philosophy flourished and the new naturalism we see in Classical Greek jewellery echoes the same naturalism that we see in Greek sculpture and architectural decoration.

Greek expansionism culminated in the conquests of Alexander of Macedon, in the latter part of the fourth century BC, ushering in what we term the Hellenistic Period. Alexander the Great is shown here in a Roman mosaic from Pompeii. Alexander's successes built on the economic rise of Macedonia under Alexander's father Philip II. While Philip of Macedon was held hostage by Greeks of Thebes in Boetia, he learned their military techniques and on his return to Macedonia, put them to use. He extended his country of Macedonia to the north and west, but wisely made a treaty with the more southerly Greeks. The Macedonian expansion brought the gold mines of mount Pangaeion under his control, providing a new source of wealth. Now a greater proportion of the Greek population could aspire to, and own, gold jewellery, and new forms and a new naturalism blossomed.

The human and animal forms that had increasingly been seen in Greek jewellery through the Iron Age, became a distinctive characteristic of Classical and Hellenistic jewellery. We now see a variety of figures that show in miniature the proportions and poses that mirror the development of naturalism in the larger-scale sculptural arts. A golden winged goddess, Nike, drives her speeding chariot or flies through the air, small naked figures of Eros dance, pluck at lyres or pour wine into cups. Remarkably, the representations exclude the Greek Pantheon of major deities, such as Zeus or Aphrodite. Such important deities really only begin to appear in jewellery – even in depictions on engraved ring-stones – in Roman times.

The animal forms in the jewellery include doves and lions, bulls and goats, though mostly their heads rather than whole bodies. The dove related to Aphrodite and the other beasts are mainly connected with the rites of Dionysus, reminding us that the choice of forms reflected underlying religious and superstitious beliefs – far more pervasive aspects of daily life then than now.

The jewellery that has survived from the Classical and Hellenistic periods is, like its predecessors, mainly from burials rather than the hoards buried for safekeeping. Hoards became more common in Later Roman and Post-Roman times. Greek burials were mainly cremations, but although some gold jewellery shows signs of having been through a fire, most is still unscathed, even delicate gold foil wreaths, so we might suspect that these were placed on the ashes at the time of interment. The burial of jewellery with the dead might seem extraordinarily wasteful, but it had been a long tradition in Greece as well as elsewhere. Actual examples, such as the amazing jewellery found in Mycenaean tombs, can be supplemented by documentary references, in a speech made by Euripides in the fifth century BC: 'Accept these gifts to deck her body, bury them with her'. It was a matter of balance and belief – the need for jewellery in the next world outweighed any desire to retain it for this. It is true that some flimsy jewellery was made especially for burial, but it is still not certain whether this was symbolic funerary gifts from mourners, a substitute for more massive day-to-day jewellery that the heirs had set their mind on retaining, or was a humble accompaniment to a deceased too poor for the real thing in life.

Of course, jewellery forms were not stagnant although styles developed far more slowly then than in our modern, more fashion-conscious times. The early Hellenistic gold jewellery, from a generation or so either side of 300 BC, still retains something of the sturdy Classical Greek styles. Mid- to late-Hellenistic jewellery , that is from the third to first centuries BC, is characterised by a tendency towards more delicate, intricate, work with a greater reliance on coloured stones and contrasting shapes and forms. This trend to the 'Hellenistic baroque' is evident right across the empire, and lingered on in the Eastern Mediterranean long after starker Roman forms had prevailed further west.

Gold jewellery after Alexander tends to show more miniscule precision than its Classical precedents, but the most noticeable change is in the use of coloured gemstones and pearls. The range of Alexander's conquests not only brought almost every known gold mining region of the ancient world under Greek control, it also stimulated the trade that began to bring other gem materials to the Hellenistic Greek world. Colour had not been absent in Greek gold jewellery, but had tended to be limited to a few materials, noticeably amber in Mycenaean and Iron Age Greek jewellery and enamel, which came into prominence after about 500 BC.

Fig.140: Detail of a Roman mosaic showing Alexander the Great at the Battle of Issus.
From the House of the Faun, Pompeii, Italy, 1st century AD.
(National Museum, Naples)
© Mimmo Jodice/CORBIS

After Alexander the Great's expeditions to the east, pearls from the Persian Gulf and India began to reach the Mediterranean and as did bright red garnets from India and green emeralds from the mines in Egypt.

This change in fashion might suggest that the Greeks embraced the love of coloured gems that had long been a characteristic of Egyptian and Persian jewellery. However, there is a major difference. By and large, the Egyptians, Persians and other Western Asiatic cultures had used opaque gem materials in their jewellery, much like blocks of pigment. The garnets and emeralds loved by the Hellenistic Greeks were brighter and transparent – properties that were still not best set off by their enclosed settings, but which gave a very different appearance to jewellery. Garnets are all but absent in gold jewellery before Alexander and the same is true of emeralds, even though these were found in Egypt in some abundance, albeit in a poorish quality. In part we might attribute this move to transparency as simply a change in taste, but is also worth noting that the gem materials employed in jewellery before about 500 BC were almost entirely limited to those that could be cut and polished, or drilled, with that most abundant of abrasives – sand. Both garnet and emerald are harder and required emery or diamond to work them. The evidence we have, both from literary sources and derived from microscopic studies of drill holes, suggests that diamonds chips were being used to drill harder stone beads by about 500 BC.

The situation with pearls is slightly more bewildering, since pearls are not only relatively soft, but come straight from the oyster in a form that requires no polishing – just drilling. One of the earliest surviving examples of pearl jewellery is a small length of pearls with gold beads and a small gold bell pendant that was excavated at Parsargadae in what is now Iran. This is part of a hoard of jewellery that may well have been concealed to hide it from Alexander the Great's advancing army in 331 BC.

The Hellenistic period saw a greatly increased fashion for signet ownership by private people. When all-gold or stone-set rings were used as signets, the sealing material would have been clay or wax. Wax was probably more usual for non-mundane purposes. The Greek historian Herodotus referred to wax seals and the Roman writer Ovid noted the practice of licking the stone in a ring to prevent it sticking to the wax – a procedure still sometimes seen when dealers make impressions from old intaglios. We can note that the lead sealings often encountered, particularly in Roman commercial contexts, would have been made with iron seals. Molten lead sticks to copper or silver and, as jewellers know all to well, causes terrible problems when it comes into contact with gold.

Not all rings, whether stone-set or all metal, that have engraved designs were used for sealing. Some were just ornamental or amuletic. Functional seals were usually accurately engraved in reverse – so the design would come out the right way round when impressed.

This pair of earrings (fig.141) hails from Eritrea in Greece and dates from about the mid-fifth century BC. The fairly flat applied filigree (wire work) decoration can be compared with that on the sixth century gold jewellery from Sindos (fig.124). The upper rosette on each earring still bears traces of the original enamel. Most of the enamel is retained in the smaller petals of the rosettes, but the large petals were probably also enamelled originally. Larger expanses of enamel were more prone to flaking off with time – not the least because the strains set up between the gold and enamel as it cooled after firing were greater. Enamel had occurred in Bronze Age Mycenaean goldwork, but it only became common from about the fifth century onwards.

The small figures on these earrings show a siren, a human headed bird. The sirens are perched on a boat-shaped form that was to become a very common later Classical and Hellenistic shape. Below hang simple loop-in-loop chains with shell pendants, the shells presumably having fertility significance.

Another similar pair of earrings from Eritrea, now in Athens, and which might be from the same workshop, have a central figure, the sea nymph Thetis in flight while Peleus tries in vain to hold her still, largely thwarted by the lions and snakes that attack him.

Fig.141: A pair of gold rosette and boat earrings with small figures of sirens. Greece, mid-5th century BC. (British Museum)
© *Copyright the Trustees of The British Museum*

Fig.142: Gold necklace with lion-head terminals and Herakles knot centrepiece. Sedes, Greece, ca 300 BC. (Archaeological Museum, Thessaloniki)
© Archaeological Receipts Fund

This gold necklace, excavated at Sedes (modern Thermi, near Thessalonica in Northern Greece) is of a well known early Hellenistic type. The heads of lions and other Dionysiac animals were the most usual terminals for earrings and necklets, and typically they had conical 'collars' decorated with filigree. The chain is a form of loop-in-loop chain, the characteristic jewellery chain type from the ancient world. The centrepiece here is a 'Herakles' knot, our reef knot, a common centrepiece on such ornaments with strong fertility significance, just as it had millennia earlier in Egypt. The symmetrical knot with its central aperture was most commonly set with blood red garnets and often had small figures of Eros or Dionysus issuing from between its folds, fertility symbolism that needs no further explanation here.

Despite the grander and even more photogenic garnet-set examples in various museum collections, this relatively humble example has been chosen for a reason. The knot itself it too shallow to allow garnets to be set within its margins, but it is unlikely that it was originally plain gold. We might expect red enamel because such knots were almost invariably red. However, the manufacture of red enamel presented an insurmountable difficulty at that period. But, there was an alternative that has only recently been recognised. Where the Greek jeweller required a red filling substance, but was unable to use enamel, he applied a red pigment – cinnabar, a mercury sulphide. This use of pigment in gold has been noted at about this period all around the Mediterranean, from Phoenician Spain to the Northern black sea. Unfortunately we cannot be sure if this necklet originally had such pigment inlay. Inlays of this type are very prone to decomposition and disappearance during burial, and in addition their ancient use has only recently been recognised and over-zealous conservators and collectors may well have been cleaning off all traces of it for centuries.

The second half of the Hellenistic period showed a more flamboyant jewellery style that is described as the Hellenistic Baroque. There was both an increased love of coloured precious stones and a fashion to set them more prominently. The ring here from Eretria in Greece is an example of a class of ring where the bezel is joined in an articulated manner to the hoop. It dates from the second to first century BC. The tiered bezel is a typical later Hellenistic form and a frequent target for forgers.

The hoop and bezel are joined by what are essentially hinge fasteners with lateral gold wire pegs. The pegs here extend from the sides of the hinges and probably originally bore pearls on their extremities. The ends of the pegs were carefully turned over to secure the pearls.

The emerald, of poor quality by modern jewellery standards, probably came from the mines in the Eastern Desert of Egypt, which were first worked during the Hellenistic Period. Emeralds were hard to polish and this one still retains much of its original hexagonal crystal form.

The hoop is set with other gems, and the one set at the back of the hoop is particularly noteworthy. Such diminutive stones on the hoop reverse crop up at various times and places in antiquity – best known being some later Medieval Islamic rings.

Fig.143: A gold and emerald ring. Eritrea, Greece, 2nd - 1st century BC. (National Museum, Athens)
© Archaeological Receipts Fund

The three rings shown here are all date from the early third century BC and were excavated at Aiginio in Greece. The bright red garnet set in one ring is unengraved (fig.144), but it might be wrong to call it wholly decorative. Garnets had fertility and other significance. This, ring although undoubtedly decorative, probably also had deeper meaning for its wearer.

This type of ring with a plain, polished oval garnet within a flat gold surround is well known, from Asia Minor as well as Greece. The garnets in Hellenistic jewellery probably came in the main from India.

The all-gold ring (fig.145) from Aiginio has a flat circular bezel that bears a diminutive figure of what appears to be the goddess of victory, Nike, naked and holding a victor's wreath. However, it is just possible that Aphrodite's attendant Eros was intended, as he was characteristically shown naked and often has fairly feminine proportions. Rings with expansive flat bezels and shallow designs are unlikely to have been primarily used as signets.

Although often described as 'cast', the solid and often quite massive Hellenistic gold and stone-set signet rings were actually carefully hammered from gold. This required extraordinary skill – indeed an elegant but plain solid all gold ring, as this example, probably required far more care than a seemingly complex jewel such as an Hellenistic earring. The latter was made up from numerous, often literally hundreds, of small separate components. These required skill to form, position and join, but such a piece-meal mode of assembly was far more forgiving than the shaping of a single piece of gold. We sometimes find similar ring forms in iron, and it is sobering to realise that the finer examples of such 'base metal' ornaments required even more skill than many a gold example.

The third ring from Aiginio (fig.146) is of a type that represents something of a puzzle. It has a totally plain, flat bezel. Rings of this type are too common from the Hellenistic world to represent unfinished rings, besides some have indications of wear. It seems unlikely that the bezels were originally painted with a design in red or black pigment, and perhaps the idea was simply a flat mirror-like surface that would reflect evil off them – there are more recent parallels for just this sort of mirror jewel. Nevertheless, flat expanses of undecorated gold are not one of the characteristics that come to mind when we think of Hellenistic gold jewellery.

Fig.144: A gold ring set with an unengraved garnet. Aiginio, Greece, early 3rd century BC. (National Museum, Athens) © Archaeological Receipts Fund

Fig.145: A gold ring engraved with a small figure of Nike. Aiginio, Greece, early 3rd century BC. © Archaeological Receipts Fund

Fig.146: A gold ring with plain bezel. Aiginio, Greece, early 3rd century BC. (National Museum, Athens) © Archaeological Receipts Fund

As we noted above, from the second century onwards Hellenistic Greek jewellery became successively flimsier and more ornate and the repertoire of animal motifs increased, so that a collection of Hellenistic jewellery can offer something of a mystical menagerie tour. However, not all amuletic or protective forms were animal or deity figures or attributes. The necklet here (fig.147), from Euboea in Greece, is of the later Hellenistic period and shows the expected use of bright red garnets and enamel. Possibly, of course, not all the pendants belonged on the same necklet originally – threads seldom survive in burials – but the range of types are interesting.

Perhaps most remarkable are the bright red heart-shaped garnets in gold mounts. This garnet form is well known in late Hellenistic jewellery and the overall shape is probably that of a vine or ivy leaf – a fertility symbol. They are the same form and colour as a modern 'Valentine' heart, although the latter is always supposed to be a far more recent invention. The two more attenuated pear-shape pendants appear to be set with bright red carnelians rather than garnets.

The central crescent pendant is a type met with far earlier in the Near East and which continued into Roman and later times – a Roman example is seen in wear in fig.148. The crescent had fertility symbolism and probably by this period always represented the crescent moon, rather than cow horns. The cow had fertility significance, as did the twenty-eight day cycle of the moon.

The tubular pendant is an amulet case, the Hellenistic version of the pendants already encountered in Phoenician jewellery (fig.99). The type, as here, continued into Roman, Byzantine and Islamic times. The two strangest pendants are those where some other object is bound up in gold wire. The object in one of those here is a piece of glass molded in the shape of a knuckle bone (second from top on left). Knuckle bones were used like dice for gambling, and like all gambling paraphernalia over the centuries have been treated as lucky or protective charms – like the furry dice exhibited by some drivers. The other object bundled up in gold wire is of uncertain nature.

Fig.147: A necklace with a variety of pendant types. Vathia, Greece,
2nd - 1st century BC. (National Museum, Athens)
© Archaeological Receipts Fund

Roman

After the baroque and often flimsy later Hellenistic jewellery, the more substantial, geometric forms of Roman jewellery are a remarkable contrast. Of course, fashions did not change in an instant and in some parts of the Empire, particularly the East, late Hellenistic rather baroque taste prevailed for centuries. However, Roman jewellery from Italy itself and from most of Europe is marked by a lack of naturalistic forms, The simple shapes, often made of few separate components unlike the intricate and multi-part Hellenistic ornaments, reveal a no nonsense approach to construction. Perhaps we might see this as jewellery more befitting the road builders and engineers of Rome than the artists and poets of Athens. Nevertheless, as documentary evidence indicates, many of the goldsmiths working throughout the Roman Empire were Greeks.

The image of a jewellery wearer shown here (fig.147) is a funerary portrait inserted in the mummy wrappings of a woman who died in Egypt in the first century AD. She wears a pair of gold dome earrings, a type well known from Egypt and Italy at this period, and a gold chain necklet with a small crescent pendant. Crescent pendants of this type are known from surviving examples, from representations such as this one and from documents such as dowry lists. The evidence indicates that moon crescent pendants of this type were linked with the Egyptian goddess Isis and were no doubt intended to provide her protection and blessing, perhaps predominantly as fertility charms – the link with the lunar cycle being self evident. Little crescents could be given to girls when still very young and were very important possessions. When there is only a single gold ornament recorded in a Roman-Egyptian woman's dowry, it was almost inevitably a crescent of this type.

Much of the ancient Roman gold that has survived to this day has done so because it was hidden during the owner's lifetime for security reasons. These were the days before banks and safes. In times of war or unrest, or simply when there was wariness of neighbours or the taxman, careful concealment of valuables was part of life.

Numerous buried hoards have been found over the years from across the Roman Empire and some spectacular Roman treasures. There are also numerous references to such hoards. We have the written record of some gold jewellery, probably been part of a dowry, hidden in box in the wall of a small house in Egypt and unworn for forty three years before allegedly being stolen by a builder in AD 28. Then there are the debates among Roman legal experts as to who was rightful owner of unclaimed buried treasure, finder or land owner? Remarkably, these debates form the basis for the Treasure Laws of England and Wales under which the ownership of Roman and other old precious metal objects found in the ground is still decided.

Alexander's conquests of Egypt and the East around 300 BC had been largely responsible for introducing the Mediterranean world to gemstones, emeralds and pearls in particular. The fashion continued in Roman times, and indeed sensible Romans decried the huge sums of gold that flowed out to the East to pay for the non-necessities of life. Earrings were a particular target for ridicule – a man in Petronuis's Satricon burdened with an earring-loving wife, said, "if I had a daughter, I'd cut her little ears off.'

At the very end of the second century AD, Tertullian of Carthage caustically observed that 'in the case of women every part of the body is weighted with gold'. The evidence of the surviving jewellery, and representations of it in wear, supports this. Later Roman jewellery tends to be more massive and more colourfully ostentatious than earlier Roman ornament. To a large extent this reflects the benefits accruing to an Empire that for more than two hundred years had ruled and exploited a large proportion of the then known world. But it was not simply a case of the rich getting richer, but also it was a case of the traditionally not-so-rich getting richer – the rise of an affluent middle class demanding the same trappings and rights as their social betters. Tertullian, an early Christian writer, was just one in a long line of those sober people who must have torn their hair out trying to stem the wearing of jewellery and other extravagancies, but he was fighting human nature.

The expansion of a jewellery-loving public is revealed even in the strict formalities of Roman law. In early Roman times, just before the time of Christ, the wearing of a gold signet ring was a privilege granted only to those of the highest military rank. By the end of the second century AD the emperor had pronounced that all soldiers might wear such rings and a century later a law was passed to allow the same for `even women'.

The two most obvious indications of the increased love of opulent jewellery in the later Roman Period are the increased use of coloured gemstones and a type of delicate pierced work, like a golden interpretation of the finest lacework (for example, figs.163 and 165). The Roman period saw the rise of more direct sea trade with Sri Lanka and thus access to sapphires of the subtlest pale blue. These were not only of a more striking colour than the darkish earlier Roman sapphires, but were generally far larger. We will meet their characteristic pear-shape form in jewellery from the Late Roman and Early Byzantine worlds.

Fig.148: Funerary portrait of a woman showing jewellery in wear.
Roman period from Egypt, ca AD 55 - 70. (British Museum)
© Copyright the Trustees of The British Museum

On the afternoon of August 24th AD 79, the attention of the Roman naval commander and naturalist Pliny was drawn to a fiery cloud of ash blasting high up above a mountain south of where he sat writing in the Bay of Naples, Italy. His 'Scholarly acumen saw at once that it was important enough for a closer inspection' – as his nephew later wrote. But what began as a scientific venture changed to a tragedy when Pliny collapsed and died, choking on the dense sulphurous fumes. His body was found two days later 'looking more like sleep than death.' Ironically, the tragedy that killed Pliny, the writer who told us more about Roman period jewellery materials than any of his contemporaries, also provided us with the jewellery. That volcanic eruption of Vesuvius claimed many lives that day, burying whole communities such as Pompeii and Herculaneum under several metres of ash. Among these bodies was a wealth of jewellery, some still in position on fingers, arms and around necks, other in bags or boxes grabbed by their owners in their attempts to reach safety (fig.109). Seldom has the archaeologist or jewellery historian had such a representative assemblage of the jewellery worn by the living in one area at one time.

The sheer quantity of Roman jewellery from Pompeii and neighbouring sites can blind us to the important fact that if Vesuvius had not erupted and preserved this jewellery, we would have almost no surviving examples of Roman jewellery of this period from Italy. Gold jewellery is almost unknown from Roman burials of the first and early second century AD. In part, this probably reflects an earlier Roman law that banned the burial of any gold with the dead other than deceased's dental work. (Actual human remains with teeth held in place with gold wires and strips have survived.). But we can also understand the state's sensible desire to keep wealth in circulation not interred with the dead. This was a sentiment in line with no-nonsense Roman thought, but in contrast to most of the earlier civilisations where economic practicalities in this life could play second fiddle to the necessities of the next.

Fig.149: Gem-set gold rings still encircle the finger of a partially excavated skeleton. Herculaneum (Ercolano), Italy, buried AD 79
© Jonathan Blair / CORBIS

The bracelet shown here (fig.150) consists of a series of linked, paired sheet gold hemispheres and is a well-known and characteristic 'Pompeian' type. Like much Roman jewellery, it lacks any obvious figural or symbolic form. Several examples have survived from the Pompeian region, but the type is very rare elsewhere in the Roman world. The only main exception being the few fragmentary examples that have been found in Egypt and which remain almost unpublished. This is a salutary lesson for jewellery historians in particular and archaeological distribution studies in general. If Vesuvius had not erupted that day, we would presumably consider this bracelet type rare but characteristically Romano-Egyptian.

Roman hollow sheet gold jewellery is often quite flimsy and so, like this bracelet type, was typically filled with sulphur to help prevent crushing in wear. Various other materials have been used for this purpose over the centuries, including pitch and resins, but sulphur served well since it could be melted and poured into place and then set hard without contraction.

The eruption of Vesuvius in AD 79 preserved for us more than just gold jewellery. It also preserved our best representation of Roman jewellers at work.

The wall painting is from the House of the Vettii at Pompeii. The goldsmiths are depicted as little figures of Amorini, attendants of Venus, goddess of love, an association between jewellery and romance that predates De Beer's advertising by almost two millennia.

The activities we see lack the precise details of processes and tools that we might like, but they do underline the main characteristics of Roman gold jewellery manufacture. At the far left one figure holds a gold ingot on a sturdy anvil with tongs while his companion beats it into sheet with a large hammer. The beating out of gold into sheet was the starting point for most Roman gold jewellery. We can leave the group with the seated woman customer for a moment and move to the next figure. This is a seated Amorini bent over a smaller anvil and tapping a small tool with a little hammer. He is shaping or cutting the gold into the required form. The next process, was to assemble the separate, shaped sheet gold components he has made into the final piece of jewellery by soldering them together. In antiquity this was done, as we see here on the far right, by soldering the parts together in a small furnace. One figure uses a pair of bellows to keep the general heat up while his companion holds the work, probably propped on a piece of charcoal, in the furnace entrance and uses a simple blowpipe to help control the heat more precisely.

Now we can return to the seated woman who we can presumably identify as the customer. The finished piece of jewellery is being weighed in front of her. Gold jewellery was priced on the basis of its weight. Often the customer provided the gold, or the money to purchase the gold, and would certainly wish to check the weight of the final piece.

The amount the woman would have paid for the goldsmiths' actual work was low by modern standards maybe around one sixteenth – 6.25% – or less of the value of the gold. In Later Roman times when gold had increased greatly in price, the maximum cost of workmanship for simple goldwork was set by law at about 0.8% of the value of the gold for basic work and 1.33% for more intricate work.

Fig.150:
Gold bracelet in the form of pairs of domes.
Pompeii, Italy, buried AD 79.
(National Archaeological Museum, Naples)
© Mimmo Jodice/CORBIS

Fig.151: Wall painting showing Putti working as goldsmiths. House of the Vettii, Pompeii,
Italy, buried AD 79. (National Archaeological Museum, Naples)
© *Mimmo Jodice/CORBIS*

These little gold earrings in fig.152 came from the Roman Empire to the East of Italy – probably Asia Minor. They date to the second century BC.

The emeralds probably derived from the mines in Egypt which were then largely worked by prisoners of war or criminals. Emeralds are harder than most of the gemstones used in the Roman period and although an increasing number were being traded across the Roman Empire from the first century AD onwards, they were usually treated fairly cursorily. Most were left in their natural form – little hexagonal crystals as we see here – and simply drilled as beads.

The little blue beads are sapphires and are also essentially 'as found', apart from the drilling which was carried out with a small diamond-tipped drill. Sapphire crystals also take a hexagonal form, though they grow in more of a barrel-like form than emerald crystals. However, the hardness of sapphire varies with direction through the crystals and so when the sapphires roll around in a river bed for 'geological' lengths of time, they wear down into the rounded little pill-shapes we see here. So far the source of these sapphires has not be identified. They are found in Roman jewellery right across the Roman Empire and are most typically in jewellery of second century AD date. From the third century onwards the paler and larger sapphires from Ceylon begin to appear, and the smaller, darker stones as on these earring fade into obscurity.

The vogue for gem-set earrings in the Roma world was commented on by Seneca in the first century AD: 'I see pearls, not single ones designed for each ear, but clusters of them, for the ears have now been trained to carry their load.'

With many hoards of jewellery it is impossible to decide whether they represent the personal ornaments of their original owner, or were the stock of a goldsmith. One remarkable and recently discovered hoard that can clearly be identified as a jeweller's stock in trade is one (fig.153) found at Snettisham in Eastern Britain. A simple and modestly-sized pot contained a large quantity of silver rings plus unset carnelian intaglios, various unfinished pieces, scrap for re-use and even a little stone burnishing tool for polishing the silver and for pressing down the edges of the settings to secure the stones.

The finished and partly finished jewellery is all silver, and the numerous all-but-identical rings show that it was the stock of a jeweller who specialised in a limited repertoire of goods, perhaps only rings. The hoard supplements our knowledge of how a jeweller making silver jewellery might operate. It clearly shows that the jeweller made silver rings for stock and didn't just make them individually to order. This, and the proof that the jeweller had actively accumulated scrap and other raw material, shows he must have amassed some capital.

The snake rings could be bent a little to accommodate different finger sizes, however, the carnelian-set rings are of beaten silver and a customer would have to have chosen one to fit. In theory a solid silver ring of this type could be made a little larger, though not smaller, by gentle hammering, but even this would have been hazardous once set with a stone.

The one hundred and ten unset carnelian intaglios, plus those already set, demonstrate the size of the potential market. Whether the stones were engraved by someone within the jeweller's own circle, or were purchased from an independent stone engraver is unknown.

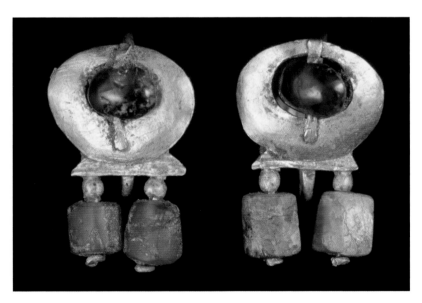

Fig.152: A pair of gold earring set with sapphires and emeralds. Probably Asia Minor, 2nd century AD.
© Jack Odgen

Fig.153: A hoard of completed and partly made silver rings, including raw materials and the pottery vase in which they were concealed. Snettisham, Britain, 2nd Century AD. (British Museum)
© Copyright the Trustees of The British Museum

This unassuming little ring (fig.154) has a significant place in jewellery history. It is the earliest surviving diamond-set ring of which I am aware.

Some diamonds were reaching Classical lands and the Near East by about 500 BC, but there is little evidence that they were valued as anything other than as hard little splinters, ideal for drilling stone beads and engraving stone seals. The first Roman indications that diamonds might be valued in their own right include Pliny's assertion in the first century that diamonds were highly valued and the inclusion of diamonds in a list of precious stones imported from India in a surviving ships log of about the same period. Then, early in the second century, the Roman writer Juvenal refers to a diamond-set ring – even if more satirically than seriously.

This little diamond-set ring comes from Tomb 2 at Vallerano, Rome and was among the fine jewellery owned by a young woman buried in the second half of the second century AD. The ring is of plain gold set with a small uncut diamond crystal of octahedral shape. Other gold jewellery from this same burial included pieces set with the dark sapphires typical of second century Roman jewellery mentioned above and which might well have come from India. It is tempting to connect the arrival of diamonds, sapphires and other Indian gems in Rome at this period with the eastern military expedition of Lucius Verus, which helped stimulate the trade in Eastern products to Rome.

This single earring, its pair long since lost, is of a type typical of Asia Minor in the third century AD, it's presence in the Byzantine Museum in Athens probably relates to its recent history more than its ancient place of manufacture or use. This example is sturdier and better made than most, but what is of interest is the use of coloured stones. The green stones in the centre of the upper rosette and those on the ends of three pendants (one missing) are emeralds left as natural hexagonal crystals, which, as we have seen, is normal in Roman jewellery,

The smaller circular inlays mid-way down the pendants are, however, green glass. This glass, now partly decomposed, was a close colour match for the emeralds. It would not have been easy, or cheap, to cut or obtain small semi-circular emeralds for such a jewel and so glass was used as an alternative. Of course we do not know whether or not the original owner was aware of the subterfuge. In an equivalent modern situation we might also ask if the retailer was aware of the true nature of the little green inlays, but in antiquity maker and seller were usually one and the same, and the person who set these stones would have undoubtedly had a good idea of what they were.

Similar Roman rosette and multi-drop earrings are known from Syria and the Levantine coast. However these more eastern examples are typically set with garnets, rarely if ever emeralds. Those from Asia Minor, as here, are rarely set with garnets. This was not fashion, but realities of trade. The emeralds came up from Egypt by sea, the garnets were traded from the east overland.

Fig.154: Gold ring set with a small diamond crystal. Vallerano, Rome, Italy, c AD 160 - 180. (National Museum, Rome)
With permission of the Minister for Heritage and Cultural Activities - Soprintendenza Archelogica di Roma

Fig.155: Gold earrings set with emeralds and green glass. Asia Minor. 3rd century AD. (Byzantine Museum, Athens)
© Archaeological Receipts Fund

The gold ornament shown here on the right was found in Tunis, North Africa and dates to the third century AD. Its original function might not seem immediately obvious, but it was almost certainly a hair ornament. We see almost identical objects worn in the hair – hanging frontally down above the forehead from a high 'bun' of hair – in the funerary sculpture from Palmyra in Syria (fig.157). It was a remarkably widespread fashion, another similar piece of jewellery was found in a child's tomb in Britain.

The Tunis example is set with emeralds and there are pearls around the periphery and hanging from the outer two pendants. The central pendant beads a pale, pear shaped sapphire, an early example of the sapphires that began to enter the Roman World from Sri Lanka in the third century and which replaced the smaller, darker stones we encountered earlier (fig.152) Incidentally the example from Britain is set with glass imitations for both the pearls and the emeralds.

Tunisia might seem a bit off the beaten track from opulent Roman jewellery, but there were major Roman cities across North Africa. Tertullian, whose caustic comments about jewellery were cited earlier, was from Tunisia.

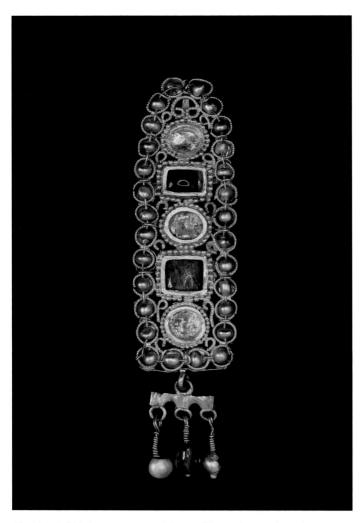

Fig.156: Gold hair ornament set with emeralds, sapphires and pearls. Tunis, 3rd century AD. (British Museum)
© Copyright the Trustees of The British Museum

Fig.157: Limestone relief showing hair ornament in wear. Palmyra, Syria, 3rd century AD. (British Museum)

One of the more extraordinary early jewellery finds for the student of gem use is that from Beaurains in Northern France. The Hoard was found in 1922 and contained a large group of gold jewellery, silverware and gold and silver coins. The coins and other evidence suggest that they were buried in about AD 315.

A gold pendant from the treasure contains a citrine, a yellow variety of quartz (fig.158). Citrine is not a particularly rare stone and it is unclear why there are only a handful of Roman examples set in gold. The unsuitability of a golden yellow gem for a gold setting might be a partial reason.

Even amethysts, as the Beauain's ornament (fig.159), were not commonly set in gold pendants or clasps, despite their obvious suitability for such a setting.

Also included among the find was one of the few surviving ancient examples of gold-set peridot jewellery (fig.160). Peridot is gemstone of a pale almost oily, lime green colour. It is a variety of the mineral olivine, and the best known occurrence in the past was on the island of St John in the Red Sea. The mines here were worked from Hellenistic times onwards, we even have a surviving inscription recording an overseer of these mines, but the surviving examples are very sparse.

Also in the treasure, but not shown here, was a ring set with an aquamarine that almost certainly came from India. This bears the names Valerianus and Paterna in niello, a black inlay material. We might assume that these are the names of the couple who originally owned the jewellery. On the basis of the commemorative coins in the hoard, a bit like modern campaign medals, we might suggest that Valerianus was a military man who served in Italy and Northern Gaul in the last couple of decades of the third century. Possibly other surviving documents will eventually allow us to identify him more closely. In any case, Valerianus and Paterna are the only known Roman gem aficionados to have left us their collection.

Fig.158: Gold pendant set with citrine (yellow quartz). Beaurains, France, 3rd century AD. (British Museum)

Fig.159: Gold ornament set with amethyst (purple quartz). Beaurains, France, 3rd century AD. (British Museum)

Fig.160: Gold pendant set with peridot. Beaurains, France, 3rd century AD. (British Museum)

The three ornaments from Beaurains show three of the types of gold surrounds that a Roman jeweller might use to enclose a gemstone. There is actually a relatively limited number of such surrounds and we see much the same repertoire right across the Roman Empire for framing gems, gem imitations and coins. Here we see a gold mount similar to that enclosing the citrine in the Beaurains Treasure, around a sardonyx cameo. This object, probably a component from a necklace, is said to have been found in Tunis, in North Africa and dates to the third century AD. The cameo is engraved with a scene showing the birth of Bacchus. A nymph, whose attire leaves a lot to be desired, shows the child to his mother Semele under the watchful gaze of a satyr.

The raised and thus white border to the cameo is typical for later Roman work, while a small perforation through the top centre of the cameo might suggest that this gold setting is not its first home.

Fig.161: Gold pendant mounted with a sardonyx cameo showing the birth of Bacchus. Tunis, 3rd century AD. (British Museum)
© Copyright the Trustees of The British Museum

Setting gold coins in jewellery is not just a modern fashion, but neither was it as prevalent in early times as some suggest. Perhaps the earliest examples of jewellery made from coins are three early silver *hemidrachms* pierced and supported on silver wire loops, that were found in Egypt. However, coin-set jewels are all but unknown from Hellenistic and even early Roman times, although there are some spectacular forgeries of 'Alexandrian' coin set jewellery from Egypt and simpler, but still often fake, early Roman necklets with coin pendants.

Discussion of Roman use of coin-set jewellery before the second or third century AD often invokes a first century Roman mention of 'old gold and silver coins which are habitually used as ornaments'. This has often been assmed to refer to coin-set jewellery. In my view it might be better understood as a reference to the well-documented use of gold and silver coins as raw materials for making jewellery.

In any case, once into the later Roman period coin set jewellery becomes far commoner and examples range from individual coins in relatively simple mounts, to spectacular and highly elaborate ornaments. Among the most elaborate is a form that consists of four strands of loop-in-loop chain passing into two sliding globular beads, thus allowing the construction to be expanded to pass over the head. Several, like that in the Walters Art Gallery, Baltimore shown here, are said to be from Egypt. The seven coins set in the pendants on this necklace range in date up to about AD 140, but the necklace itself probably dates to the end of the third century and maybe into the early part of the fourth century.

A similar necklet in the Metropolitan Museum of Art in New York has a suspension loop for the central coin in the form of a diminutive finger ring, a feature matched on a few other pieces of jewellery of this period and which might indicate some connection with marriage. Certainly such a connection is indicated by some Early Byzantine coin-set jewellery, and coin-set wedding jewellery has been a common feature in Islamic and Asian societies in more recent times.

Fig.162: Elaborate gold necklet with seven coin-set pendant. From Egypt,
c AD 300. (Walters Art Gallery, Baltimore).
© *The Walters Art Museum, Baltimore.*

The magnificent pendant shown here is part of a group of such objects, said to have originally been found in North Africa, that was split up when the group was sold at auction in London in the 1970s. The example here was finally purchased by the British Museum in 1984 with the help of the National Art Collections Fund. Others from the group are now in the Dumbarton Oaks Collection in Washington and in the Louvre, Paris.

The central coin is a double solidus that can be dated to the year 321. Surrounding this is a series of six heads in high raised relief. One head has been identified as that of the minor deity Atis, but the others are as yet unrecognised. The main field of the pendant, and the cylindrical suspension loop, are in the intricate, almost lace-like pierced work of the period. Such pierced designs were first laid out as a series of small punched holes. These holes were then 'opened out' with small triangular cutting tools to create the design. One of the hardest parts of the process was the positioning of the initial holes and some ancient examples do bear faint scratches that were part of the original planning of the layout. Whether sketches on other materials were used is unknown. Only the most skilled of modern fakers can replicate this work.

The rarity of earlier Roman set coins might have been due to a reluctance to deface them and indeed even in later Roman jewellery – such as this pendant – the coins are mounted in a way that did not damage the coin and allowed its eventual removal unharmed, if necessary. This is a contrast with Early Byzantine coin-set jewellery where the coins were not only typically soldered into their mounts, but might have their edges hammered out to increase their surface area.

Fig.163: Gold pendant in elaborate openwork with a central coin of AD 321.
North Africa, 4th century AD. (British Museum)
© Copyright the Trustees of The British Museum

Fig.164: Gold rings from the Thetford Treasure. Thetford, Britain, c AD 400.
(British Museum)
© Copyright the Trustees of The British Museum

Increased development on previously agricultural land in recent years, and the huge growth in metal detector use, has brought to light several major finds of jewellery that date from the final days of the Roman occupation of Britain. Indeed the concealment of these hoards might themselves reflect the troubled days around AD 400 when the Roman hold on Britain began to slip. We must assume that the original owners hoped that the threats were merely temporary and that they planned to return and recover their treasures. The events that sometimes prevented such reclamation are now long forgotten and we do not know if the owners fled the country alive but greatly impoverished, or died leaving modern treasure-hunters and archaeologists as their beneficiaries.

A large hoard found at Thetford, Norfolk in 1979 consisted of some magnificent jewellery and, it is said, coins. Noteworthy among the jewellery were twenty-two rings, three shown here.

Some of these rings are types well-known from elsewhere in the late Roman Empire, but others are so far unique. These rings include examples set with garnets, amethysts and emeralds.

The other jewellery in the hoard included emeralds, both loose and on the gold necklets, and green glass imitations of emeralds. Not only is the emerald colour matched, but so is the hexagonal shape typical of the natural emerald crystals.

The Thetford hoard was originally concealed in a cylindrical shale box and possibly one or more pottery vessels, but because the hoard was a metal-detector find, its exact archaeological context is uncertain. Much of the jewellery appears to be brand new and unworn, some pieces even appear unfinished. However, we still do not know whether it was a jeweller's stock or belonged to a private owner or even temple.

In 1992 a man was helping a friend find a lost hammer in a field at Hoxne, Suffolk with the assistance of a metal detector. He found a treasure, immediately reported his find and by the end of the following day archaeologists had unearthed 200 gold and silver objects and almost 15000 coins. All this originally buried in a large wooden chest.

Coins are perfect for archaeology because most can be dated pretty accurately. The latest of the coins in this hoard, all but a couple of dozen of them of gold or silver, date to AD 407-8. However, no further Roman coins entered Britain after this period, so the hoard could date to after AD 407. To put this in a historical context, Roman administration withdrew from Britain by about AD 410 – the year the Venerable Bede noted as the end of the Roman occupation of Britain and the same year that Alaric the Visigoth sacked Rome.

Who were the original owners? Some hint might be provided by this bracelet. It is one of eleven bangles in a type of intricate pierced work typical for the later Roman period mentioned above (fig.163). These bracelets have various designs, but the one shown here bears the inscription Utere felix domina Juliana which wishes well to the wearer, the lady Juliana. Several of the silver objects in the hoard also bear names and since the name Ursicinus appears on a complete set of ten spoons, it is tempting to think that he was the owner of the hoard. He might well have owned more, the absence of large silver objects in this hoard might mean that there were originally other parts to the treasure, buried separately and perhaps in different places.

The lack of earrings and the presence of only three finger rings in the Hoxne hoard is perhaps unexpected. Possibly more smaller pieces of jewellery were buried elsewhere – or, being readily portable, were never concealed in the first place. We can note, however, that earrings are not common from later Roman Britain. There were none in the Thetford Treasure either. Possibly the admonitions against ear piercing by the Early Christian fathers were having some affect, but the Thetford Treasure was ostensibly pagan, and in any case earrings were common further East, and a significant component in early Byzantine gold hoards.

One of the most extraordinary ornaments in the Hoxne hoard is this 'body chain' (fig.166). It was worn across the chest, crossing between the breasts. Other examples are known from Early Byzantine contexts and there are depictions of similar ornaments in wear from Hellenistic Greek times onwards. This fine example is made up of gold chains with animal head terminals, of a type better known in the Early Byzantine East and the centre motifs, where the chains cross, consist of a mounted coin of Gratian (367-83) on one side and, on the othe (seen here), a setting containing an amethyst surrounded by garnets alternating with empty settings. These empty settings probably originally contained pearls which did not survive some sixteen hundred years of burial in damp British soil.

Fig.165: Gold bracelet with elaborate openwork and bearing the name 'Lady Julia'.
Hoxne, Britain, c AD 400. (British Museum)
© Copyright the Trustees of The British Museum

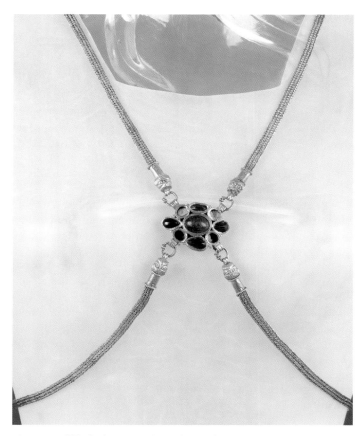

Fig.166: Gold body chain set with amethyst and garnets. Hoxne, Britain, c AD 400. (British Museum)
© Copyright the Trustees of The British Museum

The Hoxne Treasure didn't include any jewellery that would be easily recognisable as intended for male wear, but although Roman men didn't wear as much jewellery as women, they were not totally devoid of ornaments.

Apart from rings, the commonest male ornament in Roman times was the fibula or brooch that acted as a clothing fastener. We saw several examples of different periods earlier when we talked about functional jewellery. By late Roman times the most prestigious example of these was the 'crowsbow' fibula, so called on account of its cruciform shape. A fine gold example is shown below. The cross-like shape is unlikely to have had any clear Christian connotations, since the form can be traced back several centuries, but it was ultimately functional.

The cross bow brooch was worn on the shoulder with the long 'foot' pointing upwards. The high arch of the bow accommodated two layers of thickish material and the two arms to the side acted like outriggers to hold the brooch upright. The characteristic spherical or onion-shaped terminals provided smooth, rounded ends that avoided tearing or abrading what might well have been a very expensive cloak. The massive size and construction of some of these brooches, constructed from hammered components, would have made then sturdy enough to securely fasten a cloak worn by an active Roman male, but the weak link, and an aspect that challenged the maker's ingenuity, was a means to keep the pin from opening inadvertently during wear, a problem that has vexed brooch makers into recent times. The Roman goldsmith met the challenge in a variety of clever ways, from elaborately sliding sections to pins locked in place by screwing in one of the terminals. The brooch shown here has just such a screw-in terminal.

Fig.167: Gold 'crossbow' brooch. Britain, 4th century AD. (British Museum)
© Copyright the Trustees of The British Museum

Byzantine & Medieval world up to AD 1000

Eleni is famous as the mother of the Byzantine Emperor Constantine the Great, but is also regarded in her own right as possibly the earliest archaeologist. According to the legend already cited, she made an expedition to the Holy Land in order to seek the True Cross, was directed to three mounds and on digging into one of these indeed found her quarry.

Constantine, who was himself not a Christian at the time he supported his mother's quest, eventually not only converted himself, but made Christianity the official state religion. It is really only from this period – AD 324 – that we begin obvious Christian symbols and symbolism in jewellery.

This representation from Trier in Germany has been identified as showing Eleni. In addition to her box of jewellery, she is wearing what appears to be a magnificent emerald and gold necklet and is proudly holding a large pearl necklace. Jewellery, of course, presented something of a conundrum for the early Christians. The Greeks and Roman had established a serious love for jewellery and the quest for precious stones from India, Ceylon and elsewhere sapped the Empire of its wealth. But to the early Christian fathers, the problem was not so much the economic balance and trade deficits, but the difficulty of matching a widespread lust for jewels with the sobriety demanded in a religion where one was exhorted not to lay up treasures on earth. Braver souls spoke out against jewellery – such as Clement of Alexandria who said in exasperation that only foolish people `rush after transparent stones' – but it took several centuries before the Christian east took a more abstemious line on gems, perhaps shamed into doing so by the new and stricter Moslem laws.

The fourth to early seventh centuries have left us some remarkable jewellery from throughout the Byzantine Empire, from the Balkans to Syria to North Africa. Byzantium was the name of the ancient Greek city that Constantine I rebuilt in AD 330 and then renamed Constantinople, later still Istanbul. The Roman empire was now split between the capitals of Constantinople in the east and Rome to the west, a divide still represented by the Catholic church, centred in Rome, and the Orthodox Greek church, whose prelate is still based in Istanbul. Then, as we saw above, in the early fifth century Rome fell to 'the barbarians'. It was not instantaneous. Rome was not built in a day and neither could its empire be destroyed in a day, but its power was eroded and its empire contracted.

In European history, the centuries after the final fall of Rome are often called the Dark Ages. In some ways this is an apt description. It was a time of strife, a time of the migration and interaction of warlike and barely literate tribes, and a time of heroes and heroic sagas. But against this background there was also jewellery produced that at its best could rival almost anything before or since. Dark Ages are seldom as dark as they first appear, but human nature seems to like cyclical patterns in all its stories.

Further North in Europe the Middle Ages proper can be dated to the Crowning of Charlemagne as emperor of the West in AD 800. Now relatively stable kingdoms were distilling out of the chaos of the so-called Dark Ages. In Britain, there was Alfred the Great (AD 871-899), then the trauma but eventual harmonising effect of the Norman invasion of 1066.

The development of European gold jewellery during this period cannot be isolated from the other artistic changes, whether in book illumination or cathedral building. So we can approach Medieval European gold jewellery expecting to see it mirroring first the rather sombre and sober Romanesque architectural style that spread across Europe from the tenth to the twelfth century. Romanesque architecture was solid, stolid even, and geometric, and largely derived from Roman architecture, as its name suggests. It also contained Byzantine and even some Islamic overtones.

One of the earliest Christian symbols we see on jewellery, or indeed on anything, is the Cho-Rho symbol, a combination of the Greek letters Chi (C) and Rho (R), the first two letters of the name Christ. The symbol seemingly first appears in the early fourth century, probably about the time Constantine made Christianity the state religion and its symbols could be openly employed. Certain symbols we see on rings and other jewellery earlier than this, fishes and palm branches for example, might sometimes allude to Christianity, but we cannot always be certain – an ambiguity that might have suited a pre-Constantinian Christian.

The late fourth century gold ring shown here was found in Suffolk, England. The bezel bears a well defined Chi-Rho below a diminutive bird in a tree. The design was worked in a combination of engraving with a sharp metal tool and 'chasing'

with a hammer and little punch – a common combination in Roman and Early Byzantine work. A faint dotted line can be see extending past the flared end of one arm of the cross (at 5 o'clock in the illustration). This is probably a marking out line used by the goldsmith to sketch out the bezel design before beginning to engrave it. The ring was intended as a seal, as revealed by the reverse direction of the chi-rho symbol, it would appear the right way round in impression.

This is an example of a piece of jewellery that had been found and recorded some time ago, then seemingly 'lost' until it reappeared on the London market in the mid 1980.s, was recognised and acquired by the British Museum. Every year several 'lost' pieces reappear this way in dealers' hands around the world, which is one reason why it is vital for museum curators and other specialists to keep in close touch with the market.

Fig.169: Gold ring with Chi-Rho Christian monogram. Suffolk, Britain, late 4th century AD.
(British Museum)
© Copyright the Trustees of The British Museum

Some of the most spectacular - and skilful - goldwork that has survived from the Early Byzantine period is in a hoard supposedly found in the Asyût/Antinoe region in Middle Egypt around 1900. The find passed into the hands of several collectors and is now mainly divided between the British Museum, the Freer Gallery of the Smithsonian Institution in Washington, the Metropolitan Museum of Art, New York and the Berlin Archaeological Museum. The spectacular collar of set coins and the large circular medallion with pierced work border, shown here, is in this latter museum.

Tube-like torcs with coin-set pectorals and hanging medallions are among the most magnificent of coin-set jewellery from the ancient world and they seem to have been an Egyptian speciality. Three examples are known, this one in Berlin, another from the Asyût Hoard and now in New York and one further one that is from Egypt and may well have been part of Asyût Hoard originally. This latter example briefly surfaced around 1980 along with the so-called Gospel of Judas that hit the headlines in 2006, but its present whereabouts is unknown to me.

To talk of an Egyptian speciality might seem to contradict the oft-stated view that any fine quality goldwork of the early Byzantine period must have been made in Constantinople rather than 'in the provinces' like Egypt. But this rather chauvinist view has little to support it. Egypt, in particularly Alexandria, had a long and well-earned tradition of fine metalwork.

The coins set in some of the Asyût Hoard jewellery tell us that at least some pieces were not made until the early seventh century (the latest in the collar shown here is of about AD 580) and it is tempting to link the original deposition of the hoard with the Arab invasions of Egypt in AD 640. There is some suggestion that certain coin ornaments were worn by women, but we also see elaborate neck ornaments rather similar to the present example being worn by men on a mosaic of the time of Justinian at Ravenna.

It is presumably coincidence, but there is an early Christian story that survives from Egypt and tells the tale of 'Saint Claudius and the Thieves'. This was set around AD 600, but was popular for long after. It tells how three pagan `partners in theft' travelled around from Christian shrine to Christian shrine, in the Antinoe/Asyût area. They stole jewellery, gold chalices, silver objects and treasures until their progress was halted by a manifestation of Saint Claudius. The story ends, predictably, with their conversion.

Fig.170: Gold collar with elaborate coin-set centre-piece and medallion pendant from the Asyût treasure. Middle Egypt, ca AD 600.
(Archaeological Museum, Berlin)
© Archaeological Receipts Fund

The broad, cuff-like bracelet with central decorative panel or bezel was a popular form in the early Byzantine Period. The example here, said to have been found in Syria, combines a complex variety of decorative effects with early Christian iconography.

The hoop has series of alternating embossed peacocks and swans within a scrolling grape vine, and is bordered by rather cursory pierced work. The outer rim of the bracelet is plain and hollow. The peacock was an early symbol of the resurrection because after the male bird has shed its magnificent tail feathers, it grows even more spectacular ones. The peacock often occurs on early Byzantine jewellery of the sixth and seventh centuries. The swan is less often seen and can represent love and dignity, but has also been associated with divine inspiration.

The flat upper section of the bracelet consists of a circular panel, bordered by pierced work and a scalloped border, flanked by two settings for gemstones. This central section is hinged to allow it to be placed on the wrist. The central panel is an embossed sheet gold representation of the Virgin Mary with her arms raised in an attitude of prayer. She has a barely discernable halo. The halo, a disk behind the head, originated in depictions of a sun disk behind the heads of pagan deities and rulers, and initially had rays.

By the eighth century, iconoclasm had taken hold of the Byzantine world, representations of this type were forbidden,

and such a bracelet as this could not have been worn. Perhaps not surprisingly, the rise of Byzantine iconoclasm coincides with the rise of Islam with its own very strict rules against the depiction of living creatures and Allah.

The original nature of the four gems flanking the Virgin Mary can only be guessed, but from their rectangular shape may well have been emeralds or glass imitations of emeralds. The little gold disks where the settings join the central circular part are not simply decorative – they acted as reinforcements to the soldered joints. After all, these soldered joints would be subjected to the greatest stress when the bracelet was worn.

In early Christian iconography, the Virgin Mary assumed several of the attributes of the Egyptian goddess Isis who had been the mother of the 'child god' Harpocrates. There is some evidence that emeralds were associated with Isis and, in any case, their leaf-green colour made them the perfect symbol for creation and new life.

Bracelets of this general type were usually, but probably not invariably, worn in pairs. One to each wrist. The pierced work border around the Virgin's head and on the band is a simpler and later version of the delicate Roman pierced work, as in fig.166, and helps to date the bracelet to the sixth or perhaps seventh century. The halo behind the Virgin's head only became a feature of Christian art in the later fourth if not fifth century.

Fig.171: Gold bracelet with centrepiece depicting the Virgin Mary. Syria, 6th - early 7th Century AD.
(British Museum)
© Copyright the Trustees of The British Museum

The sea-born gem trade from the Red Sea around Arabia and to India had been built up by the Early Roman Emperors and was then greatly expanded in the Early Byzantine Period. Pearls and sapphires are the most obvious result of this increased in the trade in precious materials. The pearls came from India and perhaps the Persian Gulf, the sapphires from Sri Lanka (Ceylon) – as their delicate pale blue colour and other gemmological characteristics illustrate. The characteristic Byzantine pear-shaped sapphires, like those that form the drops on this earring and the lateral arms of the cross in the medallion, are probably natural water-worn crystals with minimal shaping. Sapphire and its relatives, such as ruby, are second only to diamonds in hardness, but they could be drilled using diamond chips. In theory, they could have been polished with diamond dust, but it is unlikely that fine diamond dust was available and it is more likely that the were polished using a natural tin oxide abrasive as described in Medieval texts.

The elaborate earrings and necklet are from Egypt originally and were part of the same major jewellery hoard as the magnificent necklet in fig.170. What is interesting here is the understated representational nature of the pieces. The central part of the medallion forms a cross, but in a subtle way, while comparison with other related earrings suggests that the flanking scroll-like forms of the earrings might be highly stylised dolphins.

Fig.172: Gold necklace from the Asyût treasure, set with emeralds, pearls and sapphires. Middle Egypt, 6th - early 7th century AD. (British Museum)
© Copyright the Trustees of The British Museum

Fig.173:
One of a pair of gold earrings from the Asyût treasure, set with emeralds, pearls and sapphires. Middle Egypt, 6th - early 7th century AD. (British Museum)
© Copyright the Trustees of The British Museum

The incorporation of coins into jewellery had occurred sporadically since before Roman times, but only became commoner after about the third century AD. Gold belts or girdles made of a series of linked coins are a feature of the eastern Mediterranean in the sixth and seventh centuries AD. There is contemporary and later evidence that such elaborate ornaments may have been connected with marriage and were worn by the bride. Complete examples survive, such as one from Kyrenia in Cyprus. These elaborate ornaments are made up from Byzantine solidi – a coin first minted by Constantine around AD 309 – and sometimes larger coin-like medallions.

The six solidi shown here are part of a girdle and are said to have been given to a previous owner by Pierpont Morgan and so may well be part of the same girdle as three larger medallions in Washington that formed part of the Asyût treasure from Egypt, described above. Certainly there are close similarities between these coins and the medallions in Washington, as, for example, in the way in which the beaded wire mounts are soldered directly onto the hammered-out border of the coins. There are also copper corrosion products in the hinges resulting from copper hinge pins. Copper was harder than gold and was often used to form hinge pins in early Byzantine and Medieval Islamic jewellery – much as silver had been used in Phoenician and Etruscan jewellery.

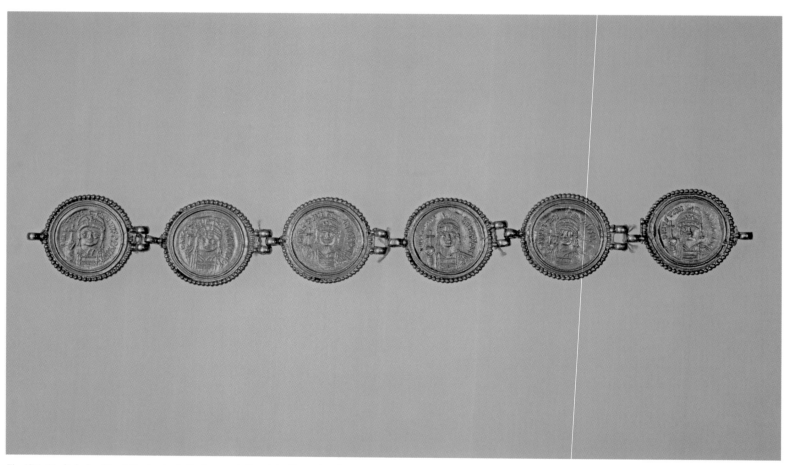

Fig.174: Six linked gold solidi coins probably from a girdle originally, and perhaps from the Asyût treasure. Egypt, 6th - early 7th century AD. (British Museum)
© Copyright the Trustees of The British Museum

One of the main characteristics of European jewellery in the Post-Roman period is the incorporation of flat cut garnets. Thin slices of bright red garnet were cut to precise angular or rounded forms and set in gold, gilded copper alloys or, less commonly, silver. The garnet slices were produced by a combination of splitting, grinding and polishing. They were then wheel-cut to shape to fit the settings, often with remarkable precision.

Jewellery set with flat garnets are often thought of as typically Northern European – for example, the extraordinarily intricate Anglo Saxon examples (fig.176). But the fashion is found far wider, from Spain to the Russian Steppes, and even in Egypt. The jewellery shown here is from the Crimea in what is now the Ukraine. It combines flat-cut garnets (upper centre and lower left and right) with oval and pear-shaped cabochons (dome shapes). Indeed, the fashion for garnet-set jewellery may well have begun in the East, perhaps in Parthian Persia.

The stylised bird heads (lower centre) have 'eyes' produced by inlaying gold into circular depressions cut into the garnets with a tubular drill. This inlaying of hard stones with gold would culminate in the Mogul inlaid jades and rock crystals (fig.231). The small pendant on the upper right is set with a single heart shaped garnet. This apparent use of a relatively modern symbol, albeit upside down here, may seem strange, but this garnet is of identical form to, and is probably a reused example of, a common component in later Hellenistic Greek jewellery (see fig.147). This Hellenistic Greek 'heart form' was probably intended as an ivy or vine leaf. The re-use of gems taken from earlier jewellery – in this case some five or six hundred years earlier, was not uncommon and is a reminder that then as now farmers or builders could fortuitously stumble on older graves or concealed hoards, and that such finds could spark off far more deliberate treasure hunts. Recycling is not a new phenomenon.

Fig.175: Gold jewellery, mostly set with garnets. Ukraine, 4th - 5th centuries AD.
(British Museum)

In 1939 the largest of eighteen burial mounds was excavated at Sutton Hoo in Suffolk, eastern Britain. It proved to contain a ship burial – the richest burial so far excavated in Europe or Scandinavia – and almost certainly that of an early Anglo Saxon king of the East Angles buried in the early Seventh Century AD. The finds were extraordinarily varied, including the necessary arms and treasures to equip a king in the afterlife. Among the finds was silverware much of which originated in the Eastern Mediterranean. As noted above (fig.48), one silver dish bears official stamps, like a modern hallmark, that date to the reign of the Byzantine Emperor Anastasius 1 (AD 491-519). Among the rich jewellery was the pair of shoulder clasps shown here.

These exquisite ornaments are among the most perfectly made jewellery of any period. The flat-cut garnets are precisely cut to fit the complex settings, particularly intricate in the animal interlaces along the outer edges. To add to the complexity, the garnets are also shaped to follow the gentle curve of the clasps. Behind the garnets are wafer thin gold foils that bear a minute latticework of raised lines to maximize the reflections through the blood-red stones. The occasional blue highlight is provided by inlaid blue glass, while the centre panels are interspersed with glass inlays of checker-board-like millefiore work.

The shoulder clasps were attached to their backing, perhaps leather, by means of numerous small loops on the sheet gold back of the clasps. The pairs of clasps were joined with the hinge-like fastener with the inserted gold pins. The pristine condition of these clasps suggest that they were never used.

In some ways, the cutting of slices of stone to fit gold settings and form part of a representational or geometric design recalls the cloisonné inlays of lapis, carnelian and other coloured gemstones in earlier pharaonic Egyptian jewellery and its Near Eastern relatives. However, this earlier jewellery made use of opaque stones while the garnets were not only transparent, but their transparency and colour was usually enhanced by backing them with shiny thin gold foil. Another difference between the earlier cloisonné inlays and the flat-cut garnets is in the way they were secured in their settings. Usually, the Egyptians stuck their inlays into their jewellery a cement of some type, often suitably tinted to make its presence less obvious around the edges of the stones. With the transparent garnets, however, any type of glue or cement would have destroyed their appearance, so they were held in place by carefully burnishing the top edges of the wall-like gold surrounds so that they extended slightly over the edges of the garnets.

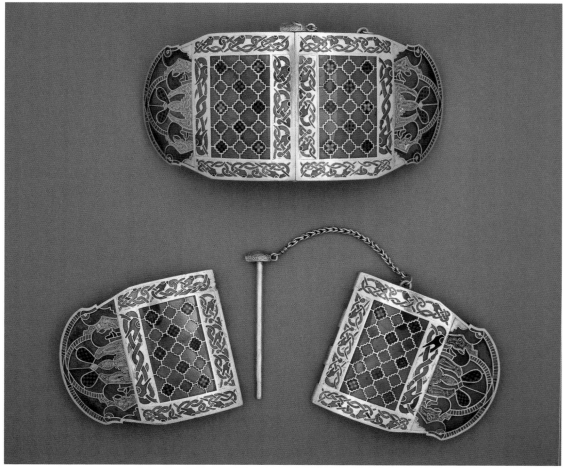

Fig.176: Gold shoulder clasps with intricate garnet inlay. Sutton Hoo, Britain, early 7th century AD.
(British Museum)
© *Copyright the Trustees of The British Museum*

Fig.177: Gold brooch with cloisonné enamel work. Probably Italy, 7th - 8th centuries AD. (British Museum)
© Copyright the Trustees of The British Museum

The flat-cut garnets just encountered are sometimes referred to as cloisonné work – because they have partitioned or cell-like settings. Cloison is French for partition. Such stone settings should not be confused with cloisonné enamel where the 'cells' contain enamel fused in place. The example of cloisonné enamel jewellery shown here, originally belonged to the Castellani family of jewellers in Rome, and was probably made in Italy no earlier than the seventh century AD and maybe a century or so later. It is an early example of true, representational cloisonné enamel. The central figure is a woman who wears earrings and a disk brooch and who might represent an empress. The central circular enamelled motif is surrounded by an enamelled decorative band and two encircling rows of partly decomposed pearls on gold wires – the pearls largely missing on the outer wire.

In fully developed cloisonné enamel of this type, the enamel was built up in several firings until it stood above the level of the surrounding cell walls. The enamel was then carefully polished down until smooth and level with the cell walls. It can be highly polished using finer and finer abrasives, or the final polish can be imparted by heat alone – the surface is just melted giving what is termed a 'fire polish'. There seems to be little evidence for fire polishing cloisonné or related enamel types before the Renaissance. The Medieval monk Theophilus, explained that enamel should be polished until you could see your face reflected in it.

At about the same time that the enamelled gold ornament just described was made in Italy, a craftsman in Ireland produced the enamelled copper alloy brooch shown here. The brooch is of the so called penannular type, the best known Irish type for several centuries, and which we have already encountered.

The red enamel seen here is typical on copper alloy jewellery in Europe from pre-Roman times until the Medieval Period. This enamel, coloured red using a copper compound, had a relatively low melting temperature, but required special firing conditions. This meant that it was tricky to combine with other coloured enamels on the same object. When other colours were wanted in combination with red, they or the red enamel could be produced as separate components, then later combined on the same object. Here the little blue and white glass motifs were separately made and then set into their cells.

The main copper-alloy components of this brooch were cast and then finished with a considerable amount of very precise hand work. The terminals are probably very stylised animal heads.

Fig.178: Copper alloy ring brooch with red enamel decoration. Ireland, ca 7th century AD.
(British Museum)
© Copyright the Trustees of The British Museum

Before the close of the eighth century, the coasts of Britain and France were being raided by a new warlike enemy from Scandinavia, the Norsemen or Vikings. For the best part of three centuries they were a force to be reckoned with. Their fast ships and navigating skills not only suited their lightning coastal raids, but established them as important traders and settlers. They founded settlements, albeit probably short-lived ones, in North America five hundred years before Columbus and served as mercenaries in Byzantium. The Norsemen who settled in northwest France in the region still called Normandy went on to carry out the last successful military invasion of England – the Norman invasion of 1066.

The Vikings have left us a vast amount of precious metal treasure, predominantly huge hoards of silver jewellery, ingots and coins from mints all over the then known world. Much of the jewellery is fragmentary, roughly chopped up, a reminder that the Vikings were looters and plunderers (fig.51). Their hoards include nielloed silver amulets from Central Asia and crudely folded Islamic silver bracelets, but a sufficient quantity of truly Viking jewellery has survived to provide us with a clear idea as to their skills and styles. A characteristic decorative effect in Viking silver jewellery is the repeated use of a small punch to form patterns of little triangles, circles and other simple geometric shapes. Lost wax casting was also often used.

The relative lack of Viking gold jewellery is noteworthy, but this is just another manifestation of the 'gold famine' experienced across most of Europe at this period. However, the gold jewellery that does survive, such as these extraordinary tenth century brooches from Hornelund in Denmark, and now in National Museum in Copenhagen, shows that in terms of intricate filigree and granulation the Viking jewellers could hold there own with those of other ancient societies.

Fig.179: Two Viking gold brooches with elaborate filigree and granulated decoration, Hornelund, Denmark, 10th century AD. (National Museum, Copenhagen)
© Werner Forman / CORBIS

Among the sparse surviving jewellery from Saxon Britain we are lucky to have two objects that seem to carry the names of rulers. The massive, though now partly crushed, nielloed gold ring shown here has the name Aethelwulf, who may well be king Aethelwulf (AD 839-858). The second jewelled object shown here bears the name Alfred who is usually assumed to be Aethelwulf's famous son, King Alfred who ruled AD 871-899.

The centre field of the gold ring depicts a stylised 'fountain of life' between two peacocks – a device we often see on early Byzantine jewellery. Niello is an inlay material, essentially a silver sulphide that is fused in place and then polished. About the time this ring was made, there was seemingly a refinement in niello production methods that allowed its wider use – perhaps the adoption of borax as a flux or the addition of lead to the niello, or perhaps both.

The so-called Alfred Jewel was probably the top of a pointer used to follow the holy words when reading from the Gospel. The pear-shaped object contains an early example of European cloisonné enamel, perhaps the head of Christ, beneath a rock crystal cover and bears around its side an openwork Saxon inscription that says 'Alfred ordered me to be made.' The complex granulated work is a clear reminder that this ancient technique had not died out with the Romans. Here the combination of granulation and wire filigree shows relationship to Viking goldwork.

The Alfred Jewel, as it is called, is not only one of the greatest surviving jewelled objects of the period, it is also an old find. It was discovered in 1693 in a field just a few miles from where King Alfred founded a monastery to mark the site where he launched his counter attack against the Vikings. The jewel was presented to the Ashmolean Museum, Oxford in 1717, just ten years after the museum had been founded.

Fig.181: The Alfred Jewel, a gold and enamel ornament that was probably an æstel (pointer for reading the Gospel), It bears the inscription "Alfred ordered me made". Britain, Late 9th century AD. (Ashmolean Museum, Oxford) © Ashmolean Museum, Oxford

Fig.180: Gold ring with niello work showing confronted peacocks and the name Aethelwulf. Britain, mid-9th century. (British Museum) © Copyright the Trustees of The British Museum

The introduction of wire drawing (pulling gold through holes in iron and steel) sometime around the ninth or tenth century made it far easier to produce long lengths of regular gold wire. One manifestation of this was the appearance of various plaited or 'knitted' wire forms, including neck ornaments. Even a braided silver wire flail survives. The armlet shown is one example of a class of armlet or bracelet made by twisting, wrapping and plaiting sturdier gold wires. The central motif – the armlet doesn't open – has a remarkably simple line and dot decoration; the armlet's impact relied on massiveness, not intricacy.

The plaited hoop form is well known in the Viking world of North West Europe, this one is from Goodrington, Devon in southwest Britain, but the type is equally at home in South Russia and east into Central Asia. Plaited hoop armlets appears in Viking contexts by the tenth if not late ninth century and seems to have survived, at least in the East, into the thirteenth. The gold example shown is dated to the tenth century. The present example, like many of its type, have a central sturdy gold wire which provides rigidity and acts as a former around which the six or eight wires are entwined. Silver examples are far commoner than gold examples .

Like the Alfred Jewel, the Dowgate Hill brooch (late tenth to eleventh century) named after its London find spot, combines cloisonné enamel and openwork filigree and granulation. However, this piece might well have been made in Ottonian Germany from whence its closest parallels come. The Saxon Ottonian dynasty, from the tenth to mid eleventh centuries and named after three Emperors named Otto, was a period of great revival in the arts, from fine manuscript illumination to monumental metalwork. Fine goldwork was produced and the love of brilliant colours that we see in miniature paintings found expression in cloisonné enamel work.

Here the cloisonné enamel represents a crowned head and thus presumably a king, but any further identification is impossible. The enamelled part was made separately, as usual, and set into a circular setting on the brooch much as a stone might be set. This type of setting was typical for enamelled components. It removed the need to fire and refire the entire object – a hazardous process. Such separate enamelled components could be re-used and even acted as objects of commerce and trade in their own right. Here the enamelled panel is convex. This complicated its assembly and polishing, but gave the object a more three-dimensional appearance.

The surround to the enamel is in openwork filigree reminiscent both of Viking and Medieval Islamic work. Although the actual wire types and their employment here is different from the Islamic, there was connection between the Medieval European and Islamic worlds, via trade and warfare. There were also close connections between the Ottonian Kingdom and the Byzantine world.

Fig.183: The Dowgate Hill Brooch, in gold and enamel. London, late 10th - 11th century. (British Museum)

Fig.182: A Viking gold bracelet with 'plaited' hoop. Goodrington, Britain, 10th century AD. (British Museum)
© Copyright the Trustees of The British Museum

The pair of bracelets shown here is among the finest examples of surviving Byzantine jewellery dating from around the tenth century AD. The bracelets each take the forms of hinged, tapering 'cuffs' and are set with panels of cloisonné enamel. Such enamel work seems to first appear in the Byzantine world in the mid-ninth century. These little enamelled rectangles, set into individual gold settings just like gems, show birds, stylised palmettes and geometric rosettes. The lack of clear Christian iconography, such as crosses, reminds us that at this period Greek goldsmiths might have had Islamic as well as Byzantine clients.

Similar enamel panels can be seen in Medieval Islamic jewellery. Indeed there are records of how the tenth century Byzantine Emperor Constantine Porphyrogenitus sent enamelled jewellery as gifts sent to Islamic princes and the following century Emperor Michael similarly sent five bracelets described as inlaid with enamel in five colours. The transparent, bright green enamel background to these enamels, somewhat decomposed in places here, appears in the ninth century and might relate to the increase in the lead content of the glass to reduce its melting temperature and bring its coefficient of expansion more in line with that of gold.

The edges of the cuffs have bands of flattened gold wire plaits. This is a decorative motif with a long history, it appears on one of Tutankhamen's daggers, for example, but it is very characteristic of gold jewellery produced in the Byzantine world in the tenth century (see figs.76 and 77)

The earrings date from the same period as the cuff bracelets and are of a type that straddle the Byzantine and Islamic worlds. Indeed some of the elaborate examples have Greek inscriptions, others Arabic. They were also very popular examples in gold, silver and copper alloy which have survived distributed from Italy and Sicily all the way east to Syria.

The examples here are enamelled and, like the bracelets, depicts birds – the commonest figural subject on jewellery of this period. The little loops along the inner curve of the crescent shape originally bore threads or wires with pearls. The larger loops to the front and rear of each earring might have originally been attachments for a chain that passed over the ear. Gold earrings from the eastern end of the Mediterranean in the tenth and eleventh centuries quite often have such attachment loops, but I am only aware of one pair on which the chains survive.

The general dearth of gold and gem-set jewellery across most of Europe between the seventh and eleventh centuries is matched in the Islamic world. Almost no jewellery has survived from Islamic lands between the time of the Prophet in the mid seventh century and beginning of the eleventh century. In part, the lack of early Islamic jewellery can be explained by the religious views against jewellery, and the fact that, contrary to practice among most earlier Old World societies, precious metal jewellery was not buried with the dead. In addition, all available gold and silver was needed to finance the most rapid and expansive military expansion the world had even seen. Within a century of Mohammed, the Islamic domain stretched from Spain to the Central Asia.

Some of the most intricate gold jewellery of the Medieval Islamic world comes from the Fatamid period. The Fatamids originated in North Africa and by the beginning of the eleventh century ruled over Egypt and the countries flanking the eastern Mediterranean up to Syria. The most noteworthy decorative feature seen in Fatamid jewellery is a type of openwork filigree as seen on the terminals of these pins. The jewellery is made up of skeletons of paired wires, with lines of fine gold granulation along the gulleys between the wires.

The examples shown are a pair of eleventh century pins, said to be from Egypt. The bend in the tang of each pin is probably deliberate as it is matched in other Medieval Islamic pins of this type. This bend probably relates to the way in which the pins used, although we still do not know exactly how they were worn. Interestingly, Elizabethan dress pins from Britain also almost invariably have a similar bend in the tang when excavated.

Fig.184: A pair of gold armbands with inlaid cloisonné enamel panels. 10th century AD. (Museum of Byzantine Culture, Thessaloniki) © Werner Forman/CORBIS

Fig.185: A pair of gold earrings with inlaid cloisonné enamelwork. East Mediterranean, 10th Century AD. (British Museum)
© Copyright the Trustees of The British Museum

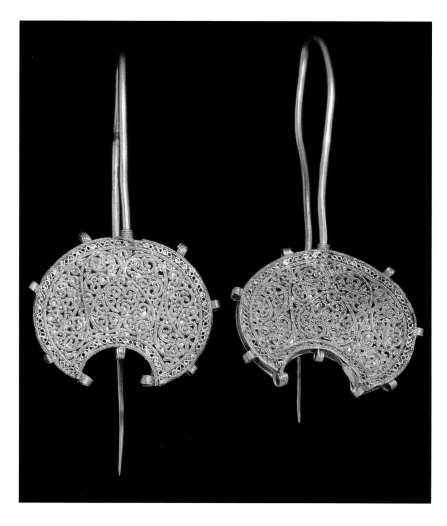

Fig.186: A pair of gold garment pins with intricate filigree terminals. Fatamid Egypt, 11th century AD.
© The Nasser D. Khalili Collection of Islamic Art (JLY1848)

An Egyptian poet in the middle of the twelfth century admired the girls by the banks of the Nile and described them as weighed down by their heavy bracelets and anklets. He was not exaggerating. A surviving list of the jewellery that formed one young woman's dowry in Egypt included a pair of gold bracelet that weighted the equivalent of about a modern pound. Islamic law probably meant that such opulent ornaments should not really be worn by women other than in private, but this didn't prevent gold jewellery from being an aspiration – as the large number of exquisite gold ornaments that have survived from this period demonstrate.

This pair of ornaments, armlets or, possibly, anklets are of the date and origin as the pins in fig.187. They are not as heavy as they might look and are actually of sheet gold which was filled with some other substance to give them support and weight. The hinged opening is also phoney – they were never intended to be opened, merely slipped over the hand or ankle. Nevertheless, the workmanship is of the highest quality and the triangular panels of decoration by the 'clasp' are in the same wire and grain technique as the pin terminals.

Fig.187: A pair of gold bracelets or anklets. Fatamid Egypt, 11th century AD.
© The Nasser D. Khalili Collection of Islamic Art (JLY 1853 & 1854)

The extraordinarily accomplished skills of the goldsmiths of the Fatamid period are best evidenced by the rings, earrings and other ornaments produced in the elaborate openwork filigree that we have just described. The intricacy is, perhaps, not on a par with the miniaturised granulation of the Etruscans one and a half millennia earlier, but the overall aesthetic effect is hard to beat. Despite their skeletal-like construction and hollowness, these ornaments were sturdy enough for use and, indeed, many examples show signs of wear and even repair work. We might trace the origins of the style to the slightly earlier and simpler openwork filigree ornaments from Eastern European jewellery, but an introduction along with the Fatamids themselves from North Africa, and perhaps ultimately Spain is also possible.

The illustration here shows the bracelets or armlets in fig.187 again alongside another bracelet and other jewellery of the same period, including beads, earrings and a ring.

The hoops to the earrings of the types shown here are frequently now missing – and often replaced in modern times. The reason being that the Islamic jewellers used silver or copper alloy hinge pins on the hoop attachments to add strength – a practice we have already encountered in Etruscan and Byzantine

jewellery. These silver and copper hinge pins have often corroded away. In some cases, the hoops themselves were of silver or copper alloy, even when the earrings were of gold. This seemingly strange practice might conceivably have originated as a subtle means of circumventing Moslem prohibitions by over-literally interpreting the instruction not to wear gold through the ears.

The ring shown here is in similar openwork filigree technique and one of a class that is both spectacular and fragile. Such rings do often shows signs of wear and even repair in one case, so they were worn. However, it would have been all but impossible to alter their finger size once made, so the assumption is that they were made to measure for a particular wearer and finger. This might be the time to point out that generally speaking few rings from the past show any signs of being re-sized to fit a finger. Why not, when ring sizing is one of the commonest activities in a modern jewellery repair workshop? We do not even know how jewellers recorded the measurements of a finger when they made a ring for a customer. All we have is the tantalising comment by the sixteenth century Italian master goldsmith Cellini that a customer supplied the 'measure of her finger' when she commissioned a diamond ring from him.

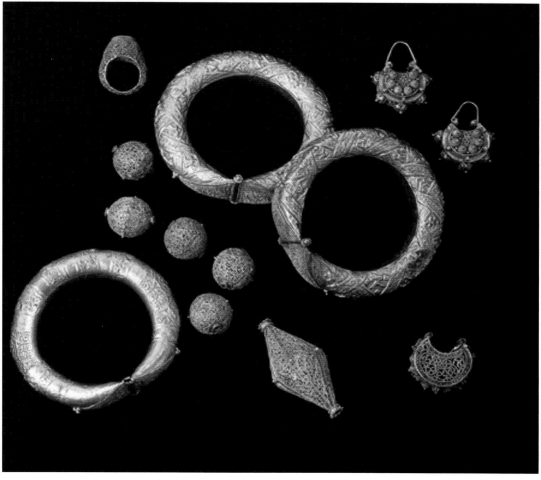

Fig.188: Gold jewellery exhibiting intricate filigree work. Fatamid Period,
East Mediterranean, 11th century AD. (The Nasser D. Khalili Collection of Islamic Art)
© The Nasser D. Khalili Collection of Islamic Art (JLY 1310)

It is unclear where the wire and granulation decoration in Fatamid Islamic jewellery originated. Technically it is unlike anything in the Byzantine world and so perhaps it was based on something brought by the Fatamids from further west, perhaps even Spain. What does seem certain is that it was not introduced from the East. Medieval Islamic gold jewellery from what is termed 'Greater Iran' lacks the intricate openwork, but it does make more use of coloured gemstones and, often, niello. The gemstones are usually set in raised settings of sheet gold taking the form of truncated cones or pyramids. We see this here on a bracelet said to have been found in what is now Syria and which dates to the twelfth century. The top setting, now missing its stone, is of pyramid shape, the ones on the sides, one now missing, are of oval cone shape. Originally, there was a hinge between the lion heads and one side of the hoop pulls out from the central setting where it is held by a peg. There is niello decoration and an Arabic inscription.

The small lions flanking the main setting, and the lion head terminals on the hoop might be unexpected in jewellery from a society where representations of nature were abhorred, but the strictness with which such rules were applied varied from time to time and place to place. Lions are one of the commonest animal forms in Medieval Islamic jewellery. The appeal of bracelets of this type, coupled with the increased interest in Medieval Islamic jewellery in recent years, have made this bracelet form a target for some ingenious forgers.

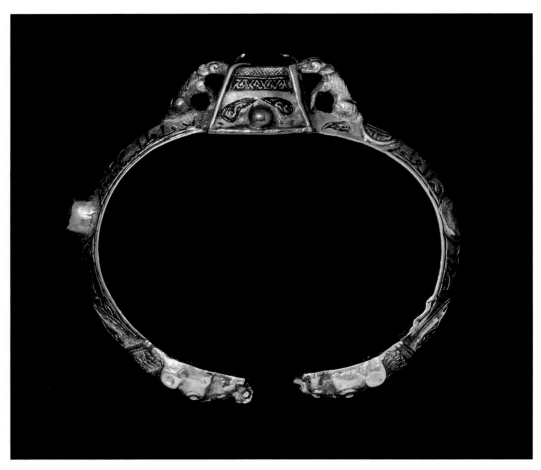

Fig.189: Gold bracelet with stylised animals and niello decoration. Stone missing.
Iran or Central Asia. Medieval Islamic, 12th century AD.
© The Nasser D. Khalili Collection of Islamic Art (JLY 1310)

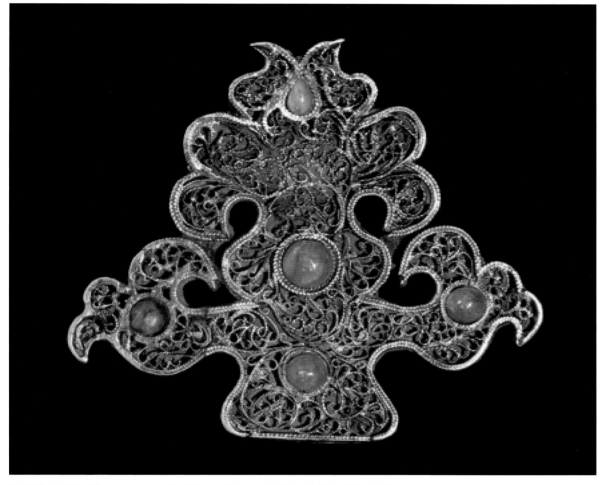

Fig.190: Gold headdress ornament with elaborate filigree work. Central Asia, 13th - 14th century.
© The Nasser D. Khalili Collection of Islamic Art (JLY 1310)

The name of the 'Golden Horde' might not be known to many readers, but some of its personalities will be. The rule of the Golden Horde was established across what is now Russia by the grandson of Genghis Khan in the middle of the thirteenth century and broken up by Timur (Tamburlaine) a century later. It was this unification of hitherto barbaric lands that opened up the Silk Route to relatively safe trade, and allowed Marco Polo to satisfy his wanderlust.

This Golden Horde ornament, possibly a head ornament, takes the form of a flame or lotus flower. It has a distinctly 'oriental' look to it although it is not unlike the Fleur-de-lis motif we see on Medieval European and Russian crowns by the twelfth century, remember, the lotus is a member of the lily family. Very similar ornaments are known from Golden Horde contexts in Russia and as far East as Mongolia. This example is said to be from Central Asia.

The front of the ornament is gold and has intricate frond-like filigree decoration. The design is in single strands of flattened wire filigree, a type of filigree often seen in medieval European jewellery but less common in Fatamid Islamic work. The back has three loops for attachment. The sides and back of the object are in silver, a feature matched in some other Golden Horde ornaments – in some case the corrosion products from the silver have coated the gold and led to the assumption that the entire object was of this lesser metal. The stones now set in it are modern replacements and the originals may have been of some material that has decayed with time – perhaps pearls or coral.

The lower left arm of the ornament had broken off in antiquity and was rather crudely repaired with iron wire. In general, Golden Horde jewellery reveals a massive and often colourful splendour with reminders, such as the crude iron-wire repair, that the owners were a no-nonsense, terrifying and nomadic people.

Later Medieval Europe
AD 1200 - 1500

This charming painted papier mâché (*cartapesta*) by Neroccio de'Landi (1447-1500) from the province of Siena in Italy shows an unknown young woman wearing a necklace with a fine pendant. The necklace may be of coral or pearl, the pendant with drops of similar materials and a set centre stone, perhaps a ruby. She was unaware of the imminent dawn of the Renaissance and no doubt more interested in the fashions of her time than the three centuries that stretched behind her, perhaps the most formative period for the development of modern European civilisation. However, another Italian, and one whose lifespan may well have overlapped with hers, did have some views about the past. The sixteenth century artist and architect Giorgio Vasari looked back at the architectural style that followed the magnificent though often rather sombre Romanesque styles of the tenth and eleventh centuries and did not like what he saw. He described it with contempt as Gothic. The name stuck, but our views on it have changed.

To some extent we can understand Vasari's point – the faultless proportions of Classical architecture were thrown to the wind and fantasy had taken over. Buildings and spires stretched to the heavens. But, lightness and space had become pre-eminent, and jewellery was just as affected as architecture. As John Ruskin noted in the nineteenth century, in earlier art ornament had decorated a structure. The decoration might be a relief on a Greek temple wall or gold filigree on a Dark Age brooch, but it was essentially applied to an underlying form. But in Gothic art ornament was the structure and the structure was the ornament. Indeed, we can look at the jewellery of this high medieval period, such as the objects in figs.194 and 198, and wonder where 'structure' stops and 'ornament' starts.

With jewellery the changes in styles coincide with the escalating importance and prominence of what we would class as 'precious gems'. This was a direct result of the growing direct and indirect contacts between Europe and the Eastern Mediterranean, and even India. By AD 1000 an increasing number of pilgrims and traders from Northern Europe were travelling to the Holy Land. Soon Italian merchants had bases in the Eastern Mediterranean and trade in oriental products, including spices and precious stones began to grow. The Crusades, for all their legacy of violence, did much to widen European horizons and encourage trade. Initially the Europeans simply acted through Arab middlemen, but gradually coloured stones and even the occasional Indian diamond began to reach Northern Europe, and gold became far more readily available. The net result was a remarkable rebirth of sophisticated jewellery in Europe from about the twelfth century onwards.

Europeans, naturally enough, wanted to seek the eastern markets themselves. Marco Polo's travels to the East around the late thirteenth century are well known and are but one recorded chapter in a period of increasing European involvement in trade with the East. Another early European traveller was the intrepid Friar Odoric of Pordenone who set off some twenty years after Marco Polo. He describes, among many other things, gold from Sumatra, a part of the world where cannibalism was rife. Here, according to Odoric, traders bought gold, spices and other goods from the locals in return for imported children destined for the pot – it was 'an evil and pestilent generation', as he notes.

Blue sapphires were a popular stone in European Medieval jewellery of the twelfth century onwards and these, at least in the main, came from Sri Lanka (Ceylon). As we have seen above, the delightful pale blue sapphires typical of Ceylon had reached the Mediterranean world – and China – by early Byzantine times (by the seventh century AD), but this trade appears to have largely ceased with the rise of the Islamic world after the mid-seventh century. The sapphires seen in some jewellery produced in Europe and the Byzantine worlds between the seventh and twelfth centuries are probably mainly reused earlier Byzantine gems.

Marco Polo described Ceylon sapphires towards the end of the thirteenth century. He even carried some to China to trade with Kublai Khan. In fact the river gravels of Ceylon contain a wide range of gemstones in addition to sapphires, including pink sapphires, star sapphires and chrysoberyl cats-eyes – charmingly called Fawn's Eyes in early sources. Rubies occur in Ceylon, but are neither fine nor common, and the best came from ever father away, in Myanmar (Burma). Not surprisingly, rubies generally appear a bit later than sapphires in Medieval European jewellery and less abundantly.

In Medieval times gem choice was limited by more than just purse or fashion. There were rules laid down. In fact, much of our information about jewellery wear throughout history comes from attempts to limit or prevent its use. Whether we look at the Jewish Talmud, early Christian writings, Islamic Hadith literature or medieval sumptuary laws, the various prohibitions and criticisms reveal much about actual practice and aspirations.

Fig.191: Painted papier mâché showing a young woman wearing jewellery.
By Neroccio de'Landi (1447 -1500), Siena, Italy, later fifteenth century.
(Victoria and Albert Museum, London)
© *V&A Images / Victoria and Albert Museum*

Medieval sumptuary laws concerning the wearing of jewellery can appear confusing and arbitrary. They varied from place to place and from period to period. For example, if we limit ourselves to pearls, in late thirteenth century Venice only the bride and one other guest at a wedding might wear pearls. In the later fifteenth century Frankish nobles serving a knight at a tournament could wear only a single string of pearls on their hats, while two centuries later professors and doctors in Saxon universities, and their wives, were forbidden to wear any pearls whatsoever. Indeed these academics were also banned from wearing any gold or silver.

We can see an underlying trend here, and some truisms of social history. The elite have always wanted something to cap the aspirations of would-be-elite, to keep indicators of their class and privileges preserved just for them. We can see much the same thing centuries earlier when Julius Caesar forbade the wearing of pearls by those of lesser rank and when Byzantine legislation that said that actresses could wear gold jewellery, but not gold set with gems. Naturally the hereditary nobility of medieval Europe wanted to continue to distinguish themselves from the growing class of affluent merchants that had begun to appear from the twelfth century onwards. The prohibitions to prevent the Saxon academics from wearing jewels must indicate that potentially they now had the wealth to do so.

An economic historian could also argue that sumptuary laws had an anti-inflationary affect and this might even have been a factor in their propagation. The economic dangers were certainly realized. For example, the more clear-headed of Romans a millennium earlier had decried the huge exodus of gold from the Roman world to the East to pander to the rapidly growing demand for gemstones.

The surviving later Medieval jewellery from Northern Europe includes brooches, used as dress fasteners, rings, and necklaces. One of the commonest forms is the simple ring brooch that served as a dress fastener of much the same type as we met earlier in this book (figs.197 and 198). Earrings, however, are almost unknown in medieval Europe except in lands fringing the Mediterranean. Possibly the lack of earrings in the west hearkens back to the criticisms of earring wear in the writings of the early Church fathers – even though earrings were common in Early Byzantium. In the eleventh century mosaics of Torcello, Venice, the 'damned' awaiting hell wear earrings, the 'saved' en route to heaven do not.

This gold ring with its small and simply-polished sapphire dates from around 1200 and is an early example of the sapphires that began to enter Europe around this period, probably mainly from Sri Lanka (Ceylon).

In form this is what we call a 'stirrup ring', from its resemblance to shape of a medieval stirrup. This particular example, from Wittersham in Kent, England, is one of the sturdiest examples, most are far flimsier, even if no less elegantly shaped.

The Medieval philosopher and theologian Albertus Magnus, who died in 1280, correctly noted that sapphire came from India and that it "makes a man chaste, cools internal heat…. brings about peaceful agreements, and makes one pious and devoted to God and confirms the mind in goodness." No wonder that sapphire rings are often associated with bishops and other churchmen. The converse was also true. There was also a belief that a sapphire might lose its colour when worn by the unchaste or unfaithful.

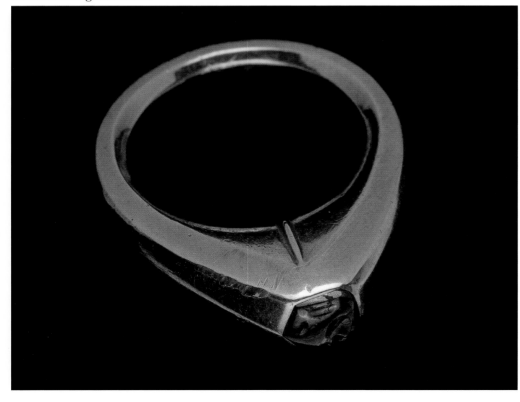

Fig.192: Gold and Sapphire ring. Kent, Britain, c 1200. (Victoria and Albert Museum, London)
© V&A Images / Victoria and Albert Museum

This second sapphire ring is a century and a half more recent than the last and makes a useful contrast. It can be dated accurately because it was found in the tomb of William Wytlesey who was Archbishop of Canterbury between 1362 and 1374. This provenance helps confirm the association between sapphires and the clergy.

The sapphire in the earlier ring in fig.192 is simply polished, the surface grooves being a typical medieval and earlier way to remove unsightly surface blemishes. The fourteenth century ring (fig.193), however, contains a sapphire that was facetted, that is polished in such a way as to provide a series of flat surfaces. Incidentally the sapphire also has a perforation drilled through it showing that it had found earlier employment as a bead.

This faceting of hard gemstones developed between the twelfth and thirteenth centuries and represents a major advance in lapidary techniques. The introduction of rudimentary diamond cutting at about this same period is part of the same trend. Diamond is the hardest natural substance in the world and, as the old saying 'diamond cut diamond' indicates, a diamond can only be cut by another diamond or by the particles of a crushed diamond. The first step was probably polishing off the pointed end of the crystal, frequently already chipped or rounded in nature, to produce what is called a 'table cut stone. By 1500 better polishing equipment had allowed the creation of more flat polished faces – facets. The slow ascent of the art of diamond cutting had begun.

The accent on gemstones and their settings in the later Medieval Period also means that we begin to find a distinction between goldsmiths and 'jewellers' after the mid fourteenth century.

The style of setting for this sapphire is also worth noting. More simply polished gemstones could be set in gold settings that surrounded them and extended up the sides of the stones to a sufficient extent to be burnished over them and hold them securely. The flat, angular facets of a sapphire like this one required a different approach, since the traditional type of setting would obscure its new fashionable qualities. Various ways to set a stone so as to reveal as much of it as possible were developed over succeeding centuries. The scalloped claw approach, as in this ring, is one characteristic of later Medieval approach.

Fig.193: Gold and sapphire ring from the tomb William Wytlesey, Archbishop of Canterbury between 1362 and 1374. Britain, 14th century. (British Museum)
© Copyright the Trustees of The British Museum

This brooch was made a generation or so before the sapphire ring in fig.193 and is set with pearls, smooth rather than facetted emeralds and rubies, as well as a small diamond top centre. This little diamond is a natural diamond crystal of the type we have already encountered in Roman jewellery. Its presence here bestows on the brooch the honour of being one of the earliest surviving pieces of diamond-set jewellery from Britain. The brooch was made in about 1350 and presented to New College, Oxford a century later. The style of gold work, the pearl clusters and the little diamond are very reminiscent of the so-called Palatine Crown now in the Residenz, Munich, one of the most elaborate pieces of Medieval jewellery to have survived from Britain.

The two figures within the arches of the M were originally enamelled and depict the Virgin Mary and the Angel. Between them is the vase which holds lilies – the flower associated with the Annunciation and typically present in Medieval Annunciation scenes. We can see similar representations in thirteenth and fourteenth century church wall paintings – such one on the North wall of the church at South Newington, Oxfordshire, probably commissioned by Margery Gifford, but with the arms of Morteyne. Despite this abundance of Oxfordshire Ms, the initial form of this brooch is generally assumed to refer to the Virgin Mary.

The settings are neatly made to hold the smooth but irregularly shaped stones. The centre stone, in contrast, is perfectly cut and polished to represent the traditional 'lily pot' and is a noteworthy example of stone-working for the period. Such complex shaped stones are rare, but not unknown in Medieval jewellery. We might mention here the elaborate reliquary ring which was part of a hoard from Thame, not far from Oxford, that is set with a single amethyst cut into the form of a double-armed cross. The Thame hoard was deposited around 1457, but contains some coins dating as much earlier as about 1350 – so a fourteenth century date might also suit the ring.

Fig.194: The Hylle Jewel or 'Founder's Jewel', set with rubies, emeralds, a diamond and pearls.
Britain, late 14th century (New College, Oxford)
© Courtesy of the Warden and Scholars of New College, Oxford/The Bridgeman Art Library

The ancient settlement at Dunstable, in Bedfordshire, England was given a new lease of life in the early twelfth century when Henry I founded an Augustinian priory there and built a palace. Just over a century later the Dominicans also arrived and established their friary. It was during an excavation at the site of the latter in 1965 that this fine swan jewel came to light. It dates to about AD 1400 and is one of the finest surviving examples of enamelled later Medieval jewellery. It is of gold with white enamelled down. In function it is a brooch, with a pin and catch on the back, and around the swan's neck is a small gold coronet attached to a length of gold chain of simple oval, unsoldered links. The chain terminates in a larger loop and may simply have served as a safety chain; it is unlikely to have supported a further ornament.

This type of all-over painted enamel on gold developed over the preceding couple of centuries, and initially may have derived from Islamic 'enamelled' glass and shared some of its compositional benefits and characteristics – namely a relatively low melting temperature and a coefficient of expansion that near enough matched the surface to which it was applied.

The significance of the swan here is uncertain. The jewel may be a livery badge, showing allegiance to the monarch or local nobility, but its high quality shows that it must have belonged to someone of considerable importance. Swans, all of which belonged to the Monarch unless otherwise marked, were associated with the house of Lancaster and became an emblem of the Prince of Wales in 1399. Possibly here there is some particular local relevance, since swans have long been associated with Bedfordshire and its river Ouse. As an aside, we can note that the Dunstable leader of the so-called Peasant's Revolt that began about the time this jewel was made, was described as the landlord of the Swan Inn.

Fig.195: Gold and enamel brooch in the form of a swan.
Dunstable, Britain, ca 1400. (British Museum)
© Copyright the Trustees of The British Museum

Trade routes had existed across the Russian Steppes and Central Asia from time immemorial, but the establishment of the Silk Route as a major and relatively safe trade artery from China to the eastern borders of Europe can be dated from the time of the emergence of the Mongol empire during the thirteenth century. An early gem product which passed along this trail may have been rubies from Burma, they are all but unknown before this period.

A well-known early traveller along the silk route was the Venetian Marco Polo in the 1270's-1290's, but his father and uncle were old hands at the Eastern trade and had earlier established business houses in Constantinople and Sudak. Sudak was the Venetian trade settlement on the northern Black Sea coast, the rival Genoese had theirs at Kaffa. The Polos were involved in the gem trade and Marco Polo's account of his twenty-four years abroad provide much information about the

diamonds and other gems he encountered. He visited Ceylon and described the pearls and gemstones from that island. This representation of searching for gems in a river in Ceylon is taken from an early fifteenth century manuscript of the travels of Marco Polo now in the Bibliothèque Nationale, Paris

By the time this manuscript was produced, European trade along silk route was about to come to end. European access through the Black Sea was effectively halted when the Ottoman Turks captured Constantinople in 1453, and about this same time major political changes further east effectively closed the Silk route. The Europeans, with their new taste for the exotic products of the east, sought their own sea routes, thus heralding a whole new period of maritime exploration in which the encounter with America had particularly significant repercussions.

Fig.196: Searching for gems in Ceylon, from a manuscript of Marco Polo's travels. French, 15th century. (Bibliothèque Nationale de France, Paris)
© Bibliothèque Nationale de France, Paris

The basic form of this brooch is one we have met earlier – it dates back to ancient times – but this is an exceptionally grand and colourful example that is probably either of English or French thirteenth century manufacture. On the reverse is a French inscription that says 'I am here in place of a friend whom I love', a charming sentiment found on other ring brooches of the period.

This brooch is set with sapphires and, again, what are probably red garnets or spinels rather than rubies. As we have seen, the gems in most fourteenth century and earlier jewellery are polished, but seldom truly facetted to form flat reflective faces. This is true here, but not entirely. The red gem at 10 o'clock, for example, is facetted to a rudimentary table-cut form. This gem, like the others in the brooch, clearly had their settings specially made to hold them. However this faceted red stone also has one end polished off flat, presumably showing that it had been in another piece of jewellery originally and, perhaps, one end was damaged and re-flattened before re-use.

The thirteenth century brooch shown here is also an example of the ring-brooch type, but is very different from the preceding object in its form and assembly. The decoration is so prominent that it takes our mind off the relatively crude workmanship with which it is made. The conical settings, for example, are formed in sheet gold with very basic overlapped joints. But, as we touched on above, where does structure cease and ornament take over? The gems are again simple cabochon sapphires and red stones that are often described as rubies, but which have more the colour of garnets or spinels.

Fig.197: A gold ring brooch set with sapphires and red stones (probably garnets). English or French, 13th century. (British Museum)
© Copyright the Trustees of The British Museum

Fig.198: A gold ring brooch with foliage design, set with sapphires and red stones (probably garnets). European, 13th century.
© V&A Images / Victoria and Albert Museum

By the fifteenth century things had changed. Gems such as sapphires and rubies began to be facetted more often, even if fairly simply, and even diamond cutting was advancing. We can attribute these changes to the increased availability of gems from the east and the spread of technical knowledge, but the most fundamental change might have been the introduction of grinding and polishing wheels with continuous rotary motion – unlike the to and fro motion of earlier bow, treadle and pole lathes.

This brooch is one of a small group of fifteenth century jewellery that was found in the River Meuse that flows through what is now Belgium and the Netherlands. It takes the form of a female amid flowers whose hands hold the side of the central setting. The cursory modelling and surface of the face, the skeletal wires forming the hands and the texturing on some of the sheet gold show that the piece was once enamelled.

The pale blue sapphire in the centre is facetted to form a hexagonal gem, almost a rose cut. Below and to each side of the sapphire is a simple polished ruby, above is a diamond. The diamond is of interest because it appears to be a diamond crystal that has been set sideways so that one of the triangular crystal faces forms the flat upper surface. This type of sideways setting of diamonds is seen in other fifteenth century jewels, and may have been an ingenious way to replicate the look of the cut diamonds that were just then beginning to come into fashion.

Fig.199: Gold brooch in the form of a woman amongst flowers set with a central facetted sapphire. At the top there is a small diamond. Originally enamelled. Flemish, 15th century. (British Museum)
© Copyright the Trustees of The British Museum

In 1966 an important fifteenth century treasure was found at the village of Fishpool in Nottinghamshire, England. It included gold jewellery and 1237 gold coins, the latter described as the largest such find ever made in Britain. The coins allow us to date the deposition of the hoard to AD 1463-64, during the Wars of the Roses (1455-85).

The jewellery consisted of four rings, two lengths of chain, a pendant cross, small padlock, a rondel and a heart-shaped brooch. The jewellery other than the gold chains are shown here. The coloured gemstones set in the jewellery include a turquoise (in the ring), a small ruby (in the cross pendant) and a sapphire (on the little circular roundel).

The style of the jewellery has been suggested to be more continental than English, but it may have been made in Britain. The jewellery and coins may represent the personal possessions of a wealthy person at the period. This was the time of the Wars of the Roses, a time when there would be ample reason to hide away jewellery to protect it from looting. The rings show evidence for wear, the other jewellery less so.

A feature of this jewellery is the use of enamel on the heart-brooch and padlock. White enamel is common on jewellery of this period, even though it does not provide much of a contrast against the gold. In this jewellery the enamel is applied within hollows cut or chased into the gold surface. On the heart brooch, the blue and white enamel also has small gold foil 'spangles' pressed into it.

The heart shaped brooch, another version of the ring brooches in figs.198 and 199, also bears the inscription 'I am yours without any diversion'. This brooch is an early use of a stylised symmetrical heart shape that is, of course, now the traditional symbol of love.

Fig.200: The Fishpool Hoard of jewellery. Nottinghamshire, England, 1463-4.
(British Museum)

This is another example of a heart shaped brooch of the fifteenth century. It is also English or French and the reverse bears the legend, in French, 'ours and always at your desire'. The front and back were almost certainly enamelled originally, although no enamel remains now. The original presence of enamel on Medieval gold ornaments can often be detected, even after it has all disappeared, by the discolouration and sometimes 'bleaching' of the gold that underlay it.

Fig.201:
A gold brooch in the form of a heart. English or French. 15th century.
(Victoria and Albert Museum, London)
© V&A Images / Victoria and Albert Museum

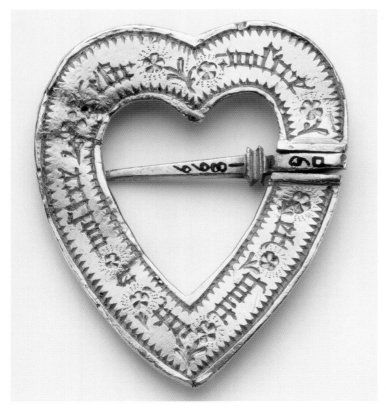

Fig.202: The reverse of figure 201,
showing inscription.
© V&A Images / Victoria and Albert Museum

Fig.203:
The Middleham Jewel, gold set with a sapphire.
England, ca 1460. (Yorkshire Museum, York)
© York Museums Trust (Yorkshire Museum)

A metal detectorist heading back to his car near Middleham Castle, in Yorkshire, found what he took to be an old powder compact and tossed it into a bag with the other odd scraps he had found that day. Once home he washed it and discovered it was a spectacular Medieval gold pendant dating from the second half of the fifteenth century. As a single stray find, it was not then classed as Treasure Trove (in which case it would have belonged to the British 'Crown') and the finder was able to sell it. The pendant sold for £1.3 million at auction and later found its rightful home in the Yorkshire Museum, York.

The pendant is of diamond shape and opens to allow the insertion of a fragment from the true cross or some such venerated relic. It is set with a large sapphire and engraved with a scene of the Trinity on one side, the Nativity on the other and has Latin inscriptions. The inscription around the depiction of the Trinity with Christ on the cross is based on the words spoken by John the Baptist when he Baptised Christ, but with additional words including 'Ananizapta'. This word in this context has been much discussed, but it is also known to have

formed part of Medieval spells against epilepsy. However, I know of no medieval associations where the sapphire is effective against epilepsy – a property more usually attributed to the emerald. 'Magical' formulae against diseases and other threats are of considerable age, but we only begin to find them engraved on jewellery around 1300, after which time they rapidly became common.

The engraved scenes were once enamelled and the enamel protected the underlying gold from cleaning, wear and perhaps original finishing operations. As a result, the empty recesses now have a slightly paler colour than the flat surfaces. This paler colour is due to the presence of silver in the gold alloy that, originally being under the enamel, was not leached out in final manufacturing processes, in use, or the initial centuries of burial.

Analysis of the gold shows that it is about 75% pure, 18 carat, and it is tempting to relate this to the introduction of the 18 carat gold standard in England in 1478. The object does indeed date from about this time.

The Rest of the World

So far in this book we have mainly been concerned with the jewellery from Europe and the Near East. It is to this goldwork that we can best trace back our more recent 'western' jewellery. However, all societies around the world that progressed past the Stone Age appear to have made some use of gold in their personal ornamentation and this deserves our attention.

The end of the Medieval Period in Europe in the late fifteenth century coincides with the development of maritime exploration and trade and, most significantly, the discovery of what to the Europeans was an entire new continent – the Americas. South America was to provide a whole new supply of gem and jewellery materials for Europe, including gold, pearls, emeralds, diamonds, amethysts, topazes and platinum. Fifteenth century mariners had set off looking for untold riches, they were not disappointed

However, by the time that Christopher Columbus first set foot on an Island in the Bahamas in 1492, the various cultures in Central and South America had been producing jewellery for many centuries. Recent archaeological discoveries has set the arrival of the earliest inhabitants of the Americas back to the hunters and gatherers who crossed the Baring Straits around 12000 BC. These new inhabitants of the continent gradually expanded southwards, reaching the southernmost tip of South America within a couple of millennia – remarkably quickly by Archaeological standards. However, it was not until 'historical times', by Old World standards, that recognizable, jewellery-producing societies had developed.

Gold working probably began in the highlands of Peru about the same time that Tutankhamen reigned in Egypt, just over 3000 years ago. The technology then gradually appears in Equador, Colombia and elsewhere, but it is unclear whether the skills spread from Peru or were developed independently in these other places. For example, the earliest gold objects from Colombia do not seem to predate about 500 BC, the time when, far away in Greece, Homer was spinning his stories of voyage and adventure. Further north, the oldest known goldwork from Panama and Costa Rica can probably be dated to about the second century AD – when far to the east, the Roman Emperor Hadrian was building his wall to keep the wild northerners out of England.

There is little to indicate that the Mexicans were using gold before later part of the first millennium – the very time that the Viking were beginning their expansion in Northern Europe and probably established short-lived settlements in North America. This is not to say that jewellery other that that of gold was not known earlier: the Olmecs in Mexcio, for example, were wearing personal ornaments in jadeite, nephrite and serpentine before the birth of Christ.

The two greatest Pre-Columbian empires were the Inca and the Aztec. At its height the Inka empire stretched through the Andean highlands, from Ecuador down through to Chile and Bolivia, while the Aztecs ruled in Central America, covering much of what now comprises Mexico.

Jewellery was deliberately presented to the gods by donating to a temple or shrine, or placing in some other sacred spot – the latter included throwing gold into rivers, wells or lakes. A famous example of the latter is Lake Guatavita near present day Bogota, Colombia which according the legend had vast amounts of gold ritually consigned to its depths. Various attempts were made over the last five centuries to drain the lake to find these untold reassures, until the Colombian government put in under national protection in 1965.

The pectoral shown here in the form of a human figure with a most elaborate headdress is from Popayan, Colombia and is made in one piece of gold by casting. Cast gold jewellery is encountered in the Andean region from before the time of Christ, but became highly advanced by the time the Conquistadors arrived.

The usual casting method was a version of the so-called lost wax casting process. A prototype of the required object is made in wax, or in Pre-Colombian work, probably a resinous plant extract. This model was coated in clay, an inlet hole was drilled down to the interior model, and then the clay was fired. The 'wax' melted and burned out leaving a negative of the model. Molten gold was then poured into this and once all had cooled sufficiently, and the gold solidified, the mold was broken and the casting removed.

As in the Old World, it was discovered that adding a proportion of copper to the gold made it flow better in the mould, thus producing far more intricate castings. The copper content caused the castings to have dark, oxide-coated surfaces, but this could be removed with natural strong chemicals such as some fruit juices or other plant extracts, leaving a nearly pure gold surface. This surface 'enrichment' of gold objects also allowed a variety of decorative effects and became a feature of much Pre-Columbian goldwork where it is termed *Tumbaga*. Some Tumbaga gold objects though appearing on the surface to be of high purity gold can actually have interiors that are less than a third gold.

Fig.204: Gold pectoral in the form of a stylised human figure. Popayan, Colombia, AD 1100 - 1500. (British Museum) © Copyright the Trustees of The British Museum

In the various ancient American societies gold jewellery was worn by the living and by the dead. Its value and importance was largely symbolic, gold was the metal of the sun. The simplest, and oldest, manufacturing approach was to hammer the gold into sheet that could be cut, bent and shaped to the required forms. The thin gold could be worked using tools of copper, stone, bone or wood implements.

The gold mask shown here, is a Chimu funerary mask from Peru. It is of sheet gold decorated with attached pendants and stone beads. The red colouration is also intentional. The Chimu were based on the northern coast of Peru, a well developed and organized culture that appeared about AD 1200. They were absorbed by the Inka Empire in the middle of the fifteenth century, just a few decades before the Europeans arrived.

The European encounter with the great civilisations of South and Central America were prompted by the attempts to find a sea route to India and China, very important trading partners.

Jewellery in China can be traced back to the simple beads worn in the Stone Age. For example, animal teeth pendants dating to before 10,000 BC have been found in a hilltop cave near Beijing. However, gold jewellery is scarce in China before the middle of the first millennium BC when there were imports and influences from Central Asia and ultimately the Greek world.

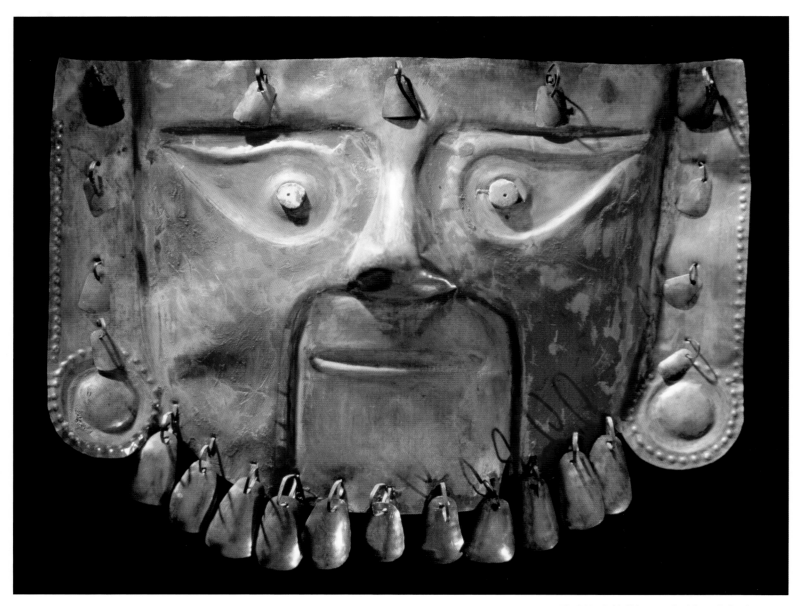

Fig.205: Gold Chimu mask with applied red pigment.
Chimor, Peru, AD 1200 - 1500.
© Gianni Dagli Orti/CORBIS

Excavations in China over the last generation have revealed an increasing quantity of gold objects that often relate to Central Asia forms and techniques. However, there is one jewellery material that China can really claim as its own - jade. Jade is hard and tough, and so difficult to shape and to polish, nevertheless, there are examples of Chinese jade ornaments that are contemporary with the Bronze Age in the Near East and Mediterranean. Remarkably, there is little evidence that Chinese jade ornaments were ever traded to the west, even though there was some use of western jade for axes.

Another area where the early Chinese excelled was in the casting of elaborate copper- alloy vessels and other objects. The Chinese were probably also the first to introduce the art of mercury gilding (see fig.55), in about 300 BC.

The elegant belt hook shown here dates to the Chinese Han Dynasty, around second to first century BC, and combines mercury gild cast copper alloy with a white jade inlay. The hook end takes the form of a dragon head, and the complex shaped jade inlay is in the form of a coiled, highly stylised dragon.

Excavations in China over the last half century have revealed an extraordinary wealth of gold jewellery. This includes some intricate goldwork produced in China at a period roughly contemporary with the Early Byzantine period in the west and which shows a mastery of intricate techniques which may even have ultimately derived from the Mediterranean world.

Shown here is a pair of elaborate hair pins dating from the Tang Dynasty (seventh – eighth century AD). The long prongs are in gilded silver, but the intricate terminals are in granulation and openwork granulation and filigree, combined with stone inlays. The wire is made in the usual ancient way as we have encountered in the west (fig.116), by twisting and rolling a narrow cut strip of gold, but the openwork granulation is remarkable by western standards since it has no backing.

Pins of this type are clear evidence for the Chinese love of elaborate hair styles. There is another similar but single pin of this type in the Metropolitan Museum of Art in New York as well as examples in Chinese collections .

Fig.206: Gilded copper belt hook with jade inlay.
Han Dynasty China, 2nd - 1st century BC.
(British Museum)
© Copyright the Trustees of The British Museum

Fig.207: Pair of gold pins with openwork granulated decoration.
Tang Dynasty China, 7th - 8th century AD. (British Museum)
© Copyright the Trustees of The British Museum

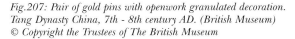

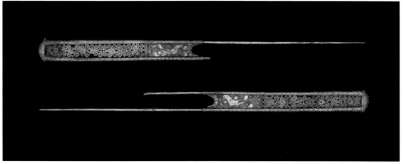

Some impressive gold jewellery survives from Korea's Silla Period that ended in the mid tenth century AD. Among these ornaments are earrings, or possibly head-dress or crown ornaments such as those shown here.

Stylistically they are fairly simple, though there is some granulation and little sheet gold leaf pendants that are attached by twists of wire and which moved when the ornament was worn. The hanging sheet gold decorations of this type might derive from the little sheet gold disks similarly attached to Central Asia and Mongolian ornaments that date from the first century AD onwards.

One feature in Korean gold jewellery of this period, is the presence of gold wire made by pulling gold through holes in a stone or metal plate. This process, termed 'wire drawing', only became common in the west by about the tenth century AD, having superceded the older way of making wires by twisting and rolling a gold strip. Wires made by drawing have been noted on Korean goldwork in several collections and suggests a rapid dissemination of the technique all the way across the then known world. Just where the technique was originally developed – in the east, the west or in the Islamic lands that lay between – still needs to be determined.

Fig.208: A group of gold ornaments for the ears or a crown. Korea, 7th - 10th century AD. (British Museum)

The culturally diverse regions of the world have provided an equally diverse range of jewellery and related personal ornaments. There is a simple but somewhat chauvinistic way in which a jewellery historian of the developed world may approach all this. It can work for all art historians: we judge all unfamiliar art on the basis of our aesthetics and taste. So beauty or some other obvious attribute is enough to entice us, even when we know little of the object's cultural background. An example would be the ear pendants, probably from Equador, shown here. They are made from feathers and beetle-wing cases. It, like so many objects made from organic materials have an aesthetic appeal , even if the materials are unfamiliar.

With such objects that have ready appeal for us, that is enough, we can dodge the tricky questions. But how might we consider, say, a necklet from the Austal Islands in the Pacific that incorporates pendants in the form of phalluses and testicles carved from human bone? Does this raise the same questions as diamonds synthesised from the carbonised remains of a dead relative, a commercial service now provided by several companies? In January 2006, the Science Museum in London hosted an event entitled 'Bio-Bling' and described as 'A groundbreaking new project - using human bone tissue to create bespoke jewellery'. Part of the rational for this bone tissue jewellery was to raise the question of the meaning and emotional content of jewellery.

I am mentioning this now because in the next section we move on to Renaissance and then later Europe. We are about to enter more familiar territory and, perhaps erroneously, think we can better enter the minds of the jewellers and their patrons. As the superstitious Middle Ages, pagan Romans and sacrificed Sumerian maidens fade into the past and we enter the age of reason and science, jewellery may hold fewer dark recesses and cultural paradoxes for us. But we must still constantly ask questions of the jewellery, or help it prompt questions. Aesthetics are not enough. After all, nobody really cares whether you think the jewellery in this books looks pretty or not apart, perhaps, from my publishers.

Fig.209: Ear ornaments in feathers and beetle wing cases.
Ecuador. (Victoria and Albert Museum, London)
© V&A Images / Victoria and Albert Museum

European Renaissance

This portrait of Queen Elizabeth 1 of England, know as the 'Ditchley Portrait', was painted by Marcus Gheeraerts the Younger in 1592, probably for Sir Henry Lee of Ditchley, near Oxford. It is pertinent for our look at Renaissance jewellery, not only because of the extraordinary quantity of gold, pearls, rubies and other gems that adorn the Queen, from her hair to the base of her gown, but also because it sums up something of the spirit of the age. She stands on, and towers above England, bringing pretty well all the world under view, and the allegorical change in the sky from dark-clouded and stormy on one side to sunlight on the other reminds us that this was a time of great change and new-beginnings.

If we had to sum up European jewellery of the Renaissance Period we might describe it as colourful, opulent and intricate while treading an adventurous path between fantasy and faith. Renaissance means rebirth. The late fifteenth century heralded a time of rediscovery of the classical world, both of its material remains and of its recorded wisdom, and it was a time of discovery on a global scale. Columbus reached America in 1492, searching for a sea route to the East. Just six years later his aim was accomplished when Vasco da Gama sailed round the Cape of Good Hope and triumphantly entered the Indian Ocean. There were 'new lands' and new riches to exploit in them; enormous potential for jewellery in new materials and in new styles. But there was another significant discovery that extended peoples horizons. In 1454, Gutenberg's Bible, the first complete printed book in Europe, had been put on sale in Frankfurt, Germany.

It is interesting in the present context to note that Johann Gutenberg had himself taught the art of 'polishing and grinding of precious stones' but his introduction of printing is rightly seen as having had the most monumental effect on almost every human art and endeavour. Printing launched the Renaissance; it was the first information revolution since the introduction of speech and writing. Knowledge could be duplicated and widely disseminated, whether Greek philosophy, translations of Arab chemistry, drawings of old ruins, maps of new lands or designs for jewellery. The availability of written information fuelled a vast increase in literacy that in turn fuelled a demand for education and knowledge on a scale never previously experienced. In jewellery design, for example, classical myths and motifs now vied with traditional Christian ones; something really only possible on a wide scale once a broader section of the aristocracy had become familiar with the Greek and Roman roots of European art.

By 1500, Europeans had wrestled emeralds, gold and pearls from the natives in South America and had opened up the direct sea route to the gem-bearing lands of the East. Gold, silver, pearls and gems now entered Europe in ever greater numbers, along with spices, textiles and other rare products. The merchants that had grown in influence and wealth across Europe in the later Medieval Period, now provided a receptive audience for new ideas. Individuality and fantasy flourished, and jewellery became increasingly associated with monetary value rather than just status or courtly rank.

Renaissance art transcended all media, from a small jewel to a tapestry to a palace. The fifteenth century Italian goldsmith Cellini was also a sculpture and goldsmith; Henry VIII's court painter Hans Holbein designed jewellery.

Perhaps strangely, the association of the Renaissance with the re-birth of classical ideas did not lead to wholesale copying of earlier jewellery forms. Despite the admiration expressed by Cellini for the works of the goldsmiths of ancient Greece and Rome, Renaissance jewellery barely casts a nod in the direction of classical jewellery, other than in the incorporation of Classical mythological subjects. However, the Renaissance did see the reappearance of those two common classes of classical ornament – the earring and the bracelet. The puritan Philip Stubbes, a contemporary of William Shakespeare, decried the 'dissolute minions' who were 'not ashamed to make holes in their eares, wherat they hang rings, and other Jewels of gold and precious stones.' One might see a reason why earrings had earlier fallen out of fashion, but it is less easy to understand why bracelets, such a staple of earlier jewellery had also almost entirely disappeared from use in Northern Europe after early Medieval times. Men also now began to wear more jewellery, a blending of the differences between the sexes that was also an abhorrence to Stubbes.

The wide popularity of jewellery is seen in the array of portraiture that illustrates the extraordinary amount of jewellery that a wealthy man or woman might wear at the time, including huge gold chains and excesses of pearls. We also find an increasing number of representations of jewellers at work. The student of jewellery technology might find few of the precise details that he or she seeks, but even absences are informative. We can note, for example, no sign of fine piercing saws or of lamps to provide the flame for soldering. Nor do we see magnification in use, other than the spectacles perched on the noses of some goldsmiths. There are also drawings of drawings. For the first time we see jewellery designs pinned to the wall. Such design drawings have survived.

DA EXPECTAT

POTEST VI ... TVR

European Renaissance 163

The embossed and enamelled gold scene on this mid-sixteenth century hat badge shows the Conversion of St Paul. The inscription around the edge is from the Acts of the Apostles and says, in Latin, 'It is hard for you to kick against the goad'. The painted enamel technique is a survivor from later Medieval times, but the postures and dress of the figures are entirely Renaissance in their borrowing from the world of Classical antiquity.

The object was made in Southern Europe, probably in Italy or Spain, and according to an inscription on a separate gold disk inserted on the reverse, it was given to the Marchese Camillo Capizucchi by Don Juan of Austria, the half-brother of Philip II of Spain, who had previously worn it in his hat. Hat jewels were a fashionable ornament for men at this time and often had Biblical scenes. The Conversion of Saint Paul was a particularly dramatic theme that was used by several Renaissance artists including Michelangelo, Caravaggio and Taddeo Zuccaro.

The windows in the building are rendered in table-cut diamonds and the two largest shields are in kite-shaped diamonds, reminders that the art of diamond cutting had progressed in the second half of the fifteenth century and greatly expanded in the sixteenth.

Signet rings had been used both functionally and symbolically as an indication of rank since the Bronze Age. They were used to seal documents and containers, and this functional use meant they could circumnavigate the various prohibitions against jewellery use through the ages. The early Christian fathers who stridently decried jewellery wear allowed men to wear signets and even the Prophet Mohammad agreed to use a silver signet ring after it was explained to him that the Byzantines would not read his letters unless they bore an official seal.

Early signet rings bore names or personal symbols. Those with heraldic devices first appeared in the later Medieval period and are encountered in Britain from the fifteenth century onwards. This example dates from the later part of the sixteenth century and is engraved with the arms of the Ravenscroft family, of Flintshire, Wales. Several members of this prominent family were Sherrifs of Fintshire in the later sixteen and seventeenth centuries and this ring may have belonged to George Ravenscroft (died 1592) who was a Member of Parliament in 1563-7 and sheriff in 1578-9. One of George's grandsons was the musician Thomas Ravenscroft whose works include the first publication of the children's song 'Three Blind Mice.' I have not traced any connection between this family and the Ravenscroft who introduced a new and improved glass for imitation gems.

Fig.211: Gold and enamel hat badge showing the conversion of St Paul. Southern Europe, mid-16th century. (British Museum)
© Copyright the Trustees of The British Museum

Fig.212: Gold signet ring with the arms of the Ravenscroft family. Britain, later 16th century. (British Museum)
© Copyright the Trustees of The British Museum

The second gold signet ring shown here dates to the late sixteenth to early seventeenth century and has an unusual feature – the centre revolves. One side bears the arms of Sir Nicholas Throckmorton a member of parliament, although a minor figure until he was adopted by his uncle Francis Carew whose arms are on the other side of this bezel. He was brother-in-law to Sir Walter Raleigh. Sir Nicholas dies in 1643.

Fig.213: Gold signet ring with a revolving bezel with the arms of Nicholas Throckmorton and Francis Carew. English, late 16th - early 17th century. (Victoria and Albert Museum, London)
© V&A Images / Victoria and Albert Museum

Fig.214: The other side of the bezel in the ring in figure 214.
© V&A Images / Victoria and Albert Museum

"I first laid down an oval framework, considerably longer than half a cubit, almost two-thirds, in fact; and upon this ground, wishing to suggest the intermingled state of land and ocean, I modelled two figures, considerably taller than a palm in height, which were seated with their legs interlaced, suggesting those lengthier branches of the sea which run up into the continents. The sea was a man, and in his hand I placed a ship, elaborately wrought in all its details, and well adapted to hold a quantity of salt. Beneath him I grouped the four sea-horses, and in his right hand he held his trident. The earth I fashioned like a woman, with all the beauty of form, the grace, and charm of which my art was capable. She had a richly decorated temple firmly based upon the ground at one side; and here her hand rested. This I intended to receive the pepper. In her other hand I put a cornucopia, overflowing with all the natural treasures I could think of. Below this goddess, in the part which represented earth, I collected the fairest animals that haunt our globe. In the quarter presided over by the deity of ocean, I fashioned such choice kinds of fishes and shells as could be properly displayed in that small space. What remained of the oval I filled in with luxuriant ornamentation."

That's how the Benvenuto Cellini described his design for this magnificent salt cellar. He made it for the King of France in the early 1540s and it was later given to Archduke Ferdinand II of the Tirol. It is the only certain surviving example of goldwork from Cellini's hand and even it came perilously close to disappearance. In May 2003 it was stolen from the Kunsthistorisches Museum, Vienna. For a time its whereabouts were unknown and fears for its survival spread along with rumours of ransom demands and bits of enamel in envelopes, and some interesting but cryptic messages on the internet. Then, on Saturday, January 21, 2006, the Austrian police were led by the suspected thief to its hiding place in a metal box buried in woods some 50 miles north of Vienna. It is said to be undamaged.

Fig.215: Gold and enamel salt cellar. By Benvenuto Cellini, Italy, c 1540. (Kunsthistorisches Museum, Vienna)
© Kunsthistorisches Museum, Wein Oder KHM, Wein

A large baroque pearl forms the body of this gold and enamel lizard or salamander pendant that dates from the later sixteenth century. In myth, that dates back at least to Medieval times in Europe, the salamander was not only resistant to fire, but lived in it. The name salamander is supposed to derive from an Arab-Persian word that means 'lives in fire'. A mundane origin has been proposed that these scale-less lizards live in cracks and crevices in logs and are seen to scurry out for safety when the logs are placed on a fire.

The choice of a salamander for this ornament is unclear. It might simply have been intended to protect the wearer from fire. Or, perhaps, it could remind its owner that true faith would withstand the martyr's death by burning which was by no means an uncommon fate in Renaissance Europe. An alternative is that the salamander was the symbol for a particular family. For example, the sixteenth century French King François I had the salamander as his symbol and the motto Nutrisco et Exstinguo (I stoke and extinguish).

In any case, this pendant illustrates a popular characteristic in Renaissance jewellery, fantastic and often asymmetric figural forms incorporating shaped pearls. It might be assumed that the pearls, large and small, that began to appear in abundance in Renaissance jewellery all hailed from the Persian gulf and India along the newly-opened direct sea routes. However, there was another new and important pearl source that became available to Renaissance Europe – America.

One of the most remarkable documents relating to the treasures from the New World is the so-call Drake Manuscript in the Pierpont Morgan Library. The 134 pages were compiled by at least two different scribes and two different artists, but it almost certainly originated among two or more of the French Huguenots whom we know accompanied Sir Francis Drake in the 1570's. The illustrations and French texts in this manuscript describe how pearls were dived for by African slaves off the coast of Venezuela, between the mainland and the Isla de Margarita ('Pearl Island'), These divers descended with a basket-like net to the bottom and, we are told, could hold their breath for up to 15 minutes.

Seventeenth century writers explained that the American pearls were not considered as good as the oriental, but even so the French jeweller and traveller Tavernier sold a large pear-shaped pearl from Venezuela to the Uncle of the Great Mogul in India in the 1660's.

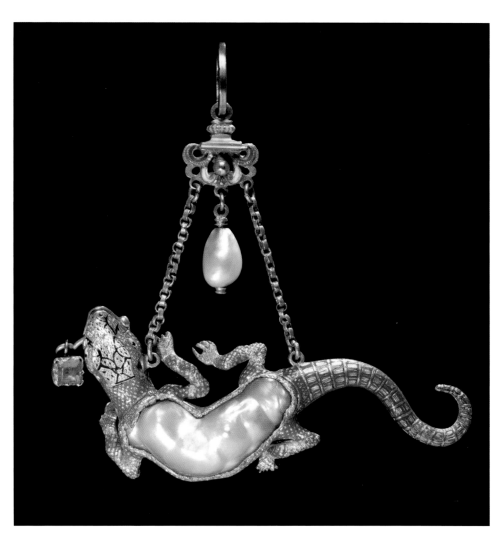

Fig.216: Gold pendant in the form of a salamander, the body a large pearl. European, later 16th century. (Victoria and Albert Museum, London)
© V&A Images / Victoria and Albert Museum

This late sixteenth century pendant is set entirely with diamonds, a contrast to the usual colourful jewellery of the period. IHS, although a common monogram in the Roman Catholic Church, are the first three letters of the name Jesus written in the Greek alphabet. This sacred monogram was popular in later Medieval times and by the sixteenth century, as here, the H is sometimes surmounted by a cross and below there are the three nails used in the crucifixion. In 1541 the Sacred Monogram was adopted by St. Ignatius of Loyola and became the emblem of the Jesuits.

The origin of this pendant is thought to be South Germany, but about a century after its manufacture it is said to have been in the hands of Sir William Howard, Viscount Stafford, who was tried and executed in 1680 for his supposed part in a trumped up Jesuit-inspired plot against Charles II. Sir William is known to have travelled in Germany.

The diamonds are cut in what is called hog-back form, a cutting style that had appeared by the late fifteenth century. The reverse of the ornament has an applied enamelled plaque that shows the symbols of Christ's passion and which might have been added to the pendant sometime after its original manufacture.

Fig.217: Gold and diamond pendant in the form of the sacred monogram
- IHS. Probably South Germany, later 16th century.
(Victoria and Albert Museum, London)
© V&A Images / Victoria and Albert Museum

The Renaissance and seventeenth centuries also saw the use of exquisite portrait miniatures set in elaborate jewelled frames. This painted miniature of Queen Elizabeth I, set in an enamelled gold container with table cut diamonds and rubies was painted by the celebrated Nicholas Hilliard around 1590-1603. The owner was presumably keen to show his loyalty to this powerful queen at a period of unrelenting religious and political plots and counter plots.

The processes of enamelling had improved greatly in later medieval times, in part due to new recipes for glass composition, and Renaissance goldsmiths could confidently apply enamel almost paint-like in thin, brightly coloured layers over undulating gold surfaces. The colour palette at their disposal was extensive, but white, black, dark and a pale blue, green and red predominate, as here on the back of this jewel. Opaque white was the base for most colours, with small amounts of other coloured glasses, or various metallic oxides, added to create the other shades.

Portrait miniatures were also often given or made as a memento or a sign of thanks. Even royalty needed to show gratitude for they too needed the reassurance that they were worthy of their position.

The sickly, Scots-born James I of England (James VI of Scotland) was particularly indebted to Thomas Lyte who, from the time of the coronation in 1603, spent seven years of toil drawing up the king's pedigree. The result of this diligent research was splendid. James's family tree stretched its branches back to the Roman Brutus, the Germanic god Woden and, conveniently, lines of Scottish, Welsh and Norman kings. A delighted James presented Thomas with this fine diamond-encrusted gold locket that bears his monogram "JR" in rubies. Inside the locket are two portraits of James I by Nickolas Hilliard, the court painter. A portrait survives that shows Thomas Lyte proudly wearing this jewel.

The jewel was presumably made in London and shows the move to delicacy and more accent on the gems that is a characteristic of the seventeenth century. Here the miniature is surrounded by table cut diamonds set in the truncated pyramidal settings typical of the sixteenth and seventeenth century. The restriction to, and the number of, diamonds is remarkable, but we must remember that James I's mother, Mary Queen of Scots, had married in 1558 wearing a wedding dress so covered in diamonds that a contemporary described it as "too dazzling to look upon".

Fig.218: Painted miniature of Queen Elizabeth I of England, mounted in an enamelled gold pendant set with diamonds and rubies.
Miniature by Nicholas Hilliard, English, ca 1590-1603.
(Victoria and Albert Museum, London)
© V&A Images / Victoria and Albert Museum

Fig.219: The Lyte Jewel, portrait miniatures of King James I mounted in a diamond-set and enamelled gold pendant. English, ca 1710. (British Museum)
© Copyright the Trustees of The British Museum

In this circular diamond and ruby brooch set in enamelled gold, the central stone is a ruby, and one specially chosen because of its resemblance to a stylised heart. This brooch dates from around 1610-1620 and was probably made in Prague. The design of a heart pierced by arrows relates, of course, to love and its reverse, with some later attachments in place, clearly shows both how much attention was paid to the back of jewellery and how it could be assembled from several parts.

Here the front and back are joined by gold nuts and bolts so that the enamelled components would not have to undergo further heat in soldering. On the pendant in fig.219, tubular rivets have been used to hold the gem settings on the front in place for the same reason. The ends of these rivets can clearly be seen and it is sobering to realise that originally these were concealed under the enamel and have only been revealed as the enamel has fractured off.

Fig.220: A gold brooch set with diamonds and rubies, including a large central heart-shaped ruby. Probably Prague, ca 1610-20.
(Victoria and Albert Museum, London)
© V&A Images / Victoria and Albert Museum

Fig.221: The back of the brooch in figure 220.
© V&A Images / Victoria and Albert Museum

Jewellery and all types of precious objects were often deliberately concealed as a means of security. In the days before strong safes or bank vaults, burying your gold jewellery in a pot in the ground or hiding it within a wall in your house was the only means you had at your disposal to best ensure its safety while away from home, or when robbers or tax authorities threatened to visit. Some of the finest assemblages of jewellery that have survived comes from hoards buried for safety, but never recovered. One of the most spectacular of post-medieval date is a hoard that seems to have been concealed by a jeweller below the floor of his house or workshop in the 1620's.

In 1912 workmen demolishing three tenement buildings in London's Cheapside uncovered the most important surviving group of early seventeenth century European jewellery. The majority of what is now known as The Cheapside Hoard is today in the Museum of London, with smaller parts of the find in the British Museum and Victoria and Albert Museum.

Shown here is most of the hoard arranged to provide an impression of how it must have looked when found. The gemstones illustrate the range of coloured stones now entering northern Europe: emeralds from Brazil, diamonds from India and perhaps Borneo, sapphires from Ceylon and rubies from Burma (Myanmar).

Despite the myriad gemstones in the hoard, it is clear that the approach to their use is very different from today. For example, the majority of stones are in gold settings with enclosed backs and some substances to 'improve' the colour of the gems. It is noteworthy that a type of setting for gemstones, especially rubies, seen in sixteenth and seventeenth century jewellery, including some objects in the Cheapside Hoard, can be paralleled right across Europe and into the Ottoman Empire in what is now Turkey and Greece. There even appear to be some re-used Ottoman gold jewellery components in the Cheapside Hoard. It must be remembered that the Ottoman Empire was one of the world's major powers during this period.

Fig.222: The Cheapside Hoard arranged to give an idea of how it may have been found.
English, late 16th - early 17th century. (Museum of London)
© *Museum of London*

The ruby and diamond bow pendant from the Cheapside Hoard exhibits the combination of delicate goldwork, coloured gems and enamel that become typical for the seventeenth century. It is also an early example of this type of bow shape in jewellery. The form might be a development of the traditional lover's knot which in turn might be traceable back to the fertility symbolism of the Classical Heracles knot – our reef knot. The lightness and delicacy of this pendant, and other pieces in the Cheapside Hoard contrast with the heavier, but grandiose flamboyancy of the Baroque styles that appear later in the seventeenth century.

The rubies here are cut in quite a sophisticated way – one in a rose cut, the other in a hexagonal form. Versions of the rose cut were used for several gem types in the Cheapside Hoard, including rubies, garnets and amethysts. Other rubies in the hoard are cut in the simple table cut with irregular outlines that were common in sixteenth century. The small diamonds are carefully chosen to match in size to form the narrow gold ribbon loops. It is noteworthy that the diamonds are still set in gold – in later centuries they would be set in silver to best compliment their colour.

The goldwork now has very much of a supporting role. From its appearance and apparent softness it is probably of relatively high purity – perhaps around the 22 carat standard (22 parts gold per 24, thus 91.67% gold) that had been re-introduced in Britain in 1575, gold of lesser purity also would have been difficult to enamel at that period. The pale rubies seen here are typical of those from Ceylon and a gemologist might prefer to class them as 'pink sapphires'.

Fig.223: Ruby and diamond bow from the Cheapside Hoard. English, late 16th - early 17th century. (Museum of London)
© Museum of London

The hair ornament here is another object from the early seventeenth century Cheapside Hoard, London, and most clearly demonstrates the move to jewellery where the gems are the predominant feature. The stones are precisely cut and must have been cut to match if not specifically for this piece. The gemstones have been tentatively identified as diamonds and if so their regularity and the complexity of their cutting would be exceptional this early.

Before the early eighteenth century the diamonds employed in jewellery had come almost entirely from India, however, the East India Company did not venture much into the Indian diamond trade until after the 1620's. So, despite the relative abundance of diamonds in this hoard, they were probably obtained via trade rather than by direct exploitation. However, the East India Company did exploit diamonds in Borneo between about 1610 and 1620, and some of the Cheapside diamonds might originate there.

There were new merchants as well as new gems in the seventeenth century. Jews were allowed to settle in England from 1650, and Huguenots after the Revocation of the Edict of Nantes (1685) had driven them out of France. There were also new problems. Measures drafted by the Goldsmiths' Company in the seventeenth century include the desire 'That no person Import into the Kingdome, or therein make, set or put to sale any false, Artificial, Counterfeit Stones, Jewelles, Pearls, Pendants, etc., upon pain not only of the forfeiture of the thing, but the punishment as by the Law…'

Fig.224: Diamond-set hat ornament from the Cheapside Hoard. English, late 16th - early 17th century. (Museum of London)
© Museum of London

The pale sapphire ring shown here is also from the Cheapside Hoard and is noteworthy for its elegant simplicity. There is no evidence that the hoop was ever enamelled. The pale sapphire is finely cut and well demonstrates the improvements in gem cutting that we see from this period onwards.

The presence of sapphire here reminds us that sapphires, though well attested in Medieval times, are less common in Renaissance jewellery and then not common until the later nineteenth century. The main source was still Ceylon and the difficulties in obtaining these stones might be best explained by the British sailor Robert Knox who was captured in Ceylon in 1659 and spent 20 years there, in captivity. He noted that "In this island are several sorts of precious stones, which the king of his part has enough of, and so careth not to have more discovery made. For in certain places where they [gem stones] are known to be, sharp poles are set up fixed in the ground, signifying that none upon pain of being struck and impaled upon those poles, presume so much as to go that way."

Robert Knox also has the dubious honour of being the first to bring to British attention 'a strange, intoxicating herb'. Today we call it cannabis.

Fig.225: Sapphire and gold ring from the Cheapside Hoard. English, late 16th - early 17th century. (Museum of London)
© Museum of London

Fig.226: Side view of the ring in fig 225
© Museum of London

The ring just described shows that although sapphires were far scarcer than rubies in sixteenth and seventeenth centuries, they tend to take pride of place when they do appear. Perhaps the dangers of their acquisition meant that only the larger specimens were worth taking a risk for. In any case, a single large sapphire also forms the main central element on this necklet that dates to the mid-seventeenth century. Here it is cut into a hexagonal form and its gem companions are a fine array of 35 table cut diamonds on the enamel-backed links and three rose diamonds surmounting the sapphire.

The gentleman shown here is Sir Bevil Grenville, painted by David de Granges, later appointed "His Majesty's Limner" (portrait painter) by King Charles II. Sir Bevil was the much loved leader of the Cornish infantry, on the Royalist side, at the Civil War battle of Lansdowne in 1643, at which he was killed. This jewel is mentioned in Sir Bevil's widow's will of 1647 and it is tempting to see it as a jewel she wore in memory of her husband. The preponderance of black enamel on the case – just visible here around the edge - here might also point to mourning use.

The gem set and enamelled case, not visible here, shows how the skulls and skeletons of sixteenth century mourning jewellery had been largely replaced in the seventeenth century by more subtle imagery including stylised flower gardens. The gems in the enamelled garden on this pendant include ten opals as well as rubies, diamonds and a large central sapphire. Opals are very uncommon in surviving sixteenth and seventeenth century jewellery, although there are also surviving examples in the Cheapside Hoard.

Fig.228: The portrait miniature of Sir Bevil Grenville set in the 'Grenville Jewel'. English ca 1643. (British Museum)
© Copyright the Trustees of The British Museum

The growing European trade with India during the sixteenth and seventeenth centuries led to the transport of techniques and styles as well as raw materials. The seventeenth century pendant here, from Mogul India, can be compared with jewellery from the Ottoman Empire in Turkey and the Balkans, and right across Europe. We see the same prominence of rubies and a diamond, and an intricate use of enamel. The question, of course, is in which direction did the influences travel?

The use of enamel in Mogul jewellery was probably due to European influence and Jaipur became the major centre – and still is. The tulip, which we see in some Renaissance enamels was a flower introduced into Europe from the Ottoman world in the mix sixteenth century.

The rubies here are set in thin gold foil in a technique typical of late sixteenth and seventeenth century Mogul Indian jewellery and which is termed Kundan work. The rubies are bedded in lac or similar resin and very thin, high purity gold foil is burnished down over them. The rubies in both Mogul and much European Renaissance jewellery are of a bright red colour that suggest they come, in the main anyway, from Burma (Myanmar). It is likely that many of those in Renaissance European jewellery were traded via India. The records of Fort St George, now Madras, in India for 1681 refer to a small vessel belonging to a Portuguese merchant that had 'arrived from Pegu [Burma] upon which cam severall Ruby Merchts with considerable quantitys of Rubies.' We see identical, irregularly shaped flat-cut rubies in European Renaissance, Ottoman and Mughal jewellery, strongly suggesting that these were often cut in the east. Indeed, a seventeenth century report says that Burmese rubies were never cut in Burma, but only in India.

Fig.230: The reverse of the pendant in figure 230, showing elaborate enamel work.
© *Copyright the Trustees of The British Museum*

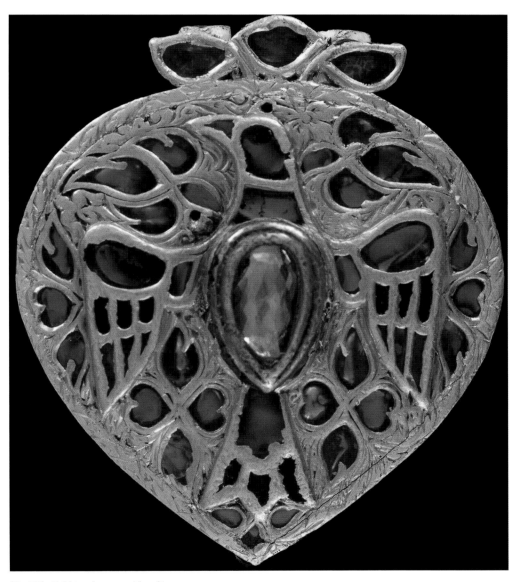

Fig.229: Gold pendant set with rubies.
Mogul Indian, 17th century. (British Museum)
© *Copyright the Trustees of The British Museum*

This Indian inlaid white jade pendant is shown here to demonstrate how similar forms could appear in different materials. This shape is a popular Mogul one and may derive from the arrowhead which was a protective amulet. The pendant also demonstrates the Mogul skills in inlaying of hard stone – here pale nephrite jade, with gold and gems. The rubies and emeralds are set into recesses carved into the jade using a version of the kundan setting technique as seen in fig.229. Below the pendant hangs a pale emerald – perhaps one of Indian origin.

This pendant dates from the early seventeenth century, the heyday of inlaid hardstones, although they do occur earlier contexts. Originally it probably hung as the centrepiece of a necklace, attached by means of a lateral perforation along its top. On the reverse of the pendant is inscribed a verse from the Koran, a reminder that the Moguls were converts to Islam and that, despite the beauty and refinement of Mogul and Indian art, the gradual extension of Mogul control over India at this period was accompanied by bloodshed on a scale that is unpleasant to comprehend.

Fig.231: An inlaid jade pendant of similar shape to that in figure 229.
Mogul Indian, 17th century. (Victoria and Albert Museum, London)
© V&A Images / Victoria and Albert Museum

Fig.232: A later gem and enamel encrusted elephant goad.
Indian,19th century. (Victoria and Albert Museum, London)
© V&A Images / Victoria and Albert Museum

This section ends with an object that jumps chronologically by some two and a half centuries and is by no stretch of the imagination jewellery. It is an elephant goad made in India around 1870. But it illustrates well the relative conservatism within India at the very time that Europe in general, and jewellery in particular, was undergoing a huge transformation with the Industrial revolution and the evolution of a relatively affluent, jewellery-loving middle class.

The goad is highly intricate, and a masterpiece of the goldsmiths art. It employs much the same techniques as the Mogul jewellery in figs.229 to 231. It is covered in diamonds, bears highly elaborate enamel work with hunting scenes and tigers, and even its steel 'business end' is kundan set with rubies – a refinement no doubt lost on the elephants.

If a jeweller serving the seventeenth century Mogul court had miraculously travelled forward in time to stand at the shoulder of the man who made this goad, he would have seen little to surprise him. If the unfortunate jeweller who buried, but never retrieved, the Cheapside Hoard in early seventeenth century London had rematerialised in a Birmingham jewellery factory in the 1870s he would have been flabbergasted.

3
The Emergence of
the Modern World

3

Europe and the Industrial Revolution

One period stands out as a time of rapid transformation in contrast to the usual conservatism of the jeweller's craft: the eighteenth century. Not only was it a time of change in style terms, from exuberant Baroque to restrained Neoclassical, it was a time of significant developments in materials, technologies and society.

The portrait shown here sums up something of the period. It was painted around the 1730s by Gabriel Mathei and depicts Maria Theresa of Austria, then a young woman. The symmetrical diamond brooch, with its three pear-shaped drops, and the matching earrings are well contrasted against the gold embroidery of her dress. This was the period at which diamonds were becoming more abundant and the gem par excellence. And, of course, Maria Theresa (1717-1780) was a woman, but she still became one of the most powerful rulers of eighteenth century Europe. She even became the Holy Roman Empress. She also epitomises trade because the silver thaler (dollar) bearing her portrait became the most important and most trusted trade currencies in the Islamic world. It continued to be struck and used long after her death. The Maria Theresa silver thaler was the raw material for silver jewellery produced throughout the North African and Near Eastern world.

The Rococo style that dominated early eighteenth century European design can be seen as the lighter, exuberant offspring to the more dramatic and pompous Baroque. The full Rococo with its asymmetrical curves, scrolls, shells and flowers, even mythological and pastoral scenes, is far less evident in jewellery than in silverwork. But, although jewellery tends to remain more restrained and more symmetrical than many other art forms, the naturalistic element becomes increasingly evident as the eighteenth century progresses.

Against the theatrical, even self-indulgent, backdrop of Rococco courtly life, and those that aspired to it, there were the momentous social and technical changes of the Industrial Revolution. This eighteenth century revolution not only changed jewellery production technology, but it also provided a whole new social stratum of jewellery buyers – wealthy capitalists. At the same time, the discovery of abundant diamonds in Brazil quite literally brought a whole new sparkle to the jewellery trade. Parures, whole sets of matching jewel, necklets, earrings, and so on, found their way in every woman of note's jewel box, not just those of the nobility such as Maria Theresa. Meanwhile their men folk wore gem-set rings, fastened their jackets with jewelled buttons and carried richly worked snuff boxes, watches and canes.

Naturally the new rich needed instant fashion sense, to match in years what had permeated through European nobility for centuries, and this was provided by published design books. These, the style gurus of the period, created uniformity across national and media boundaries, and distanced designer from craftsman. Now not only might a London goldsmith be asked to realise a design by a French draftsman, but the scrolling floral decoration chased onto a tea pot could be the same as that embroidered on Maria Theresa's dress.

To some extent the very flamboyance of the Rococco style fended off uniformity in jewellery, but then came Neoclassicism.

The eighteenth century saw a reawakened interest in the monuments and cultures of the classical world – the Greeks, Etruscan and Romans. The improving security of travel and communications across Europe permitted young men to educate themselves on the Grand Tour and scholars began to excavate such fertile sites as Roman Pompeii, buried by the eruption of Vesuvius on the Bay of Naples in AD 79. The greater understanding of Classical art and ideals, including republicanism, democracy and asceticism, neatly meshed with the lesson of the Industrial Revolution that man could better his situation by his own mental and physical effort. The result was a reaction against the flippancy of courtly excesses that at one extreme took the flourishes out of jewellery, at the other took the head off Maria Theresa's daughter Marie Antoinette.

By the late eighteenth century the extrovert Rococco spirit barely survived in the repetitive motifs neatly framed in elegant but no-nonsense Neoclassical frames.

These two ribbon bow bodice ornaments (figs.234 and 235) help set the scene for our look at 18th century jewellery. They belong to the second half of the 17th century. The one set with brown topazes and diamonds has matching earrings and was possibly made in the Netherlands. The second is set with emeralds and has been tentatively attributed to Spain.

Topazes and emeralds were both South American gem materials. Europeans had encountered fine, deep green emeralds almost as soon as they stepped onto the shores of Colombia, but only located the mines and began direct exploitation in the 1550s. The history of topaz export from South America is less certain, the gems begin to appear in Spanish and Iberian jewellery in some quantity in the 17th century and were popular in the 18th.

The emerald ornament is all set in gold, which best sets off their fine and remarkably uniform colour. The other ornament, however, employs both silver and gold. The former metal sets off the diamonds, gold is used for the topazes. This use of silver to set diamonds is an early example of a practice that became normal during the eighteenth century. The diamonds are cut in simple table and rose forms. The polishing and cutting of diamonds had been practiced for several centuries, but it was only in the later seventeenth century that polishing became more commonplace and regular facetted forms such as the early brilliant cut were developed.

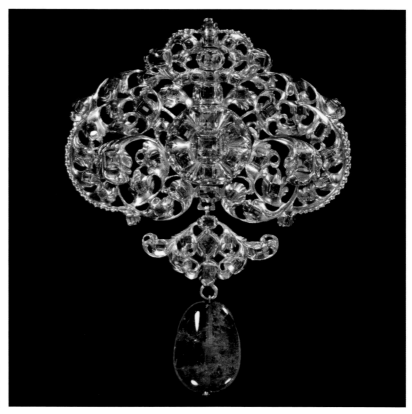

Fig.234: A diamond and topaz ribbon bow bodice ornament mounted in gold and silver with matching ear pendants. Possibly Netherlands, ca 1650-1675.
(Victoria and Albert Museum, London)
© V&A Images / Victoria and Albert Museum

Fig.235: An emerald ribbon bow bodice ornament mounted in gold. Possibly Spain, ca 1650-1675.
(Victoria and Albert Museum, London)
© V&A Images / Victoria and Albert Museum

This magnificent suit of three bow-shaped brooches from the Russian crown jewels were made in around 1760, probably in St. Petersburg and perhaps by Louis Deval, a Frenchman. They were worn in a line between neck and waist line and are rare surviving examples of the formal diamond jewellery of the period. Although diamonds had began to reach Europe in some quantity from Brazil by the 1730s, little eighteenth century diamond-set jewellery has survived the cycle of breaking up and reusing jewellery materials that has fuelled the trade through the centuries.

The jeweller set these three diamond brooches in silver because diamonds look their best in a white setting. As we have seen, by the later seventeenth century diamonds are sometimes in silver settings, the coloured gems in gold. The next stage, the use of gold backs for the silver settings of even all-diamond jewellery became more common after about 1760. In part this was for aesthetic reasons, but it also prevented the skin or clothing from being stained by the inevitable tarnishing of the silver.

The settings here are still enclosed at the back. Setting diamonds with open backs, described in the past as 'transparent' settings, are sometimes encountered by this period, but really only became common in the nineteenth century.

The relative lightness of the settings are noteworthy. In earlier times diamonds and other stones had settings almost like architectural plinths and most jewellery was more metal than stone. During the seventeenth century there had been some fining down, but with the greater accent on, and availability of, diamonds in the eighteenth century, settings were relegated to very much of a supporting role and eventually became the merest skeletons consistent with adequate strength. The lighter and more airy designs coupled with the new naturalism also meant that stones could be set at varying angles, no longer were they set in serried planes, all exactly face-on to the viewer. Look how the sides of the bows curve over. The net result is even more sparkle as the wearer moved.

Fig.236: Set of three diamond-set bow-shaped bodice ornaments set in silver.
Perhaps by Louis Duval of St. Petersburg, Russian, circa 1760. (Victoria and Albert Museum)
© V&A Images / Victoria and Albert Museum

Facetted diamonds undoubtedly look their best under multi-sourced artificial light. However, holding a ball for diamond-festooned guests under the smelly, sooty, dripping and unreliable light of tallow candle chandeliers was unthinkable. Significant improvements in candle and other lighting only became widespread late in the eighteenth century, but from early in the century the rich could increasingly afford, and had access to, the more expensive bees wax candles in quantity. So the wealthy now owned both daytime and evening jewellery, guests glittered around the ballroom and conversation genuinely sparkled across candelabra laden dinner tables.

The ruby and diamond brooch illustrated here is from Russia in about the 1750's. It shows the asymmetry typical of eighteenth century floral jewellery and contrasts with the more conservative regularity of the three bow brooches. However, these flowers and the bows all demonstrate the new lightness in appearance of gem-set jewellery in the seventeenth century.

Fig.237: Ruby and diamond floral spray brooch set in gold and silver, and decorated with enamel. Russian, 1750-70. (Victoria and Albert Museum, London)
© V&A Images / Victoria and Albert Museum

This sapphire ring dates to around 1760. The hoop, bearing an inscription against a white enamel background, is in yellow gold, the settings for the sapphire and its diamond surround are in silver. The combination of gold and silver on a single object complicated the manufacturing process and prompted new approaches to soldering and solder alloys.

Sapphires, highly esteemed in Medieval times, as we have seen, are actually rather rare in seventeenth to earlier nineteenth century jewellery. Prior to the later 19th century, the main source of sapphires was Sri Lanka, probably the origin of this stone. The wonderful deep blue sapphires of Kashmir only first appeared on the market in the 1880's and other major sources were also unknown before more recent times. For example, sapphires were only noted from Montana, USA in the 1860s and those of Australia slightly a few years after that. Sapphires are also found in Burma (Myanmar), the traditional source of the best rubies, but these sapphires do not appear to have reached Europe in any significant numbers in the past.

We had a clue to why even Sri Lankan sapphires were rare in seventeenth and eighteenth century jewellery in the report of Robert Knox (see fig.226). The larger-scale commercial exploitation of Sri Lankan gems really only developed in the nineteenth century. The island formally became a British Colony in 1802 and that other major Sri Lankan commercial product, tea, only became a commercial crop in the 1860's.

This ring is in the so-called Giardinetti ('little garden') style, a popular eighteenth century ring type that reflects the naturalistic, asymmetric style of the period. A range of gems were used in this type of ring, but most popular were emeralds and rubies. The emeralds were in the main from South America, the rubies from Burma (Myanmar). Sri Lankan sapphires were, as we have just seen, not common at this period.

The diamonds in this type of ring are typically set in silver while the settings for the coloured stones and the hoop are in gold. However, there are exceptions, as here. Here the diamonds, rubies and emeralds are all set in silver.

Coloured stones, of course, mirror the colours of the flowers they represented – emerald green leaves, ruby red roses. This 'painting with gems' was not a new phenomenon, but it was very much an eighteenth century characteristic and had resulted from the increasing number of gems reaching Europe from the East and the New World. The use of enamel to render the colour realism in jewellery, as had been usual in former centuries, was less feasible with the soldering constraints encountered when jewellers wishes to combine gold and silver components. The solders necessary to join gold and silver had to have a relatively low melting temperature and these could be a bit too close for comfort to the melting temperature of some enamels.

Fig.238: Heart-shaped sapphire and diamond cluster ring set in silver and gold, with enamelled hoop. European ca 1760. (British Museum)
© Copyright the Trustees of The British Museum

Fig.239: Giardinetti or 'little garden' ring in diamond, ruby and emerald. European, mid-18th century. (Victoria and Albert Museum, London)
© V&A Images / Victoria and Albert Museum

In general enamel became far less prevalent in jewellery after the end of the seventeenth century, in part due to the greater availability of coloured stones and diamonds, in part for technical reasons, as we have just seen. But enamel never totally disappeared and indeed made a come-back in the later eighteenth century, perhaps due to the increased availability of low-melting temperature glass, and is then typical of much memorial and sentimental jewellery. The introduction of gas-fired furnaces in the early nineteenth century gave enamel another lease of life.

The naturalistic Spanish floral spray brooch illustrated here illustrates the renewed interest in enamel in the later eighteenth century and one solution to the assembly problems.

The diamond-set silver components were attached to the piece after enamelling.

Similar methods were used to assemble eighteenth century enamelled gold boxes. Enamelling jewellery components always raises problems of relative melting temperatures and the order of work. The last thing the jeweller wants is for the gold to melt when he enamels it, or for the enamel to melt when he solders the components together. Renaissance enamelled jewellery had employed all manner of rivets, pins and even nuts and bolts to avoid soldering. The delicate mounts and gem-laden jewellery of the seventeenth and eighteenth centuries generally relied on more subtle approaches.

Fig.240: Enamelled gold and diamond bodice ornament in the form of a floral spray. Spanish, late 18th century. (Victoria and Albert Museum, London)
© V&A Images / Victoria and Albert Museum

The little dragonfly is attached to this mid-eighteenth century garnet flower ornament by a thin wire so that that it trembled in wear. This type of springy setting is described by the French term as *en tremblant*. The principal was known to the Hellenistic Greeks, but it became popular in some mid-eighteenth century jewellery where, as here, movement perfectly suited the new naturalistic forms. In some nineteenth century jewellery we find diamonds set 'en tremblant' (fig.283).

This jewel was originally worn in the hair or on a hat and is set with bright red garnets that were now beginning to come into fashion as an alternative to rubies. The brightest garnets were 'Bohemian' garnets from what is now the Czech Republic. These garnets had been used in jewellery since antiquity, but became very popular again in the eighteenth and nineteenth centuries.

In the eighteenth century bracelets were still usually worn in pairs, just as they had been in Greek and Roman times. This pair of bracelet clasps (opposite page) dating to about 1770 are in gold and silver, set with diamonds and with oval blue glass panels. As the view of their backs show, they have been adapted into brooches in recent times.

One bears the initials M and A, traditionally linked with Louis XVI's Queen Marie Antoinette, the other a dove feeding another, a quiver and a torch – a comprehensive symbol of love.

The deep blue enamel is typical of the period as are the simple 'cut down' settings for the little brilliant cut diamonds.

Fig.241: Garnet-set hair ornament in the form of a floral spay and dragonfly. English, mid-18th century. (British Museum)
© Copyright the Trustees of The British Museum

Fig.242: Pair of diamond and blue enamel bracelet clasps.
Probably French, ca 1770. (Victoria and Albert Museum, London)
© V&A Images / Victoria and Albert Museum

Fig.243: Reverse of the clasps shown in figure 242.
© V&A Images / Victoria and Albert Museum

The later eighteenth century saw a renewed interest in all things Greek and Roman. The wholesale replication of ancient forms and techniques in jewellery did not occur until the mid-nineteenth century, but in the later eighteenth century there was increasing use of more formalised classical decorative motifs in jewellery. The straight lines and repetitive beaded or guilloche borders of Greek architecture not only reflected the simpler dress styles of the period, but also were particularly suited to replication in miniature using the new-fangled rolling mills and engine turning lathes. This classicism was coupled with the trend for embracing sentimentality, for life, love and death.

We saw love symbolism in the previous ornaments, the pair of bracelet clasps. Now we meet death. Death-related jewellery was an old tradition, but in the later 18th century new secularity and emotion were bolstered by classical urns and lyres. The weeping widow replaces the grinning skull. One cannot view memorial jewellery of this period without recalling the pathos of a classical Greek funerary stele, both artistically and emotionally. The personal sorrow of loss is expressed, not simply by the apprehension of inevitable death nor the anticipation of resurrection.

The late 18th century mourning brooch (fig.244) shows a young lady seated beside a sepulchral pedestal and holding a mirror. The bracelet clasp of the same period (fig.245) shows two conjoined flaming hearts on a column up which a snake is climbing. The inscription above says 'In Spite of Envy'.

Fig.244: Mourning brooch with sepia miniature depicting a woman beside a sepulcre. Probably English, late 18th century. © Christie's Images Ltd. 2002

Fig.245: Mourning brooch with sepia miniature showing a column with conjoined hearts and a serpent. English, late 18th century. © Christie's Images Ltd. 2002

Rings were the commonest mourning jewellery, sometimes called 'burying rings' at the time. The three rings shown here were made between 1785 and 1792 and are in the typical attenuated oval and marquise shapes of the period. Two show urns in true Neoclassical style and that with the blue enamel was in memory of a jeweller – Gabriel Wirgman of London. According to the report of a theft in 1769, Gabriel Wirgman's stock included enamelled watch dials as well as gold and silver pendants, confirming his involvement with enamels. Wirgman, was born in Gottenburg, Sweden, and died in 1791.

Enamel is often used in mourning jewellery, black for married persons, sometimes royal blue, but white was used when the mourned were young or unmarried as with the ring on the right here, which was for a two-year old child. The rose buds against the enamel background reinforce the poignant inscription 'nip't in the bud'.

Mourning rings of this type are often of 18 carat or lower gold fineness and are frequently in the copper-containing 'red gold' so popular at this period. However, gold jewellery of this sort of composition was tricky to enamel and the enamelled components were thus often separately made and enamelled in higher purity gold, and then attached, often simply with an adhesive.

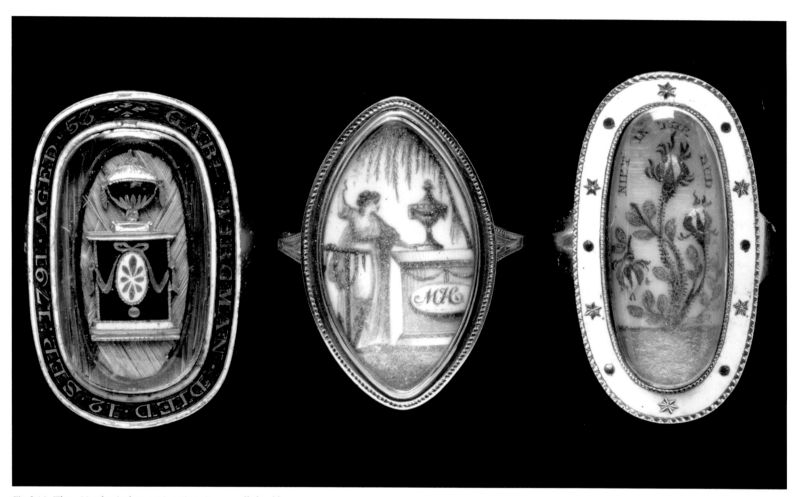

Fig.246: Three Neoclassical mourning rings in enamelled gold.
English, 1785 - 1792. (Victoria and Albert Museum, London)
© V&A Images / Victoria and Albert Museum

Mourning jewellery was one manifestation of the sentimental jewellery that came into favour towards the end of the eighteenth century. Possibly this sentimental approach was a balance to the increasing rationalism of the 'Age of Reason', but in any case it is found with jewellery both for the living and to commemorate the dead. A variety of symbols provided appealing shorthand for universal emotions – love, hope, trust, faithfulness – while mementoes of family or loved ones could take both tangible and representational form. The former includes the various types of jewellery made from or incorporating human hair, while the latter included portrait miniatures and silhouettes.

Most intriguingly enigmatic of the portraits are those that show only the eye – concealing the identify of the subject, but still providing the wearer with the window to soul of the subject of their attachment. Eye jewels of this type became popular in the last couple of decades of the eighteenth century and seem to have been simply love tokens. The two examples here, dating to 1800 or soon after, are both English, even though the fashion appears to have originated in France.

Just as diamond and gem-set jewellery came into their own under flickering candles, so rich gold surfaces and enamels looked best by day. Nowhere is this better seen than among the semi-functional ornaments such as chatelaines, watches and boxes. These objects, primarily for daytime use, were particularly popular among the middle classes as ostentatious evidence of wealth and fashion sense, much like owning the latest mobile phone might be today.

Chatelaines were the pre-eminent lady's accessory of the eighteenth century. Like some sort of forerunner to the Swiss Army knife, they kept a range of useful implements within easy reach. They hung by a hook on the reverse from the waist and bore such things as a watch, as here, tweezers, pencils and even folding scissors. They were made of gold or gold plated copper alloy, or even cut steel, and ranged from highly elaborate and finely chased enamelled examples to simple repetitive repoussé or saw-pierced panels – the latter a then newly introduced technique. As can be seen in the example shown here, made by John Rowe of London in 1758, the two dimensional form and choice of materials means that the flamboyant Rococo style is more evident is this type of object than in most mid-eighteenth century jewellery.

'Daytime' objects such as chatelaines and watch cases were also ideally suited to decoration that utilised individual motifs in subtly varied colours of gold. The characteristic yellow of gold can be modified by alloying it with other metals. Adding silver makes it paler and eventually a greenish shade, adding copper makes it red. But in addition to these well known variations, the goldsmiths in the second half of the eighteenth century used other hues – for example a little iron or even arsenic, could make the gold a bluey-grey colour.

Fig.247:
Brooch with an eye miniature and a surround of purple paste.
Ca 1800.
(Victoria and Albert Museum, London)
© V&A Images / Victoria and Albert Museum

Fig.248: Pendant with an eye miniature and a surround of seed pearls.
Ca 1800. (Victoria and Albert Museum, London)
© V&A Images / Victoria and Albert Museum

Fig.249: Gold chatelaine by John Rowe. English, 1758
(Fitzwilliam Museum, Cambridge) © Fitzwilliam Museum, Cambridge.

The significant improvements in steel manufacture in the early eighteenth century that propelled the industrial revolution and changed warfare for ever, also had a more frivolous offshoot – steel that could be cut and polished for jewellery. It was a British invention, Britain, after all, was the cradle of the Industrial Revolution, and by the 1760's cut steel ornaments were being made in several parts of the Kingdom. From Britain the fashion spread to France and other parts of Europe and cut steel was worn in the highest society. The cut steel chatelaine shown here is probably French and dates from the early nineteenth century.

Cut steel should not be confused with the cast iron jewellery (fig.28), often of extraordinary delicacy, that appeared about 1800 and continued to be made into the middle of the nineteenth century.

One singular feature of eighteenth century personal ornament is the shoe buckle. At the close of the seventeenth century the more conservative elements in society complained that 'foolish young men have lately brought about a new change in fashion. They have begun to fasten their shoes and knee bands with buckles, instead of ribands, wherewith their forefathers were content.' Conservatives railed against such 'effeminate and immodest ornaments' and appealed to the clergy 'to tell these thoughtless youths, in a solemn manner, that such things are forbidden in scripture.' Naturally, these grumbles fell on deaf ears. The fashion spread and shoe buckles became larger and more opulent as the century progressed. Many were made of silver and set with paste, there were even some diamond set examples. Then, almost as quickly as it had arrived, the fashion died. Laces took over. So much so that in 1791 bucklemakers petitioned the Prince of Wales to do something to halt the trend and help 'the distressed situation of thousands in the different branches of the buckle manufacture'. Despite the Prince wearing buckles and commanding all those in his household to do the same, the influence of the young fashion setters was too strong and buckles faded from the scene.

The fine shoe buckles shown here are of silver set with paste (glass) and with steel fittings. They were made around the 1780's and belonged to Admiral Sir Rupert George.

Fig.250: Châtelaine in cut steel. Probably French, early 19th century (with some later additions) (Victoria and Albert Museum, London) © V&A Images / Victoria and Albert Museum

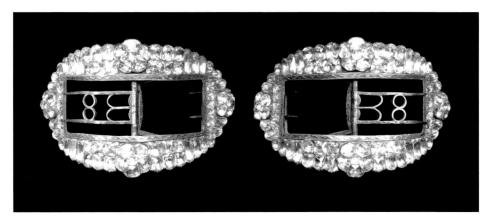

Fig.251: Gold and paste shoe buckles worn by Admiral Sir Rupert George. English, ca 1780-90. (Victoria and Albert Museum, London) © V&A Images / Victoria and Albert Museum

Fig.252: Paste bodice ornament set in silver. Probably English, ca 1720. (Victoria and Albert Museum, London)
© V&A Images / Victoria and Albert Museum

Paste, as we encountered in Sir Rupert's shoe buckles, is another word for glass.

The imitation of gemstones in glass dates back to the second millennium BC, but the eighteenth century fashion for jewellery laden with gems, and the demands of the new middle classes led to a rapid requirement for these glass alternatives. The need to match cut and brilliance as much as colour was served by the development of glass with a higher lead content that was reassuringly heavy and sparkled almost as much as a gem when facetted.

Lead glass was not a new invention, but the fashion reached its height in the Eighteenth century. In the later seventeenth century George Ravenscroft in Britain patented his lead-glass production method and launched his new product with what modern observers would describe as excellent marketing. Outside of Britain, a forerunner in fine paste jewellery was Georges Frédérick Stas who was producing his paste by the 1720's and within a decade or so had premises in Paris.

The best paste was cut by hand and set in silver with the same intricate care as the genuine gemstones. This care can be seen in the shoe buckles (fig.251) and in this fine 'Stomacher' made in about 1720, probably in England.

These little lace or cravat pins also exemplify the paste of the late eighteenth century. Although paste was initially used to copy diamonds and other gems, it soon took on a life of its own as a jewellery material. It was not just a cheap substitute for the real thing, illustrious sellers and wearers were unashamed to be associated with it. Paste jewellery bears witness to the types of more precious jewellery in vogue in the eighteenth century, but which have long since been broken up and their diamonds and coloured gems re-used.

Settings for pastes were enclosed on their backs and were often foiled, just as had been traditional for diamonds and real gems. Foiling is the ancient practice of placing a highly reflective foil, or even coloured paper, behind a gem to augment its apparent sparkle or colour or both. Pastes were usually foiled with coloured foils, but these often discolour, and not always evenly, with time. Diamonds were often foiled with a smoked, thus black, foil. What would now be considered fraud, was then an acceptable enhancement.

The acceptance of jewellery set with humble pastes ties into the eighteenth century fashion for other materials that recall nature, or classicism or both. At one extreme we find jewellery set with agates with all sorts of natural patterning, some reminiscent of the woodland grottoes popular in full-blown Rococo art; at the other extreme we see neat, Neoclassical Wedgwood porcelain cameo plaques, as here.

This pendant dates from about 1790 and is in blue enamelled gold with a central blue and white Wedgwood panel depicting the Greek goddess Hygeia. Hygeia was one of the daughters of Aesculapius, the Greek god of medicine. Hygeia symbolized healthy living and the prevention of ill health while her sister Panacea represented treatment. This ancient Greek distinction between preventive and curative medicine was beginning to be reappraised in the eighteenth century and by Victorian times Hygeia – from the same Greek word as our hygiene – had become a common name for hospitals and hotels in fashionable spas. Hygeia was a symbol not simply of health, but of healthy living and thus also, to the Georgian and Victorian mind, spiritual health.

The only clue to the original owner of this pendant is a compartment on the reverse containing hair and the initials CB in seed pearls.

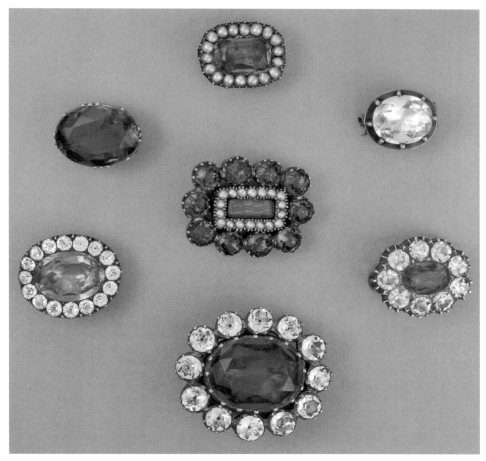

*Fig.253: A collection of lace or cravat pins in paste. Late 18th century.
(British Museum)*

Fig.254: Gold mounted pendant set with a Wedgwood panel, with enamel, seed pearls and human hair. English, ca 1790.

The Nineteenth Century

This portrait of Susan Beckford, Duchess of Hamilton painted by Willes Maddox in the mid 1830's introduces us into the nineteenth century. She wears pearl and diamond earrings and a forehead ornament that would not have been out of place a couple of generations earlier, but about her wrists are two very typical nineteenth century ornament types, large gold bracelets, one with what appears to be a painted miniature, the other a large cameo.

In the nineteenth century the jewellery industry flourished. There was greater affluence further down the social scale, there were new methods of production, new sources of materials and even new materials. And there were counter reactions against all these.

The neoclassicism of the later eighteenth century had continued into the early nineteenth. The neat linear style perfectly complimented the simplified modes of dress that followed the French Revolution. Then the clean, elegant lines of the Neoclassical gave way to busier filigree work in the early decades of the century, pursued by a revival of naturalism with roses and other blooms supplementing the grape vines and lilies drawn from the Neoclassical repertoire.

The post Industrial Revolution factories had provided the wealth to create a new, affluent class of jewellery buyer, while the empires of the European powers provided the precious raw materials. The same factories also provided increasingly mass produced ornaments for those with jewellery aspirations but without the funds to match them.

The second half of the nineteenth century in particular saw the increasing use of mechanisation in the jewellery industry. Factories in centres such as Birmingham in England, and Newark in New Jersey, produced large quantities of machine-made chains and die-stamped brooches and earrings to supply the ever increasing demands of the new middle classes. Charles Dickens described gold chain making machines in Birmingham in the 1850's and from about this period onwards there is a great increase in patents for ingenious new methods of jewellery construction and manufacture. But not everything was mechanized and the women burnishers who polished those same chains worked hard and long hours to keep up with the production machines.

A contrast was made between the fine handmade jewellery of London and the cheap, mass produced 'Brummagem' ware from the factories of Birmingham. Though, as Dickens pointed out,

"Fine gentlemen and ladies give, in London shops, twice the price for Birmingham jewellery that they would pay, if no middlemen stood, filling their pockets uncommonly fast, between them and the manufacturer; and they admire the solid value and great beauty of the work; but as soon as they know where the articles were wrought, they undervalue them with the term 'Brummagem'.

Meanwhile, the American jewellery industry was also beginning to blossom. The puritanical abhorrence of jewellery that had affected much of seventeenth and eighteenth century America was dissipating and, for example, the first jewellery factory opened in Newark, New Jersey in 1801. By the middle of the nineteenth century manufacturers of Newark and entrepreneurs such as Charles Tiffany were making the United States not only essentially self-sufficient in jewellery, but also creating a new, highly discerning and voracious market.

In Britain, the production of jewellery in the new factories meant to some the loss of both craft and craftsmanship. The role of the artist/designer/craftsman jeweller was seen as threatened by automaton-like workers sliding sheet gold under the steam-driven stamps to produce an endless stream of identical components to be assembled into so-called jewellery in equally soulless production lines.

There was a reaction. The stamped jewellery might be gold, but so what? True jewellery wasn't about intrinsic value, it meant design and art, the loving and inventive creation of unique pieces in which beauty and innovation were pre-eminent. Like most counter movements, this so-called Arts and Crafts revolution took some extremist views that would have sent shivers down Cellini's spine. Finish was unimportant – innovation ruled and roughness was fine. Intellect was more important than intricacy.

Naturally, as time passed, approaches mellowed and it is hard to see any echoes of an abhorrence for intricacy for intricacy's sake in the exquisite jewellery of, say, René Lalique, even though the roots of his Art Nouveau styles lay in those same reactions against mass-production and concepts of intrinsic value.

The pre-Raphaelite movement's celebration of the craft of the jeweller, the intricate filigree of the 1820's and the lingering influences of Neoclassicism formed a perfect combination to spawn the archaeological jewellery fashion that took flight around the mid-nineteenth century.

Fig.255: A portrait of Susan Beckford, the Duchess of Hamilton. By Willes Maddox, ca 1835. (Hamilton Collection, Lennoxlove, East Lothian) © The Hamilton Palace Trust

Paying homage to classical forms was nothing new. The Renaissance goldsmiths worshipped classical goldsmiths, even though they didn't slavishly copy them, and the neo-classical movement in the later eighteenth century had permeated some jewellery design. When Napoleon was crowned self-proclaimed Emperor Napoleon I of France in 1804 he used two crowns. One was his 'Crown of Charlemagne' actually a replacement for the ancient crown of France destroyed in the French Revolution, the other a laurel crown of ancient Greek and Roman type. The use of the crowns of both Charlemagne and the Roman Emperors says much for Napoleon's sense of self importance.

In any case, at the forefront of the new mid-nineteenth century fashion for copying of Greek and Etruscan forms was the firm of Castellani in Rome and whatever its antecedents, the new Archaeological Style was also very much a shrewd commercial response to the new wave of tourism to Italy. European politics had quietened down after half a century of Revolution, Napoleonic Wars and other upheavals, and the improved comfort, speed and safety of travel meant that wives and daughters would now accompany menfolk on what was by then a far more genteel Grand Tour. Women were drawn to souvenir jewellery in the archaeological style, especially the fine 'ancient' craftsmanship of Castellani's jewellery.

As the nineteenth century progressed the diamond was increasingly confirmed as the epitome of gems, especially after the discoveries of the new diamond sources in South Africa in the 1860's. Improving technology, and technological understanding, allowed the development of new jewellery materials, from platinum to early plastics, and even, for a short period, aluminium. At the same time demand for cheaper jewellery and the increasingly competitive nature of what was becoming a global market led to a reduction in the permissible qualities of gold. 9, 12 and 15 carat gold was introduced in Great Britain in 1854 and similar lower levels were introduced in other parts of Europe around this same period.

Legislation in 1738 had exempted most gold jewellery from Hallmarking. 'Mourning Rings' were one exception. This legislation was seemingly not applicable to the more complex late eighteenth century forms with their miniatures and glass-fronted bezels. But the simpler enamelled band types of mourning rings were hallmarked, such as this 18 carat one for James Pennington who died in 1831 and which bears the hallmark for the same year. The maker was Barber, Cattle and North of York, a company best known for silver flatware. Hallmarking was sometimes a time consuming process and so jewellers could keep pre-hallmarked 'blank' mourning rings which could be quickly engraved and enamelled as required.

In this class of ring, the enamel was applied directly to the gold and after hallmarking, to avoid jarring and fracture. This practical necessity to enamel after hallmarking is evidenced by instances where enamel is applied right over a hallmark – for example in some objects by Fabergé that were sold in England.

Fig.256: Gold and enamel mourning ring for James Selby Pennington.
English, 1824-25. (Victoria and Albert Museum, London)
© V&A Images / Victoria and Albert Museum

The ancient art of filigree – designs made up from small scrolls and coils of wire, often highlighted with small gold spheres – is not common in later eighteenth century jewellery from North West Europe. Its inherent fussiness was in contrast with the refined and elegant Neoclassical forms. However, there was something of a filigree rebirth in the early decades of the nineteenth century, possibly due to the greater exposure to Mediterranean cultures in the Napoleonic period. In any case, the fashion for filigree is best seen in the so-called *Cannetille* work that derives its name from the gold-thread embroideries on military uniforms.

In the finer examples, the filigree is an almost organic, albeit regular, array of small scrolls and nest-like coils assembled to provide a distinct feeling of depth and lightness. The poorer examples, in contrast, are flatter, repetitious patterns of loops and little spiral coils that at best form serviceable borders.

One of the most spectacular examples of this type of jewellery is the necklace and earrings shown here that date to the 1820's and were probably made in France. Cannetille work often surrounds coloured gemstones, but the wide range of coloured gems used here and their carefully planned distribution is particularly noteworthy.

Fig.257: Gold and gemstone necklace and earrings in Cannetille work.
France, ca 1820. (Victoria and Albert Museum, London)
© *V&A Images / Victoria and Albert Museum*

This Cannetille work bow brooch is set with bright blue turquoise and pearls. A feature here is the use of lines and scrolls of little gold spheres, granulation, in graduated sizes.

Turquoise found some use in antiquity, though not as much as might be expected and it is conspicuous by its absence in Hellenistic Greek and Roman jewellery. The gem is more common in Medieval Islamic jewellery, but not held in any great esteem. One twelfth century writer says that 'many kings hardly have a desire to wear a turquoise, because the vulgar frequently use it as a seal.'

There are occasional turquoises found in Renaissance and later European jewellery, but they really only came into fashion again in the 1820's and 1830's.

Fig.258: Gold and turquoise bow brooch in Cannetille work. English or French, ca 1820 - 30.
(Victoria and Albert Museum, London)
© V&A Images / Victoria and Albert Museum

Whether we are dealing with romance, mourning or witchcraft, the possession of a sample of a person's hair has always been seen as providing a direct bond with the person themselves. The use of a lock of hair concealed in a ring or other piece of jewellery as a memento certainly dates back to the seventeenth century and locks of hair are included in many later eighteenth century mourning rings. However, the use of human hair on a larger scale, often seen as slightly morbid today, was very much a nineteenth century phenomenon. Whole components were plaited or woven from hair, such as the bracelet shown here which dates from about 1825. The hair here is in three different types of twists or braids and these appear to vary slightly in colour – perhaps the hair came from three different people.

Although hair jewellery was one of the few types of jewellery that was acceptable in mourning, it was by no means always so associated. Hair jewellery was also a link with the living. After her engagement to Prince Albert, Victoria always wore a piece of jewellery containing a lock of his hair.

Some specialists excelled at making hair jewellery, but it could also be made at home and several nineteenth century books described the art.

The shell cameo mounted on the clasp is in the Classical taste and the depiction of a Greek warrior and his consort, plus a diminutive Eros holding a torch, suggests that this bracelet was intended as a love memento. Perhaps the hair was that of a couple's children. The gold surround to the cameo and the two rectangular gold terminals are very finely worked with floral designs.

Fig.259: Bracelet in plaited and twisted human hair, with gold clasp set with shell cameo. Probably Swiss, ca 1825. (Victoria and Albert Museum, London)
© V&A Images / Victoria and Albert Museum

The scrolls of the Victorian rococo revival, seen around the cameo on the hair bracelet (fig.259) and on the bracelets worn by the Duchess of Hamilton (fig.255), border the garnets in these matching gold and garnet brooch and earrings which were made in Britain in about the 1830's.

This type of stamped sheet gold ornament was perfectly suited to the increasing use of mass production – the labour-intensive filigree work of the previous decades most certainly was not.

Machines to stamp gold and silver sheet had been introduced in the Industrial Revolution of the mid eighteenth century, but initially such mass production was largely reserved for items required in quantity, such as buttons. The newly rich industrialists still wanted their jewellery, like their properties, to be unique and individual.

By the 1820's jewellery was being made by soldering together several separate stamped sheet gold components. This allowed a pick and match approach to jewellery where a limited range of stamped components could be assembled in different ways to provide a wider variety of finished items. The garnet-set jewellery here exemplifies this type of construction.

Fig.260: Gold brooch and earrings set with cabochon garnets. English, ca 1835.
(Victoria and Albert Museum, London)
© V&A Images / Victoria and Albert Museum

After the mid-nineteenth century there was a trend to even greater mechanization, often resulting in fewer individual stampings being used in the assembly of a piece of jewellery. Factory made jewellery was now less a collage of separate stamped motifs assembled with some freedom and ingenuity, but a carefully planned construction of precisely formed and well-fitting components.

This trend marginalized even further the mental input of the assembler, thus reducing labour costs, but it necessitated a larger overall demand to warrant the extra capital costs of the more complex steel stamping dies – factors well in tune with the changing economics of the time.

The brooch, and its constituent parts, as shown here was made in 1875 by the well-known Birmingham jewellery company T. and J. Bragg. They were later awarded the Royal Warrant.

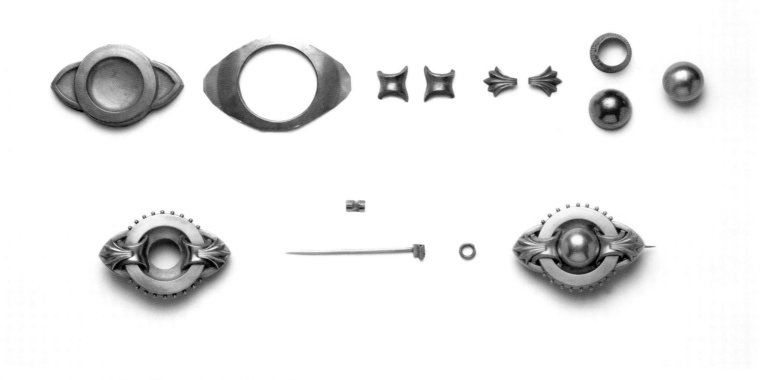

Fig.261: Demonstration model of a machine-made brooch with its 13 gold components. T&J Bragg of Birmingham, England, 1875. (Victoria and Albert Museum, London)
© V&A Images / Victoria and Albert Museum

Serpent armlets and snake-headed bracelets are often seen as being archetypal 'ancient Egyptian'. However, although the concept dates back to antiquity, the earliest examples are actually found in Western Asia and from thence spread to the Greek world, including Egypt after Alexander the Great's invasion of that country in the fourth century BC. The Romans were especially fond of snake rings and bangles, and some form realistic coils around finger, wrist or upper arm. The snake had fertility associations, which hardly required Freud to explain, and also represented rebirth and new life because of the way in which a snake periodically sheds its skin.

After Roman times snake jewellery largely fell out of favour, not least because to Christians the serpent was an associate of the Devil, the cause of man's fall and expulsion from the Garden of Eden. It is unclear what led to the snake's rehabilitation in the nineteenth century when Queen Victoria herself had a snake engagement ring. The fertility and 'rebirth' associations of the classical prototypes may have been a factor, but perhaps the protective aspects had come to the fore, mirroring the cobra's protective guise in Britain's Indian Empire.

This enamelled and diamond set bracelet, perhaps more dragon-like than snake-headed, was probably made in the 1840's and represents an early example in the history of Victorian snake-headed jewellery. This was made before the introduction of the new flexible, scale-like linkages and before the full development of steel springs within bracelets and bangles. Thus it relies on a traditional double hinge flexibility and a closure where the heads overlap.

The components are enamelled in royal blue, a traditional choice, and the heads are set with diamonds.

Snake heads allowed some interesting design approaches, but the main challenge to the jeweller lay in replicating the flexibility and scaliness of the body in a functional way. The second half of the nineteenth century saw a wide variety of approaches to this, with patents granted for several ingenious link constructions.

The necklet shown here (fig.263) dates from about 1850. The flexible construction and the combination of blue enamel and diamond for the head is typical. Here the head is also embellished with a cabochon garnet and there are smaller garnets in the eyes. The presence of the larger garnet might relate to the legend of the precious stone on a snake's forehead, Garnets also commonly embellish snake heads in Greek jewellery.

Fig.262: Gold serpent bangle with diamonds and blue enamel. ca 1845.
© Christie's Images Ltd. 2003

Fig.263: Gold snake necklet with blue enamel and set with diamonds and a large cabochon garnet. ca 1850.
© Christie's Images Ltd. 2003

The flexibility that so suited the snake necklet would not serve for bracelet forms where springiness was desired. This required a different approach to construction. The second half of the nineteenth century, from the 1870's onwards in particular, saw significant development in jewellery constructions and components incorporating small steel springs. In particular, a variety of new clasp and hinge forms were introduced.

The snake shown here was made in about 1875 and takes the form of a springy coiled bracelet that could be wound onto the wrist, but which was rigid enough to stay in place. The head is set with a rose-cut diamond and there are rubies in the eyes and decorating the tail.

The turquoise-set eagle brooch shown here is one of the twelve that Albert, Prince of Saxe-Coburg and Gotha, presented to the bridesmaids when he married Queen Victoria in 1840. This use may have contributed to the enormous popularity of the gem in 1840's-1860's – supply improved, no doubt, by the Suez Canal opening in 1853. The workmanship here is exquisite, as you might expect. The talons clasp pearls and the eye is of ruby, the beak minute rose diamonds.

These eagle brooches are particularly fine examples of the turquoise and half-pearl set bird brooches, often swallows, that become common in the second half of the nineteenth century. Some are entirely covered by massed settings of turquoises, others retain some gold surfaces that are engraved to replicate feathers and other details. The qualities of workmanship vary greatly. In the finer examples the turquoise are well set, often with precise grain or carved settings, and the feathers and other details were carefully engraved in the gold before the turquoise were set, then neatly retouched after the turquoise were in place. With the more poorly made versions the settings are the simplest of drilled holes and any engraved detail cursory at best.

Fig.264: Gold snake-coil bracelet set with diamonds and with ruby eyes. ca 1875.© Christie's Images Ltd. 2003

Fig.265: Turquoise-set 'Coburg Eagle' brooch, a bridesmaids' gift at the marriage of Queen Victoria and Prince Albert. 1840. (British Museum). © Copyright the Trustees of The British Museum

The name Castellani is almost synonymous with the Classical revival jewellery of the second half of the nineteenth century.

Fortunato Pio Castellani opened his workshop in Rome in 1814 producing jewellery in the fashions then in vogue in France and Britain. However, he became intrigued by the ancient Etruscan jewellery then being excavated in Italy and with the support of Duke Michelangelo Caetani began to produce jewellery inspired by, and sometimes copying, the ancient. It is likely that his workshop did some restoration work on genuine pieces, but we have no conclusive proof that they produced deliberate fakes.

From the 1850's Fortunato's sons Alessandro and Augusto took over the running of the firm, producing an ever wider range of archaeological style jewellery to sell to the affluent tourists then beginning to flock to Rome. They exhibited their jewellery at several international exhibitions in Europe and in even in America, and became famous for their Greek, Etruscan, Medieval and Renaissance style jewellery employing filigree and granulation and sometimes incorporating cameos, enamels and minutely intricate mosaic work.

The brooch shown here is based on a Greek type earring of about 300 BC excavated at Kul Oba in what is now the Ukraine. This brooch was made in various versions by the Castellani firm and might be best described as a modern interpretation of the ancient. There was no attempt to slavishly replicate the original.

The Castellani family were early adopters of the art of marketing and helped set a major trend – they were a jewellery company where the owners were celebrated by name and had become part of the very society they served.

Fig.266: Gold brooch by Castellani based on a Greek earring excavated at Kul Oba burial on the Northern Black Sea coast. Italy, ca 1870-80. (Private Collection) Private collection, New York. Photo by Maggie Nimkin.

In practice, the bulk of Castellani jewellery, though finely made, lacks the precision and slight irregularities that give the truly ancient so much of its character. The brooch in fig.266, for example, is on a far more grandiose scale than the original and incorporates much of its own age.

It is important to separate the more commercial Castellani jewellery, like the last, from the exhibition pieces. The necklace and pendants shown here are masterful copies of the originals which, like the last, were excavated at Kul Oba to the North of the Black Sea 1864. Fine 'exhibition pieces' such as these ornaments, are of extraordinarily workmanship and we might suspect here the hand of Alessandro's gifted protégé Giancinto Melillo.

The accuracy with which the Castellani exhibition and test pieces such as these replicated the originals is in direct contrast with the ideals of John Ruskin who believed that the true artist should never slavishly copy something of past times without incorporating some new, inventive aspects. In his memorable words, written in 1853, "No painter has any business to be an antiquarian." Alessandro would have disagreed with him.

Nevertheless, the inability to reproduce the most intricate Etruscan style granulation particularly vexed Alessandro who had devoted considerable effort to attempting to rediscover the secret of its production. He never fully succeeded.

Fig.267: Castellani's copies of a Greek necklace and pair of large disks excavated at the Great Bliznitza burial mound on the Northern Black Sea Coast. Rome or Naples, ca 1870-80. (Victoria and Albert Museum, London) © V&A Images / Victoria and Albert Museum

The rather stark, no nonsense jewellery of the Romans generally had less appeal for the Castellani and their clients than Greek and Etruscan styles. But nevertheless, some Castellani copies of Roman jewellery exist, such as this pair of gold and pearl earrings.

They are closely modeled on a Roman earring type of the third century AD, although one far more common in the Eastern Roman provinces of the Levantine coast than in Italy itself.

These earrings accompanied a pearl and gold wreath and a gold and pearl festoon necklet and the set is said to have been made 'from the design of Michelangelo, Duke of Sermoneta, in conjunction with Castellani'. This was Michelangelo Caetani who indeed worked with the Firm of Castellani in their early days. The simple design of this jewellery parure might well suggest that it belongs to the early days the Castellani firm.

Fig.268: A pair of earrings made by Castellani, based on a Roman style of the 3rd century AD. Rome, probably ca 1860-70.
(Victoria and Albert Museum, London)
© V&A Images / Victoria and Albert Museum

This magnificent necklace in the Etruscan taste is by Carlo Giuliano, an Italian jeweller who worked in the archaeological and Renaissance styles and who had connections with the Castellani firm.

Guiliano, originally from Naples, had settled in London, opening a workshop in Frith Street, Soho, around 1860. From here he supplied London retailers. In 1874 he opened his own shop on Piccadilly which in due course passed to his son. Perhaps surprisingly, Giuliano was applying his monogram to jewellery even before he opened his own retail shop.

Giuliano seems to have been far less fixated by the challenge of replicating fine granulation than Alessandro Castellani, but there are some fine examples that bear his monogram. In her 1878 book, 'The Art of Beauty' Mrs Haweis commented on a Giuliano necklace 'of his own design and workmanship' where 'The grain work (each piece being made in gold and laid on separately, not imitated by frosting) was finer than any I saw.'

His work is often very close to that of the firm of Castellani and we might suspect that Giuliano had some of his jewellery made in Naples – possibly even in the Castellani workshops.

Fig.269: Gold necklace with a Bacchus mask pendant, by Carlo Giuliano. Naples or London, ca 1860 - 1880. (Victoria and Albert Museum, London) © V&A Images / Victoria and Albert Museum

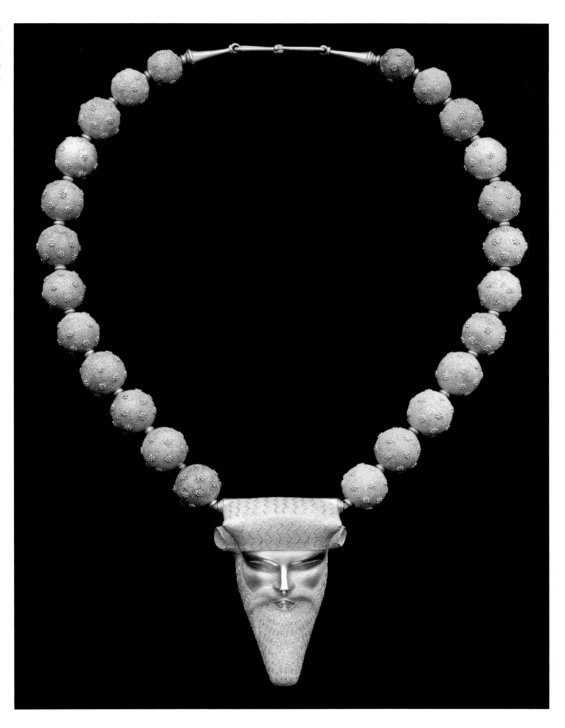

The archaeological revival in jewellery of the second half of the nineteenth century is often seen as a classical revival. However, although copies and interpretations of Greek, Etruscan and Roman jewellery were the most ubiquitous products, other ancient societies also provided inspiration. The bracelet here incorporates an ancient cylinder seal and the gold replicates a relief showing the Assyrian king Ashurbanipal that was excavated by Sir A.H. Layard and brought to the British Museum.

The bracelet is by the firm of John Brogden and dates from around 1860. The company passed through three generations and in the 1850's and 1860's was well known for its fine workmanship and enamel, and its jewellery in the archaeological taste. It was recorded that 'to each of the articles are small tickets explaining the history of the things imitated' – a thoughtful touch.

An advertisement in the Illustrated News in 1882 says 'The attention of the public is respectfully directed to the great advantage of purchasing from the bona fide manufacturer at really wholesale prices for ready money, thereby superseding co-operative stores.' This blatant 'buy at wholesale' pitch surely jars with the earlier high repute of the firm and it closed a few years later when John Brogden died.

Fig.270: A gold bracelet in 'the Archaeological Taste' incorporating an ancient cylinder seal and with embossed designs based on Assyrian reliefs. John Brogden, London, ca 1860. (Victoria and Albert Museum, London) © V&A Images / Victoria and Albert Museum

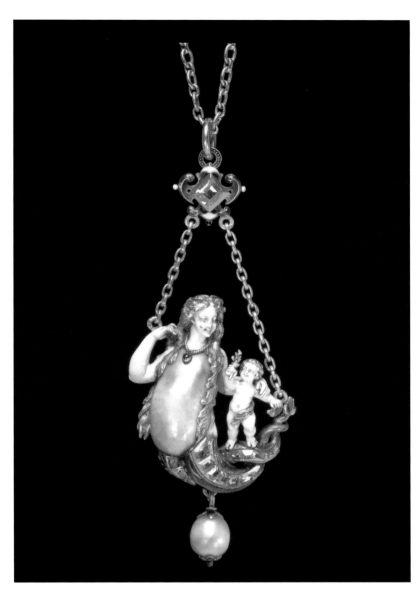

Fig.271: A enamelled gold and diamond-set mermaid pendant in the Renaissance style. By Louis Wièse (1852 – 1923), Paris, ca 1890. (Victoria and Albert Museum, London) © V&A Images / Victoria and Albert Museum

Rrecent years have seen a large number of 'Renaissance' jewels reassigned to the nineteenth century. One significant prompt in this on-going act of art historical backpedalling was the discovery in the Victoria and Albert Museum, London, of a large group of designs from the workshop of the German goldsmith Reinhold Vasters (1827-1909). The drawings made it clear that a remarkably large number of objects hitherto taken as Renaissance or earlier, had been created in his workshop. Many had been made for the collector/dealer Frederic Spitzer and it is still a little unsure as to who was duping whom. The Vasters' copies are remarkably well made and are by no means always readily identifiable, even with close examination. However, more technical studies, such as analysis of the enamel and solder compositions, are providing a growing databank of information to help the forensic jewellery historian. The reader might object to the use of the term forensic here, since it applies to application of scientific knowledge in a legal context. However, forgery is a crime.

But not all nineteenth century versions of Renaissance jewellery were intended to be passed of as fakes. Several well known jewellers, including the Castellani family and Carlo Giuliano, made items in the Renaissance taste and some were very clever pastiches of the real thing. This well-made, albeit rather coy, little mermaid here is by Louis Wièse (1852-1923) who followed on in his father's, Jules Wiese's, footsteps. It was made and sold as what it was – a nineteenth century and attractive and wearable interpretation.

Jules Wiese had worked with Froment-Meurice in Paris until he started his own independent workshop. Louis is famous for his jewels in the Renaissance style and this pendant, of about 1890, is a fine example. It has a large baroque pearl body and enamelled gold set with table-cut diamonds and a cabochon ruby.

As with many of the nineteenth century copies of Renaissance jewels, the table cut diamonds here have the same irregular outlines, and thus irregular edged settings, as in the Renaissance originals. This might suggest that nineteenth century goldsmiths had access to fairly substantial supplies of diamonds from earlier centuries, perhaps in many cases broken up ecclesiastical or civic ornaments.

Coral had been used for jewellery since early antiquity, but it began to come into greater prominence in European jewellery in the later eighteenth century and became hugely popular in the nineteenth, particularly after about 1850. Naples was the main centre for coral carving and the coral jewellery of this period includes a variety of cameos as well as smaller pieces set in jewellery.

The suite of gold and coral jewellery shown here was made in about 1860 and comprises a necklace, a brooch and a pair of earrings. All are set with turned coral drops in an attenuated pear shape. The fringe-like form of the necklace recalls classical Greek forms and although this suite is not truly in the 'Archaeological style', it bears some relationship to it.

Recent years has seen a depletion in coral with pollution and, probably, global warming, threatening an increasing number of coral reefs. Many types of coral are now covered by international legislation relating to the trade in materials derived from endangered species. Coral jewellery is thus also an endangered species.

Fig.272: A set of gold and coral jewellery, Suite of jewellery comprising of a necklace, brooch and a pair of ear-pendants, coral mounted in gold, circa 1860.
© Christie's Images Ltd. 2003

The Victorian cross pendant here is of another organic material that might fall foul of modern endangered species legislation. It is of tortoiseshell with gold filigree decoration and was made in about 1825. Tortoiseshell was a popular material in the nineteenth century, but the hawksbill turtle, the most popular source of the shell, is now endangered.

Here the gold filigree is applied to the tortoiseshell surface and incorporates pearls and turquoise. The gold wire is pinned into the tortoiseshell. This technique is somewhat different to so called piqué work where the gold decoration is inlaid into the tortoiseshell.

Fig.273: Cross pendant in tortoiseshell with applied gold filigree decoration. ca 1825.
(Victoria and Albert Museum, London)
© V&A Images / Victoria and Albert Museum

As we saw earlier, jet jewellery had a long history in Britain, a prehistoric jet necklet was illustrated in fig.76. The manufacture of jet jewellery and jewellery components began in earnest again in Whitby, on the coast of North East England, in the early nineteenth century. It had become a significant local industry by the middle of the century and a very substantial one after the death of Queen Victoria's husband Albert in 1861 had initiated a vogue for black mourning jewellery.

The jet suite shown here dates from the 1870's-1880's and shows how the Whitby workers had by then joined in the craze for the classical revival – here jet cameos in the Roman style. Linked chains like that on this necklace can in theory be carved in one piece, but in most cases the workmen cheated by opening the links then gluing them together after assembly.

Naturally a widespread fashion for jet led to a whole host of imitations in everything from black glass (often termed 'French Jet', even today) to Vulcanite (a form of rubber) and even a vile sounding substance made from sawdust, blood, black dye and glue.

Another wood derivative was Irish Bog Oak. This was often incorporated in nineteenth century jewellery with Irish themes such as the shamrock and a harp. Dark brown Bog Oak could be carved, but it was also shaped by softening in boiling water and then pressing between dies.

Fig.274: Jet mourning parure consisting of a necklace and pendant, bracelet, earrings and brooch. English, ca 1870-85.
(Victoria and Albert Museum, London)
© V&A Images / Victoria and Albert Museum

Cameos are designs carved in three dimensional relief, the figurative or other design being raised above the surround area. Cameos are thus the opposite of intaglios where the design is sunk into the material.

Cameo first appear in jewellery in the closing years of the Hellenistic period and only became commoner in Roman times (fig.161). In antiquity they were almost invariably carved in stone, usually agate or onyx, rarely molded in glass and only exceptionally cut in shell.

All cameos are rare after the end of the Byzantine period and with the exception of the occasional Byzantine and Medieval example, only reappear in the Renaissance when classical forms and imagery became popular. The Renaissance examples are again, almost always, in stone.

The heyday for cameos in recent times was in the Victorian period, particularly after the 1850s when Classical themes in general became common. The Victorian cameos are commonly carved out of shell, the varied colouring of the layers allowing the colour contrast in the design. The cameos are usually cut from the large 'Helmet Shells' from the Mediterranean and carved in Naples where the industry had been introduced in the early years of the nineteenth century. Typically the scene or figure is in white against a pale pinkish or yellowish background. The designs are generally based on classical themes and most frequently show the profile head of a young woman with varying degrees of artistry.

The finest Victorian shell cameos are of high quality, but many are repetitive and unimaginative, just like the poorer quality modern equivalents that fill jewellers' windows to this day.

In the cameos seen here we see a variety of subjects. One, in the finely worked Victorian brooch (fig.275), shows a person of some importance, but the subject has not been identified. A classical theme is shown by the winged woman who holds a goblet and the sun (fig.276). Possibly she is intended to be Hebe, the Greek goddess of youth and the daughter of Zeus and Hera. Hebe is often shown in Greek art holding a goblet of intoxicating nectar and possibly this representation also alludes to how her husband, Hercules, barrowed the "goblet of the Sun". The other cameo (fig.277) is a personification of 'night and day', a popular Victorian subject.

Fig.275: A gold-mounted shell cameo brooch depicting a woman's head in profile. Mid to late 19th century.
© Christie's Images Ltd. 2003

Fig.276: A gold-mounted shell cameo brooch depicting a Hebe.
Mid to late 19th century
© Christie's Images Ltd. 2003

Fig.277: A gold-mounted shell cameo brooch depicting Night and Day.
Mid to late 19th century
© Christie's Images Ltd. 2003

Not all nineteenth century Naples' cameos were in shell, many were cut in what is usually described as 'lava'. These cameos again typically depict classical heads and were produced in quantity in Naples for the blossoming tourist industry. The colours include various shades of beige and grey, a reddish brown and yellow. The bracelet shown here is a typical example with its oval cameos mounted in simple, linked gold settings.

It was a masterstroke of marketing to associate the cameos with the lava that had been spectacularly ejected from the erupting mount Vesuvius and buried Pompeii, but it may not have been accurate. Most of these cameos seem to be in a type of local fine grained limestone and some might be of other materials – some may even be molded. The colours were sometimes produced by staining. Victorians might have been misled; modern collectors should not.

From the time gold coinage was first introduced around 600 BC, it was a highly convenient source of raw material for jewellers. Coins were a legitimate way for a person to obtain precious metal in standardised weights and purity. There is ample evidence that coins were so used in antiquity, from the coins and coin fragments found in goldsmiths' hoards to documentary mentions. As an example of the latter, the Medieval Islamic writer al-Adili al Tusi describes walking down a street where 'A charming girl is cutting gold coins into bits inside a house'.

It was seldom in the state's interest to allow such melting down and re-use of its coinage and various legislation was attempted over the centuries to prevent this. However, even in Victorian Britain the practice was very common. The British gold coin of the period was the Sovereign, an 1875 example is shown here, that had replaced the gold Guinea (named after the country we now spell Ghana on the 'Gold Coast' of Africa) in 1816. The Sovereign weighed 7.98 grams and had a fineness of 22 carat. Half sovereigns were also minted.

Even at the time Sovereigns were first minted 'The melting down of coin and the manufacture of plate was a leading feature of the Birmingham industry' to quote a writer of the period. The practice increased during the nineteenth century, and there were good reasons for it. The Sovereign was of regular weight and purity and, most importantly, was worth exactly its face value in gold – the gold price was fixed in those days. So jewellers could simply obtain gold in coin form from the banks and avoid paying the small profit margin on gold obtained via bullion dealers and refiners. Also it was still the practice for customers to provide jewellers with the gold from which to make a wedding ring and a half sovereign fitted the bill here perfectly – a reason why the gold wedding ring is still traditionally of 22 carat gold in Britain.

Needless to say, the practice worried the Government and the mint, but it was only in 1920 that legislation was introduced to remedy the problem and make it illegal *'to melt down, break up, or use otherwise than as currency any gold or silver coin which is for the time being current in the United Kingdom or in any British possession or foreign country.'*

Even so, during the Second World War, and the period of austerity that followed it, hoarded Sovereigns and other gold coins were being made in wedding rings by what were described at the time as 'Pirate jewellers with hide-out workshops'.

Fig.278: A gold-mounted 'lava' cameo bracelet.
Cameos Italian, mid to late 19th century
© Christie's Images Ltd. 2005

Fig.279: Front and back of a gold sovereign.
British 1875
© Spinx and Son Ltd.

Before the early eighteenth century the diamonds employed in jewellery had come almost entirely from India – Borneo being the only other 17th century source of note. The discoveries of diamonds in Brazil and their entrance into the European market around 1730 increased tenfold the quantities of diamonds available to jewellers and their customers. Their was an inevitable drop in prices initially, but from then on diamond jewellery played a far more prominent part in the jeweller's repertoire. The rise of rich merchant classes in the wake of the Industrial Revolution in the Eighteenth Century provided a widening customer base and diamond tiaras, necklets and bracelets vied for maximum glitter around the candle-lit ballrooms and dining rooms of the opulent new country houses.

Then, just after the middle of the nineteenth century diamonds were discovered in South Africa. The first diamond recognized for what it was in South Africa was probably the

Eureka, a stone of 21.25 carats, found by a young Boer man from a farm by the Orange River, Hopetown. It came to the notice of the Colonial Secretary and was eventually exhibited in the Universal World Fair in Paris in 1867/8. This pebble, for which the finder's family had refused any payment, was the beginning of the great diamond rush in South Africa. It is perhaps a sad testament to human nature and greed, that while nature had made Africa one of the richest parts of the world in terms of natural resources, including gold and platinum as well as diamonds, it is still a continent with some of the poorest inhabitants in the world.

The illustration shown here is from an article entitled 'Life in the Diamond Fields' from Harpers New Monthly Magazine in 1873. This article noted that out of the 4000 diamonds and pieces of diamond unearthed daily only a handful became 'pure water brilliants.'

Fig.280: Early diamond mining in South Africa. From Harpers New Monthly Magazine, 1873

In the later seventeenth and eighteenth centuries, diamonds had been cut to be brilliant in appearance, but also to retain optimum weight from the crystal rough. The resulting diamonds possess variations in proportion and sparkle that gives older diamond jewellery a pleasing character all of its own. An example is the bow here which was made at about the time of the first African diamond discoveries. As was by now traditional, the diamonds are flatteringly set in silver, but the backing is in gold.

The bird brooch, also silver set with gold backing, dates from around 1880 and shows that despite the increasing quantity of diamonds now entering the world market, not all jewellery owners could aspire to the best stones. Here simple little rose diamonds are used, often cut from diamond fragments or little pieces cleaved off larger stones.

Despite the use of little rose diamonds, the workmanship is still good and this brooch shows the combination of naturalism and symbolism that inspired many later nineteenth century jewellery forms. Here is a swallow in flight. From its ruby-set collar hangs a single pearl drop. The swallow was a popular motif in Victorian jewellery and could symbolise love and

motherhood. The swallow always returns to its same abode, a tendency that might have been reassuring to a Victorian woman whose husband had been separated from her by business or military duties.

Feathers have always been used as personal ornaments, from the Equador ornaments in fig.209 to the feather in a huntsman's hat, but here the form is reproduced in diamonds with a ruby centre. The brooch was made in about 1890 and, as usual, has the diamonds set in silver, the emeralds and central ruby in gold. The piece is mounted 'en tremblant' along a spring, to provide movement when it is worn, a naturalism reinforced by its asymmetry and the irregularity and even overlapping of some of the feather barbs.

The feather is that of a peacock, hence the coloured gemstones. The peacock had long symbolised love and pride as well as immortality and the soul – we saw an early use of peacock imagery in the Byzantine bracelet in fig.171. The peacock, and its plumage, continued to play an important role in Art Nouveau jewellery.

Fig.281: Bow brooch of old-cut diamonds mounted in silver and gold. ca 1860.
© Christie's Images Ltd. 2005

Fig.282: Swallow brooch in diamonds with ruby collar and pendant pearl, mounted in silver and gold. ca 1880.
© Christie's Images Ltd. 2005

Fig.283: Peacock feather brooch set en tremblant, central ruby with emeralds and diamonds, mounted in silver and gold, English, circa 1890.
© Christie's Images Ltd. 2005

The Tiffany company had its origins in a New York store, Tiffany, Young and Ellis, selling what would be classed today as a variety of gift and fancy wares. In 1848 a buying trip to Paris led to the significant purchase of diamonds from the impoverished French nobility and a move into the higher diamond and gold jewellery market, as well as design and manufacture, not just retailing. In the early 1850s Charles Tiffany opened a Paris office, bought out his partners and renamed the New York shop Tiffany and Company.

Japanese art styles had become popular in USA by the 1870's and jewellery in the Japanese taste was being produced or imported from Europe. The gold ornaments in the Japanese style shown here were sold by Tiffany in the 1860's, although they may well have been imported from Paris.

The silver book brooch has a butterfly reminiscent of Japanese art on one page and, surprisingly, rather stylised ancient Egyptian hieroglyphs on the other, making this a particularly early example of the Egyptian influence upon jewellery.

The bracelets (fig.285) and the little brooch depicting a heron standing in a pool (fig.286) are noteworthy because the white metal flowers on the bracelets and the pool on the brooch are platinum. The bracelets bear an inscription with the date 1882 and These are early examples of platinum in jewellery. But they are not the earliest. There are some references to platinum jewellery before 1820 and George IV bought a gold and platinum chain in about that year. In 1829 the manufacture of jewellery in gold and platinum was officially sanctioned in France.

Even so, platinum jewellery really only came into its own in the early twentieth century and as late as 1892 one observer described platinum as 'Unsuited by its unattractive appearance to the jeweller's purposes.'

Fig.284: Silver brooch in the form of a book, a butterfly on one page and stylised Egyptian hieroglyphs on other. ca 1860
© Copyright the Trustees of The British Museum

Fig.285: A pair of gold bracelets with applied gold and platinum floral decoration. Tiffany & Co. New York (but perhaps made in Paris), dated 1882.
© Copyright the Trustees of The British Museum

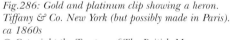

Fig.286: Gold and platinum clip showing a heron. Tiffany & Co. New York (but possibly made in Paris). ca 1860s
© Copyright the Trustees of The British Museum

This brooch was produced by Tiffany and Co in New York around 1890 and consists of a cameo, probably a re-used earlier one, set behind gold bars and within a diamond link surround. It's overall form recalls Renaissance forms, as does both the inclusion of a cameo and its subject – Eros, the young, winged son of Venus, goddess of love. Here Eros is imprisoned and sits looking dejected behind bars. Below the bars is a diamond key among forget-me-nots. This type of playful romantic motif is not unusual in Tiffany's jewellery. The imprisonment of Eros crops up in various myths and stories over the centuries – usually ending with his escape and the obvious moral that one cannot lock-up love.

The photo is of the British actress Lily Elsie. She was born Elsie Cotton and became what has been called as 'one of the best known, and most loved, faces in England.' This image, from a postcard from about the time she married in 1911, shows her wearing jewellery in the style of the period. It might be imitation 'stage' jewellery or the real thing, after all her new husband was the son of a Lancashire textile millionaire. By the time she died in 1962, and pearl and diamond jewellery and a Cartier clock were listed in her will, she had seen many changes in jewellery styles.

The steady march of mass production had permeated the jewellery trade since the mid-eighteenth century. Also, successful lobbying by jewellers and, in particular, watchmakers had led to lower standards of gold being acceptable in much of Europe. The end result was cheaper and more abundant jewellery, churned out in quantity to serve a growing middle class to whom the Victorian love of over adornment or bland sentimentality was still appealing.

Inevitably, there was a backlash.

In the view inspired by John Ruskin and his followers, true art had died with Raphael in 1520. So when William Morris began to design and produce furniture, furnishings and even jewellery he did so in a quasi-Medieval style that was soon joined by a repertoire of Celtic motifs. As befitting the whole philosophy, the value was in the craft not the materials. Silver was commonly used and diamonds and other valuable gems typically scorned in favour of cheaper stones and enamels.

Since John Ruskin's views had such an influences on the Arts and Crafts jewellery movement it is worth briefly looking at what he said in the 1850's. To him manufacture was essentially degrading to the worker unless it involved some innovation on his or her part. Thus, although cutting precious gems involved skill, it required little mental faculty and so "Every person who wears cut jewels merely for the sake of their value is, therefore, a slave driver." In contrast, "the working of the goldsmith, and the various designing of grouped jewellery and enamel-work, may become the subject of the most noble human intelligence."

To Ruskin, invention was more important than execution.

It was mistaken to think that 'one man's thoughts can be, or ought to be, executed by another man's hands...'. Rough work should be chosen over smooth work since one should "never imagine that there is a reason to be proud of anything that may be accomplished by patience and sandpaper."

This 'Arts and crafts movement' lasted from the 1880's to 1910. Much of the jewellery has a sensible and symmetrical nature, often of worthy craftsmanship but – and this is remarkable considering the private lives of many of the style's proponents – it lacks the sensuality that became such a feature of French Art Nouveau.

European and Western trade with Japan had become established by the 1860's and the fascination that Japanese artists had with the natural world, particularly plant motifs, soon found a ready acceptance in the West. Art Nouveau largely grew out of a combination of the archaism of the Arts and Crafts movement with an oriental impressionism where asymmetrical and free flowing lines delineated the movements and rhythms of nature – plant forms, flowing hair, waves and female curves. Realism became secondary to dream-like fantasy with a harmony of form and colours. In its sensuous imagery of women, Art Nouveau managed to mirror their growing freedom of expression. This blending of Art and Crafts forms with oriental influences lead into the so-called Art Nouveau movement. The name of the style Nouveau derives from Samuel Bing's Parisian Oriental art shop that was renamed L'Art Nouveau in 1895. One exhibitor at this relaunch was the Parisian jeweller René Lalique.

In the years after 1900 jewellery in the Art Nouveau style had become available in most of the major Parisian jewellery houses, including Boucheron and Chaumet. Only Cartier seems to have largely spurned the style. They were predominantly interested in diamond-set platinum.

The arrival of diamonds from South Africa in closing decades of the nineteenth century and development of usable platinum alloys around this same time had a significant impact on how jewellery was made and what it looked like. There was also an increasing number of wealthy people with the means to indulge in luxuries of all types, including jewellery and foreign travel. In particular, there was the new bourgeoisie of North America; the growing ranks of industrialists and businessmen who were discriminating buyers, insisting on the finest stones and best cutting. A book on diamonds published in 1887 noted: 'As a nation, the Americans are the finest judges of diamonds in the world. American buyers insist on getting the finest stones and the most perfect cutting.'

The jewellery manufacturers and sellers expanded on the proceeds of this new trade, and soon companies became famous, often identified with a particular style and the flare or charisma of an individual. Jewellery houses like Tiffany, Cartier and Fabergé became synonymous with style, good taste and wealth.

Fig.287: Brooch set with a carved agate cameo of Eros imprisoned, with diamond surround. Tiffany & Co., New York, circa 1890. © Christie's Images Ltd. 2004

11427 B ROTARY PHOTO E.C.   MISS LILY ELS'E

Fig.288: Lily Elsie (Mrs. Bullough). Portrait on a postcard, ca 1910. © Courtesy of the National Portrait Gallery, London

The mechanization of production and other changes in the jewellery industry began to generate a counter reaction even as early as the mid nineteenth century. Craftspeople and their customers hankered after the old days when jewellery was a craft, pieces unique and when wearers were proud patrons of the arts, not simply glitter junkies.

This 'Arts and Crafts' brooch shown here is of various metals with blue and green enamel. The oval stone mounted in its centre is so-called 'Eilat stone', an intergrowth of turquoise with the green mineral malachite.

The case for this brooch bears the legend 'The Guild of Handicraft, Ltd.' and gives the works address as Chipping Campden in Gloucestershire, England. The Guild of Handicraft had moved to Chipping Campden in 1902 after being founded in Whitechapel in London 1888. The guild was a practical craft cooperative modelled after the Medieval British guilds. The concept developed out of lectures on Ruskin given by Charles Robert Ashbee and aimed at the working man. The Guild would produce hand made goods and train apprentices.

Charles Robert Ashbee himself was the designer of the enamelled copper brooch (fig.290) and the stylised dragonfly brooch in mother of pearl, amethyst and enamel also shown here (fig.291).

In the context of Ruskin's ideas, it is worth noting that Ashbee is also well known to jewellery historians as the translator, in 1884, of *The Treatises of Benvenuto Cellini on Goldsmithing and Sculpture*. Cellini was perhaps the ultimate example of Renaissance designer and craftsman, and a stickler for perfection and perfect finish – hardly things to please Ruskin.

Fig.289:
Brooch in mixed metals with enamel and Eliat stone.
From the Guild of Handicraft, Chipping Campden, early 20th century
© Christie's Images Ltd. 2002

Fig.291: Brooch of enamelled white metal set with pearl and an amethyst. Designed by Charles Robert Ashbee and made by the Guild of Handicraft, ca 1890 - 1910.
© Christie's Images Ltd. 2001

Fig.290: Brooch in enamelled copper decorated with silver wire, blister pearls and baroque pearl drops.
Designed by Charles Robert Ashbee and made by the Guild of Handicraft, ca 1896. (Victoria and Albert Museum)
© V&A Images / Victoria and Albert Museum

The growing freedom of expression among women around the turn of the century, as reflected by the Art Nouveau, opened by a crack the door that would eventually allow women to follow professions traditionally within the male domain. Nothing could sum this up more than this extraordinary gold buckle in two colour gold. It shows a scantily dressed woman holding a lion's head and pelt, designed by the celebrated jewellery designer Antoine Bricteux of Paris, and is said to have been inspired by a woman lion tamer.

The woman was Claire Héliot, the 'Lady of the Lions', a famous performer in the USA and Britain until she was badly mauled by one of her twelve lions in 1907. She died in poverty in Germany as recently as 1953.

The Art Nouveau suite in gilded silver was made by Janvier Quercia in Paris in about 1900. The suite comprises a comb for the hair, a large buckle and a necklet with pendant. The motif on each is in the form of a woman's head with long symmetrical flowing hair. As in other works by this maker, the gilding is used ingeniously. Here the flesh on the three faces has been lightly abraded to reduce the thickness of the gilding and provide a paler, more mottled flesh-like appearance. Conversely, the hair has been reddened slightly, perhaps by the application of some other substance over the gilding.

The three heads were produced by casting. The largest head, on the buckle, is well modelled in the round and was probably a one-off lost wax casting with surprisingly little subsequent hand finishing – a feature that no doubt would have pleased Ruskin. The two smaller heads are more cursorily modelled and lack some of the detail of the larger one – most noticeably the star on the forehead. Possibly these two smaller heads were cast from wax antitypes made by pressing wax into a metal die

The chain of the necklet is of simple, scrolling links.

Fig.292: Gold buckle showing a woman holding a lions pelt. Designed by Antoine Bricteux of Paris, French ca 1900. (British Museum)

Fig.293: Art Nouveau gilded silver comb, buckle and necklet. Janvier Quercia, Paris ca 1900. (British Museum)

In 1899 a Grandson of Queen Victoria and a keen supporter of the Arts and Crafts movement, Grand Duke Ernst Ludwig of Hess, invited selected artists to Darmstadt in Germany to establish an artists colony there. One of these was the interior designer and jewellery designer Patriz Huber (1878 – 1902).

Like other examples of Huber jewellery, this buckle was made by Theodore Fahrner, a Pforzheim manufacturer who collaborated with the Darmstadt colony. It was sold by Liberty's of London having been imported through Mürrle Bennet and Company of London and Pforzheim, whose mark it bears. It also bears the London British Hallmark for 1902 – a reminder that buckles were a class of precious metal ornament not exempted from Hallmarking.

The silver buckle is set with four green cabochon stones and has a deliberately blackened 'oxidised' finish, a colour combination found in other Huber jewellery.

Huber committed suicide shortly after the three year contact at Darmstadt ended.

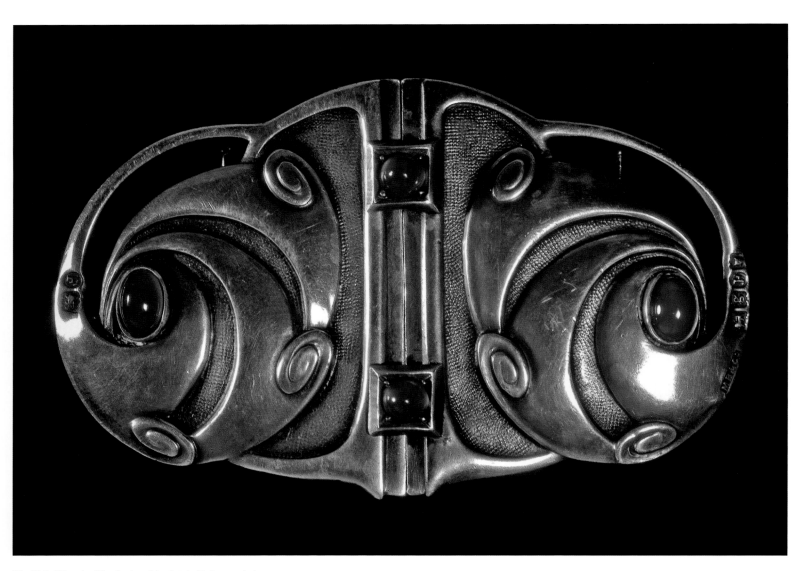

Fig.294: Silver buckle. Designed by Patriz Huber, made by Theodore Fahrner of Pforzheim and sold by Liberties of London, 1902. (British Museum)
© Copyright the Trustees of The British Museum

The newly discovered repertoires of Japanese art had begun to reach the west from the 1850's onwards. Japanese influence introduced a vibrant new colour palette and a naturalism eminently suited to jewellery materials and jewellery techniques. Indeed, Tiffany & Co. had imitated decorative Japanese *Shakudo* and *shibuichi* metalwork since the 1870's.

The firm of Falize in Paris was an early adopter of the oriental style. Alexis Falize opened his first workshop in Paris in 1838 and rapidly became renowned for his cloisonné enamelled

work. He exhibited cloisonné enamel jewellery at the 1867 Exposition Universelle in Paris and international customers had included Tiffany & Co. The pair of cloisonné enamelled cuff links shown in fig.14 were made in about 1870.

The extraordinary suit of jewellery shown here, made by Falize in about 1900, owes its inspiration to middle Byzantine art – as a glance at fig.184 will prove. The bracelet, clasp and brooch show birds among a scrolling vine in vibrant cloisonné enamel.

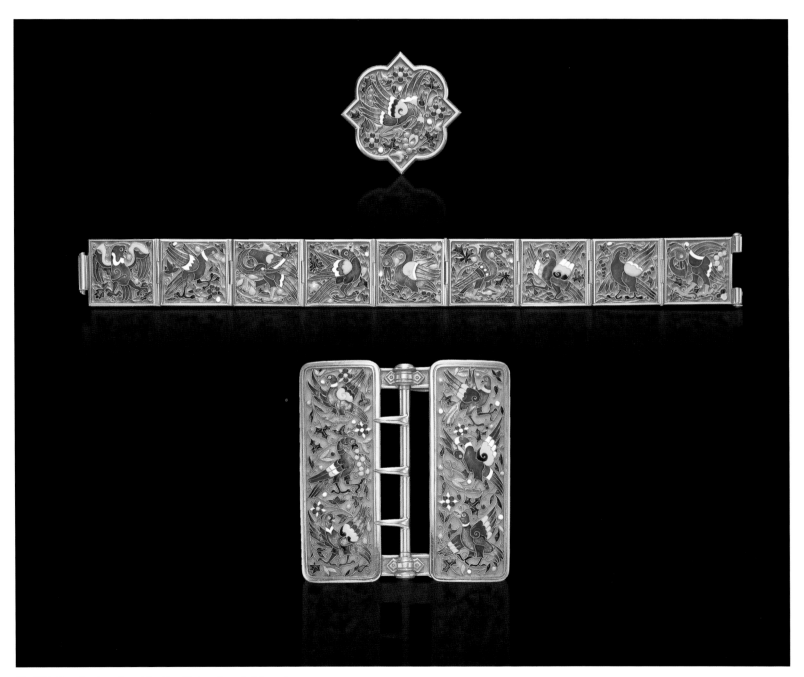

Fig.295: Bracelet, brooch and buckle with translucent cloisonné enamel panels mounted in gold. Falize, Paris, ca 1900
© *Christie's Images Ltd. 2002*

The pendant shown here is by Lucien Falize, Alexis' son, and is in the Renaissance style. It was exhibited at the Paris Universal Exhibition in 1900. The finely made enamel, sapphire and diamonds pendant with 'grapes' of dark pearls, a grey pearl drop, and a sapphire and pearl embellished chain is a perfect example of Falize's mastery and of the type of jewellery that had come into vogue among the fashionable rich by the turn of the century. The design shows Joshua and Caleb bringing back grapes from the promised land to show Moses.

As we have seen (fig.271) gold and enamel figural pendants in the Renaisance style were copied extensively during the nineteenth century, indeed objects that were once accepted as Renaissance originals are being reclassified as fakes or reproductions with monotonous regularity.

Fig.296: Gold pendant in the Renaissance taste with vari-coloured black pearls, sapphires, diamonds and enamel, Falize, Paris, 1896. © Christie's Images Ltd. 2001

René Lalique (1861-1945) had trained as a conventional jeweller, as his surviving jewelry from the 1880's shows. He sold to major Paris houses such as Cartier and Boucheron, but by the late 1880's a new element of fantasy was appearing. Indeed Boucheron rejected an 1887 design for a flight of swallows as too avant guard. Lalique produced it all the same, and Boucheron not only then sold it, but reordered it in various versions. Cartier also bought a version. His business was now doing well, and in the early 1890's he concentrated in breaking away entirely from the traditional forms and ideas, abandoning diamonds and adding enamel and new naturalistic and figural forms. Among the latter were naked female forms which were greeted by reactions from admiration to calls for outright bans. The bodice ornament and tiara shown here are less controversial floral forms in bone, glass and topaz – a clear demonstration that appearance was more important than intrinsic value.

Fig.297: Tiara comb and bodice ornament in glass, topaz, horn and enamelled gold. René Lalique, Paris, ca 1903-04.
(Victoria and Albert Museum, London)
© V&A Images / Victoria and Albert Museum

By the second half of the 1890's Lalique was highly celebrated in France and his jewellery met with international acclaim at the 1900 International Exhibition in Paris. This extraordinary wasp pin was purchased at that exhibition by the Danish Museum of Decorative Arts, Copenhagen. It depicts five gold, diamond and enamel wasps on an opal flower and epitomises Lalique's approach to design and the use of varied materials. The design and execution are superb, the realism extraordinary.

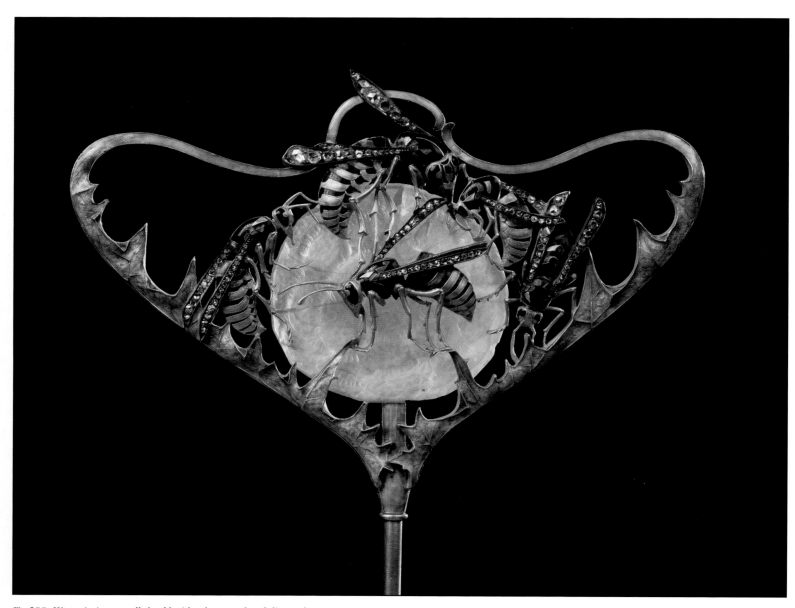

Fig.298: Wasp pin in enamelled gold with a large opal and diamonds.
René Lalique, Paris ca 1900. (Danish Museum of Decorative Arts, Copenhagen)
© *Danish Museum of Decorative Arts, Copenhagen*

Although Lalique was pre-eminent among French Art Nouveau jewellers, he was not alone. Particularly influential was the firm of Vever that had been founded in Metz 1821 and had moved to Paris half a century later when Alsace-Lorraine was annexed by the Germans. Paul and Henri Vever took over the firm in 1881 and greatly expanded its international reputation and, like Lalique, exhibited jewellery in the Art Nouvean style at the International Exhibition in Paris in 1900.

Like Lalique, they used a variety of materials including enamel and ivory. The gold and enamel buckle shown here was made about 1900. It depicts a grasshopper on a sheaf of wheat in raised relief against a green enamel background. The prongs on this buckle appear to be of a pink or 'rose' coloured gold – this may have been for aesthetic reasons or for practicality, gold-copper alloys can be tougher than the more usual gold-silver alloys.

Vever also used more conventional gems. The diamond pendant illustrated made by Vever at the beginning of the twentieth century is set in platinum. The old style of the cutting of the diamonds used here and in many other turn of the century jewellery suggests that they may have been re-used from older pieces, in some instances unfashionable jewellery owned by customers.

The delicate style is typical for the period and in part reflects the use of platinum for the settings. Platinum was hard, tough and bright, when correctly alloyed, perfect credentials for delicate mounts for diamonds. Such jewellery was made at a time when, relatively speaking, labour was cheap and diamonds and platinum costly.

At present there is a resurgence of this type of turn of the century and 'Belle Époque' jewellery. This time made viable by either cheap but increasingly skilled labour in Asia or by the now almost perfected practice of casting diamonds and other gemstone in situ in the mounts, even platinum mounts.

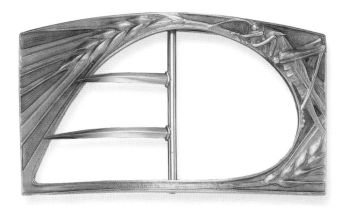

Fig.299: Yellow and rose gold grasshopper buckle with enamel. Henri Vever, Paris, ca 1900.
© Christie's Images Ltd. 2005

Fig.300: Diamond pendant mounted in platinum and 18 ct gold. Henri Vever, Paris, ca 1900.

The two brooches here were made by George Fouquet. The house of Fouquet, founded in the nineteenth century, produced some magnificent Art Nouveau jewellery with Desrosiers and then the Czech painter Alphonse Mucha as designers. It then gained high international acclaim for their post – World War I jewellery, helping to spear-head the Art Deco jewellery movement, before bankruptcy in the financial upheavals of the 1930's.

The brooch with the lotus flower and bee was designed by Charles Desrosiers, made by Georges Fouquet and purchased by the Victoria and Albert Musuem, London from the Salon de la Société des Artistes in Paris in 1901. It perfectly epitomises the finer Art Nouveau jewellery, with its flowing lines and naturalistic forms.

The second brooch, maybe a year or two later, has a frame of diamonds and it is interesting to see how this encloses and cuts off the mistletoe or laurel leaves.

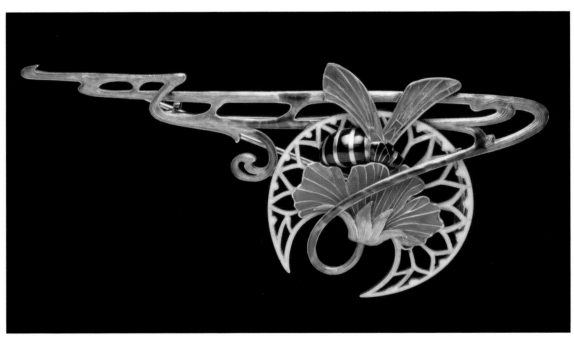

Fig.301: Bee brooch in enamelled gold with plique à jour enamel wings and petals.
Designed by Desrosiers and made by Fouquet, Paris, ca 1901.
(Victoria and Albert Museum, London)
© V&A Images / Victoria and Albert Museum

Fig.302: Diamond and seed pearl brooch mounted in gold with enamelled leaves. Fouquet, Paris ca 1900. (Victoria and Albert Museum, London)
© V&A Images / Victoria and Albert Museum

In recent centuries in the west, silver jewellery has often been seen as the poor relation to gold, but some of the greatest designer have chosen to use silver. This was particularly true in the Arts and crafts movement when the concept of preciousness was often scorned in favour of art, imagination and craftsmanship.

The silver belt buckles here were both sold by Liberty and Company of London. This London firm, whose name has become almost synonymous with the Celtic Revival, Arts and Crafts and Art Nouveau design in Britain, was founded in 1874 with the deliberate intention of setting rather than following fashions. The founder, Arthur Lazenby Liberty, was later knighted.

The buckles owe much to Celtic interlace, but Celtic interlace as seen through the filter of late nineteenth century aesthetics. With early Celtic and Saxon interlace, the intertwined creatures are both omnipresent but concealed, their weaving together serving to keep them tense but restrained. In the nineteenth century revival, the sensuous curves and tendrils are almost growing, like lush vegetation, ready to embrace wearer or bystander within their folds.

The opal set buckle was made for Liberty's by the firm of Hasseler in Birmingham and was owned by the wife of John Llewellyn a director of Liberty's whose own Welsh ancestry may have influenced the launch of their 'Cymric' range of Celtic revival jewellery.

Fig.303:
Silver clasp set with an opal. Made by Haseler's of Birmingham and probably designed by Oliver Baker, English, ca 1899. (Victoria and Albert Museum, London)
© V&A Images / Victoria and Albert Museum

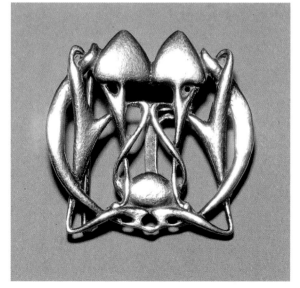

Fig.304: Silver belt buckle. Liberty and Co., stamped Birmingham, Cymric silver, English, 1901.
© Christie's Images Ltd. 2001

The enamelled orchid brooches, one in white and pinkish enamel the other in pink alone, were made by Tiffany & Co. between about 1890 and 1900. Orchid jewels had first been exhibited by Tiffany & Co. at the 1889 Paris Exposition and secured the grand gold prize for jewellery. All twenty five of their botanically-based enamelled brooches had been sold by the second day of the exhibition.

Their perfection in both technique and representation attracted great admiration from observers at the time and were a tribute to the skills of Tiffany's designers Paulding Farnham and Edward C. Moore. The orchids are indeed accurate representations of specific varieties – the white and pink one is of the *Laelias* variety, the pink one a *Calanthe veitchi* – a *Calanthe vestita* and *Calanthe rosea* cross.

The association between Tiffany & Co. and enamel work was boosted when Charles Tiffany's son, Louis Comfort Tiffany, born in 1848, began to pursue his own interests as jewellery designer, glassmaker and enameller in the 1890's, perhaps inspired by Lalique's work.

Fig.305: 'Calanthe Veitchii' enamelled gold orchid brooch. Tiffany and Co., New York, ca 1890.
© Christie's Images Ltd. 2004

Fig.306: 'Laelias' enamelled gold orchid brooch. Tiffany & Co., New York, 1900.
© Christie's Images Ltd. 2001

In Germany and Austria the Art Nouveau (Jugendstil) jewellery had appeared by the mid 1890's and, like its French counterparts, abandoned traditional forms in a search for abstract shape and movement. A major manufacturing centre was Pforzheim.

Vever decried the German work as tasteless and although the finest examples are equal to the French, many pieces lack some of the ethereal quality of the best French work and are more solid and symmetrical than free flowing. Some have an almost Renaissance look of somber fantasy about them.

However, the rather linear and abstract forms that developed in German jewellery after about 1900 were the precursors of the post World War I Art Deco style. This can be seen in the diamond and gem-set brooch shown here which was designed by Joseph Hoffmann in 1904 and executed by the Wiener Werkstätte. It is in gold and silver, set with diamonds, moonstones, lapis lazuli, coral and opal. Hoffmann was one follower of the 'Vienna Secession', a modern movement that deliberately sought to counteract Art Nouveau naturalism with more geometric modern art. Others involved in the movement included the artist Gustav Klimt.

Fig.307: Silver and gold brooch with rose-cut diamonds, moonstones, lapis lazuli, coral and hardstone plaques. Designed by Josef Hoffmann for Mrs. Fritz Wärndorfer, Austrian, 1904.
© Christie's Images Ltd. 2000

The firm of Fabergé really needs little introduction. Carl Fabergé took on his father's languishing jewellery shop in St Petersburg in 1870 and with the realisation that money was more likely to result, from focusing on design and craftsmanship rather the intrinsic value of the materials, began to build his business.

The pink topazes in this cross pendant by Fabergé might well have come from the Russian deposits of this attractive gem. The rectangular topaz is bordered by small diamonds on the right with lower edges providing almost a three-dimensional 'drop shadow' effect. There is a single larger diamond in the cross's centre.

This piece was made in the decade before the Russian Revolution and once belonged to the Grand Duchess Zenia Aleksandrovna, one of Faberge's extensive circle of royal and influencial clients.

The locket shown here was produced by Fabergé and has pink enamel over an 'engine turned' background. This type of background was produced using a mechanised engraving machine with several cutting edges that produced a series of sharp lines in wavy or radiating patterns that could produce almost a watered silk effect.

The engine turning technique surfaced out of the Industrial Revolution in the second half of the eighteenth century and soon became popular for watch cases, gold boxes and the like. The initial decoration of this type was largely limited to flat bands of decoration to which the term guilloche was often applied – a term that is sometimes applied, perhaps wrongly, to all engine turning. The technique was particularly popular around the early twentieth century when the more complex three-dimensional curved surfaces could be decorated in this way. The Fabergé workshops were masters in this technique. Even so, when covered by enamel a variety of short cuts could be used without ready detection – sometimes we even find 'engine turning' that is really just thin stamped foil underlying the enamel.

Fig.308: Pink topaz and diamond cross. Fabergé, St Petersburg, ca 1908-1917.
© Christie's Images Ltd. 2001.

Fig.309: Pink enamel and diamond pendant locket. Fabergé, St Petersburg, ca 1896-1908.
© Christie's Images Ltd. 2003

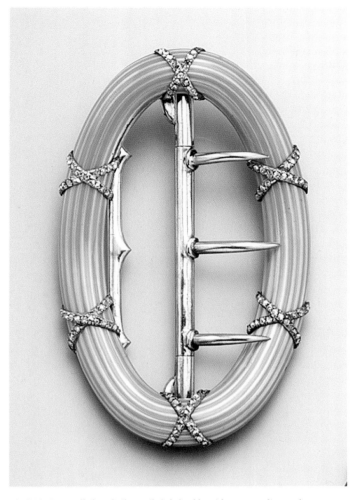

Fig.310: Enamelled and silver gilt belt-buckle with rose-cut diamonds.
Fabergé (workmaster Michael Perchin), St Petersburg, ca 1896-1908.
© Christie's Images Ltd. 2002

This Fabergé belt buckle is in pink enamel over silver. Some of the exposed silver is gold plated, and the crossed ribbon ornamentation is in rose-cut diamonds. It bears the mark for 1896-1908.

It might appear inappropriate to produce an exquisitely made rose-diamond and enamel decorated buckle in silver, especially when the maker is such a renowned company as Fabergé. However, the firm of Faberge, like the other great houses, were well aware that different colours of transparent enamel required different coloured metals underlying them to show off their subtle colours at their best. In 1880 Lucien Falize pointed out that "the color and overall appearance of transparent enamels will depend on the nature of the underlying metal."

In fact the Fabergé firm was demonstrating its virtuosity by enamelling on silver. It is far trickier to enamel over silver than gold, especially with transparent enamel, since the strong heat required can oxidise the silver, playing havoc with the subtle hues of the enamel.

In 1913 the Romanov dynasty of Russia celebrated its 300th anniversary. In 1613 Russian nobility, still smarting from the horrors and excesses of the mad, mass murderer Ivan the Terrible, sought a new Imperial dynasty. However, they did not stray far from the blood-line, Michael Romanov, elected tsar by a National Assembly in 1613, was the grandnephew of Anastasia Romanova, the first wife of Ivan the terrible. In fact, the death of Ivan's beloved Anastasia, possibly she was poisoned, may well have been a contributory factor in his madness.

For the occasion of this 300th anniversary, the Fabergé firm was commissioned to produce a range of jewellery pieces that might be presented as gifts by the Emperor or Empress to officials, members of the court and other dignitaries. Among these gifts were a series of rings bearing the Imperial Russian double-headed eagle and the dates 1613 and 1913. There are records of such rings being distributed, but few have survived and it is unfortunate that we do not know the original recipient of this ring.

Fig.311: Romanov Tercentenary ring in gold mounted with of diamonds. Fabergé, St Petersburg, ca 1913.
© Christie's Images Ltd. 2003

Fig.312:
© Christie's Images Ltd. 2003

In this photograph taken in about 1925, the actress Kendall Lee is wearing a selection of jewellery by Cartier including an onyx and diamond brooch and earrings, and bracelets and a matching ring in one of Cartier's signature designs – the interlocking 'rolling' bands. Kendall Lee had ample access to such jewellery, as she was married to Jules Glaenzer, who was vice-president and then later president of Cartier.

The photo cannot have been taken before 1924 because that was the year in which Cartier first introduced their triple 'rolling ring'. However, it is somewhat remarkable that the firm, almost synonymous with platinum jewellery, launched these rings and the matching bracelets in three colours of gold – yellow, red and white.

The firm of Cartier was founded in Paris in 1847 by Louis-Françoise Cartier, but only in around 1900 did it begin to create its own pieces, rather than simply acting as a retailer for other manufacturers and designers. This change can be linked with the company's move to a new grander location in Paris in 1899. The first decade of the twentieth century was one of growth in its business and its international reputation for exquisite design and quality materials. Cartier opened branches in London (1902) and New York (1909) and clients ranged from American millionaires to Indian Maharajas.

In their pre-First World War jewellery, diamonds predominate. There are spectacular necklaces, tiaras and bracelets consisting of numerous perfectly cut diamonds, often with oriental pearls, in intricate but delicate platinum settings. The styles, perhaps pandering to both the old rich and the new rich, hearkened back to the stately grandeur of eighteenth and early nineteenth designs with barely a nod to the Art Nouveau styles then so much in vogue.

What was new was an ability to produce diamond jewellery that combined strength with almost lace-like delicacy. This had been made possible by the introduction of platinum settings, an innovation largely pioneered by Cartier.

Colour also played an important part. We see diamonds combined with fine rubies from Burma and sapphires from Kashmir, sometimes Colombian emeralds, sometimes enamel and not infrequently black onyx. Such use of colour increased during the years running up to the First World War and then become far more prevalent in the 1920's. In particular, the discovery of the tomb of Tutankhamen in the Valley of Kings, Egypt in 1922, led to a whole new wave of Egyptomania and Cartier produced a wide range of jewellery that drew on Egyptian motifs and, characteristically, incorporated small but genuine ancient Egyptian objects and fragments.

Cartier jewellery is also closely linked with the rise of the Art Deco movement, a largely geometric art style that might be seen as a predictable reaction against the more ornate and sensuous naturalism of Art Nouveau.

The years following World War I also saw new materials in jewellery – most noticeably white gold – and huge social changes ranging from the increasing emancipation of women to the the near-death of the apprentice system.

Fig.313: Kendall Lee holding a Persian-design brooch of onyx and diamonds and wearing matching bracelets and ring in three-coloured gold. Jewellery by Cartier, photo ca 1925. © Condé Nast Archive/CORBIS

It is noteworthy that although the firm of Cartier had largely scorned Art Nouveau influences, it was in the forefront of the Art Deco jewellery fashion.

Cartier also drew heavily on even more easterly design ideas. They produced jewellery, cigarette cases and other objects inspired by Mogul India and Persia, and a whole range of pieces in the Japanese and Chinese tastes. The latter often incorporating Chinese jades – from simple jade disks, as here, to ancient Chinese jade belt hooks. These jadeite, diamond, ruby and black enamel earrings were sold by Cartier around 1920.

Chinese jadeite, here a carved panel, is also used in this lapel watch by Cartier circa 1925. Again, the platinum and gold ornament is also set with diamonds and cabochon rubies and embellished with black enamel.

The rainbow hues of the jewellery in ancient and oriental styles led to the development of the striking colour combinations seen in Cartier jewellery from the mid 1920s up until the Second World War. A combination of diamonds with black (enamel or onyx) was common, often also embellished with red (rubies or coral) and sometimes, as here, green jade.

The use of bright red coral with black onyx or black enamel became almost a hallmark of Cartier style. Platinum remained the precious metal of choice for the settings.

The initially geometric form of Art Deco softened in time to allow some stylized naturalistic forms. The little flowerpot brooch by Cartier, London, dates to around 1925 and is an early example of this trend. The coloured gems here include amethyst, garnet and citrine flowers in a black onyx vase.

Fig.315: Lapel watch in carved jadeite with diamonds, pearls, rubies, emeralds and black enamelled beads, mounted in platinum and gold. Cartier, Paris, ca 1925
© Christie's Images Ltd. 2001

Fig.316: 'Giardinetto' brooch in carved onyx, citrine, amethyst and garnet. Signed Cartier London, ca 1924.
© Christie's Images Ltd. 2002

Fig.314: Ear-pendants in jade, diamonds, rubies, onyx and black enamel, mounted in gold, Cartier, Paris, ca 1920.
© Christie's Images Ltd. 2004

As noted above, Egyptian influence upon jewellery had been developed sporadically since Napoleon's expedition there in the early nineteenth century, but a craze for all things Egyptian followed the 1922 discovery of Tutankhamen's tomb. The diamond, emerald and ruby pendant and necklet here is one of the more spectacular of Egyptianising jewels and was produced by Van Cleef and Arpels in Paris in 1924. Two similar necklets are recorded as having been produced, but the whereabouts of the other is unknown.

The figure in the centre of the pendant depicts the Egyptian Goddess Maat, sometimes described as the Goddess of 'truth', but in fact represented a more general concept of judgement and equilibrium. Before her is one of her symbols, a feather. After death the deceased's heart was weighed against this feather and if it were heavier, the deceased would not pass into the afterlife.

The border around Maat has lotus flower motifs. The lotus flower opens each morning when the sun rises and the lotus was thus thought to represent the birthplace of the sun. The chain has a series of panels with the sky god Horus in the form of a hawk and the clasp is in the form of a winger scarab. Such a scarab propelled the sun on its daily journey across the sky.

Fig.317: Pendant in diamonds, rubies and emeralds. Van Cleef & Arpels, Paris, 1924.
© Christie's Images Ltd. 1998

These two clip brooches are in the characteristic geometric forms of the Art Deco, both were produced by Cartier in about 1930.

The first is a diamond clip in which narrow, rectangular cut baguette or 'baton' diamonds play an important role in the design. This diamond form was one of the new styles of cutting introduced in the early twentieth century. It was first used around the time of the First World War, but was uncommon before the mid 1920's and it really came into its own in the 1930's where its rectangular form fitted perfectly with the Art Deco style then in vogue. The same is true of the little trapezoidal diamonds and half moons.

The second brooch is also of platinum, but here set with bright almost metallic blue-green aquamarines as well as diamonds. Aquamarine was a rarity in jewellery until relatively recent times. It was not unknown in antiquity, but generally speaking its colour was unsuited to gold mounts and it really came into its own with the increasing use of platinum after about 1900 and, a couple of decades later, white gold.

Fig.318: Diamond brooch, mounted in platinum, Signed Cartier London, ca 1930.
© Christie's Images Ltd. 2003

Fig.319: Aquamarine and diamond clip brooch mounted in platinum, Signed Cartier London, ca 1930.
© Christie's Images Ltd. 2003

The long established firm Fouquet of Paris was particularly well known in the post First World War years for its Art Deco designs. The ring shown here is in gold and platinum set with black onyx, amber and jade and dates from the early 1930's. Black onyx and jade were, as we have seen, popular in Art Deco jewellery, but the use of set amber is unusual, especially amber set in platinum. However, the use of opaque gemstones, outside of the usual glittering repertoire of diamonds, sapphires, rubies and emeralds, was a characteristic of some Art Deco jewellery and sometimes can almost give it an Arts and Craft feel.

Fig.320: Ring of amber, black onyx and jadeite set in platinum and gold,
Designed by Georges Fouquet, French, 1930-1935.
(Victoria and Albert Museum, London)
© V&A Images / Victoria and Albert Museum

The geometric neatness of Art Deco was succeeded by what we might describe as a reluctant naturalism. Jewellery designers wanted to return to more flowing and less rigid forms, but were anxious to demonstrate an allegiance to contemporary abstract art and show that they stood aloof from, even despised, the lush representationalism of traditional earlier jewellery. Nature might inspire, but it should no longer dictate. It was a new world, the atom had been broken apart, as had many social traditions. A brooch was no longer a leaf, say, but could be the merest essence of a leaf. At best this allowed the production of some truly inspired jewellery, at worst it provided a repertoire of bland, unsure forms by designers and makers whose eagerness to join the bandwagon outpaced their skills or discernment.

The brooch here is a magnificent floral form in sapphires and diamonds mounted in yellow gold and platinum. It was made in about 1940 by Van Cleef and Arpels and bears a number indicating it was sold in New York where the company had opened its first boutique in 1939.

The colour of the sapphires suggest that they might have come from the mines in Montana, a source discovered in the later nineteeth century.

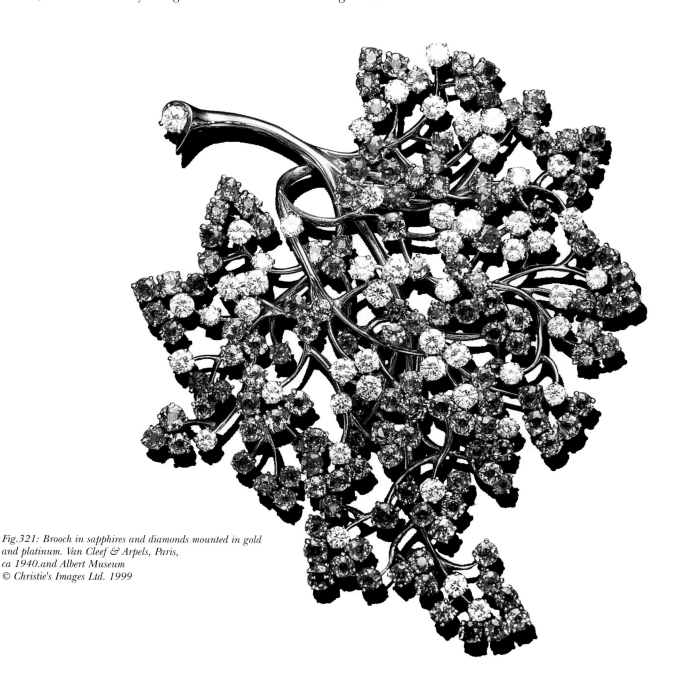

Fig.321: Brooch in sapphires and diamonds mounted in gold and platinum. Van Cleef & Arpels, Paris,
ca 1940.and Albert Museum
© Christie's Images Ltd. 1999

Fig.322: Gold ear ornament reminiscent of cubist design.
South India, early 20th century.
(Victoria and Albert Museum, London)
© V&A Images / Victoria and Albert Museum

This single gold earring is included here as something of a trick. To the uninitiated it appears to represent jewellery in the European cubist styles as developed by Georges Braque and Pablo Picasso before the First World War. As far as dating goes, this is not far out, but this earring is actually an example of a gold ear ornament from Tamil Nadu, south India. The abstract design incorporates naturalistic forms including an animal head.

Post World War 2

With the end of the Second World War this survey comes to an end. The myriad trends and processes encountered in jewellery since the mid-twentieth century deserve a separate study. It would be a somewhat different type of study to the present one. We are close enough to the jewellery produced over the last sixty years or so, and to many of the designers, makers and wearers, to have copious information for the historian, but we are perhaps too close to view the jewellery objectively and dispassionately. We need a breather before we can see it in the context of 5000 years of jewellery development.

Contemporary jewellery cannot be considered in the same way that we study jewellery from the past – anymore than we could apply sensibly apply modern architectural criticism to the great pyramids of Egypt. With recent jewellery, we can react instinctively to aspects that we like or find interesting, or are repelled by, but we approach it from a different intellectual perspective than older pieces. A medieval brooch attracts our interest because of how it fits into its historical and artistic context, because of how it is made, the extensive trading patterns that its materials might demonstrate, that it survived at all, and even perhaps on the basis of that most paradoxical of aspects – it reminds us of something from our own times. A modern brooch by a celebrated designer must be judged differently. Understanding how an individual piece or its material or technique fits into and contributes to the on-going development of jewellery is not the same as passing judgement on its aesthetic and technical merits.

The nineteenth century dichotomy between designer/craftsman and mass-produced jewellery continued through the twentieth century. As has been made evident in this study, developments in jewellery technology and materials played major roles in stimulating new forms over the passing millennia. Particularly relevant in a post Second World War context are advances in jewellery casting processes. The basic casting technique used by the jewellery industry through some 6000 years was the lost wax technique as described with fig.204. But there were two significant advances that only came into widespread use after the Second World War. The first was the adoption, from the dental industry, of centrifugal and vacuum casting processes that allowed far more detailed castings. The second advance was the introduction of flexible rubber moulds for the serial production of wax models. Now a large number of identical pieces could be manufactured.

High definition casting provided the artist designers with a ready way to convert concept to the final piece or pieces and, in particular, allowed a range of unusual and irregular surfaces to serve as an intentional part of the design. In talented hands this gave rise to some wonderful effects, but not all involved had the wisdom, taste and restraint to realise that 'irregular' was not necessarily a synonym for 'modern', or that being new or startling was better as a by-product of good design, not as an end in itself.

Advanced casting technology also brought to the fore again the arguments about craft that Ruskin had raised a century earlier. More traditional jewellery makers and retailers belittled cast jewellery as inherently inferior to hand-made pieces. But, good cast jewellery is surely better than shoddy hand made pieces. All that was happening was that the 'craftsmanship' aspect was being shifted upstream, in production terms, to the wax model rather than the metal components.

Gold, both yellow and white, have remained the jewellery metals par excellence, and platinum has undulated in and out of fashion, but new metals have also come on the scene. Perhaps the most significant here is titanium. Titanium has only been commercially available in metallic form since the 1950s and came to the notice of jewellers in the 1960s. Titanium is light and the thin and durable protective oxide layer that it rapidly forms in air can be developed electrolytically to provide brightly coloured surfaces.

With gemstones, there have been several significant new discoveries of gems, new synthetic gems and numerous advances in methods to 'improve' gemstones. For example, poor quality rubies made to look far finer by being impregnated with glass and sapphires can be diffused with beryllium to generate some very interesting shades. New methods of pearl culturing have reduced some classes of cultured pearls to little more than cheap costume jewellery. However, perhaps the most marked change has been with diamonds. The once rare diamond has burst onto the scene from a plethora of new mines, from Australia, Botswana, Canada, and all the way to Zambia, and in quantities that would have astounded earlier observers.

Much of what that has just been said can be seen as part of what has been called the democratisation of jewellery. Who in, say 1955, would have guessed that the world's largest retailer of jewellery half a century later would be a mass-merchandiser and discount store – Wal-Mart? Now many supermarkets offer diamond-set jewellery and the internet has allowed customers to compare, price and buy jewellery with far more information at their disposal than ever before.

*Fig.323: Jill Ciraldo and Grace Flynt admiring the McLean Jewel Collection at Harry Winston,
New York, 1949. The Hope Diamond is upper left, the "Star of the East," upper right.*
© Bettmann /CORBIS

One feature of jewellery has always remained to the fore. Jewellery is worn as a symbol of status or allegiance. This can be straightforward, such as the wedding ring that shows your married status, but it can also be far more subtle and even unconscious. Traditionally styled or antique jewellery provides a modern wearer with the veneer of a certain social status from the past – whether or not it is deserved. On the other hand the wearer of contemporary jewellery is demonstrating a more forward looking and independent approach.

The idea that jewellery represents wealth has manifested itself less and less by the wearing of tiaras by the old aristocracy, but more and more by the wearing of jewellery by the new aristocracy, rock stars and other celebrities. Wearing a heavy gold chain or a large diamond on your finger, or even in your tooth, demonstrates that you, or someone close to you, can spend. You are above subsistence level, you have a surplus. Such a surplus only comes with power. It is tempting to equate this with the treasuries of ancient Sumeria or Athens, say, but there are differences. For almost all of jewellery history, jewellery and other treasures have been a store of surplus and readily convertible to cash. However, with the taxes, production costs and marketing expenses of the developed world, most jewellery now becomes negative equity the moment it is purchased. Jewellery is now a symbol of wealth, no longer wealth itself. So, the two classes of traditional and contemporary jewellery have been joined by a third class, luxury branded jewellery that ensures peer respect without making any great demands on an individual's level of artistic discernment. Against this background, it is not surprising that designers are either tempted to startle or amuse observers into recognition, or simply rely on reworking forms from the past in the hope that these might stir some nostalgic longings.

So, how will jewellery historians view jewellery from the second half of the twentieth century a couple of hundred years from now? Will our celebrated designers and celebrated jewellery have stood the test of time? More importantly, how will this jewellery be classified and defined so that it forms a coherent chapter in our history.

There was some intentional use of variations in the colours of gold in the eighteenth and early nineteenth centuries, but thereafter decorative use of contrasting gold colours was surprisingly rare until they became a fashion trend over the last decade or two. The colours used today are typically yellow, pinkish, white and green, and these can be seen right across the jewellery stage, from the cheapest of mass produced chains to Cartier's triple 'rolling ring' which is still in production after 80 years – though in deference to the importance of branding, it now bears the Cartier stamp in full view on the outside.

Of course, Cartier was not the only major jewellery house to have employed coloured golds during the twentieth century, Fabergé, for example was another. And then there is this spectacular example, a diamond-set bangle in pink gold that was made by Boucheron, Paris in about 1945.

The pink colouration is normally produced by the addition of copper, but as well as affecting the colour, copper can cause problems with the structure of the alloy. In particular, care has to be taken to avoid brittleness. The cheaper 'red gold' chains from the 1990s can sometimes crumble like cookies, especially if cleaned in an ultrasonic cleaning bath.

The advances in coloured gold alloy production, and the ability to troubleshoot the problems when they arise, are tied into the great advances in the science of metallurgy. Scientific advances that impact on jewellery, from mining to finishing to the recycling of waste, have revolutionised the industry in recent decades, but not always in a way that is beneficial to society or the earth. For example, the modern cyanide process for gold extraction, invented just over a century ago in 1887, is the commonest means of gold extraction today, but is increasingly being viewed as environmentally unfriendly. The protests against such processes, manifested in the current 'Dirty Gold' campaign, are part of an increasingly vociferous criticism against jewellery and mining industry practices that are deemed unethical, environmentally problematic or both. These issues range from child labour in jewellery factories to the funding of civil wars by illicit diamond mining. The industry is reacting with several initiatives that range from establishing codes of best practices to establishing 'Fair Trade' jewellery, much on the lines of Fair Trade coffee that at the time of writing commands as much as 5% of the coffee market in some cities. Some individual companies take a stand, such as Tiffany's refusal to buy Burmese rubies because of the poor human rights in that country; sometimes new industry bodies are formed, such as the recently launched Council for Responsible Jewellery Practices.

It is too early to say how all this will affect jewellery and the jewellery industry through the twenty-first century, but affect it all it most certainly will.

Fig.324:
Pink gold and diamond bracelet. Boucheron,
Paris, ca 1945.
© Christie's Images Ltd. 2002

Jewellery manufacture and gem dealing has always been a profession that suited itinerant craftsmen. The raw materials were portable or supplied by the client as were the tools to work them. The jewellers on the move ranged from the tinkers that trudged round from town to town, to jewellers that transported their entire businesses to distant countries. This has been true throughout history. Records of Greek jewellers have been found in Southern France and the Fabergé family were originally French Huguenots. The reasons for these migrations varied considerably. Sometimes they were prompted simply by the search for new or less well served communities, sometimes by the tumultous events that shaped history. All this raises certain questions about the nature of the jewellery industry and the nature of those who have followed it. For example, is the frequent persecution of Jews through history, from the expulsion of Jews from sixteenth century Portugal to the events of 1930's Europe, one reason why gem dealing and working has so often been seen as a traditionally Jewish profession? To say that gem dealing simply suited the widespread diaspora and close knit nature of jewish communities around the world begs the question. That diaspora was often the result of forced migrations.

The interlinking between large and small scale migrations and jewellery history remains to be written, but it is clear that the movement of jewellers have had an enormous effect on the development and transmission of jewellery styles through history. We encounter one of two alternatives. Either the migrant craftsman has considerable difficulty pursuing his profession in his new environment, or he is feted as a novelty and adopted by the rich and famous. Much depends on skill, of course, and it can be argued that a great craftsman or innovator will find his niche regardless of the society into which he decides to integrate.

There are numerous instances of transplanted jewellers of note that we might cite. One would be Fulco di Verdura. He was born in Palermo at the end of the nineteenth century and after having produced jewellery for Coco Chanel in Paris in the years after the First World War, he headed to America in the 1930's, first Hollywood and then he opened a studio in New York in 1939. His clients between the 1930's and 1960's were the sophisticated rich and his designs have been aptly described as baroque, colourful and voluptuous.

The brooch here, in 18 carat yellow gold, and platinum with about three carats of diamonds, is in the form of a woven ray, all-gold examples were also made. Celebrated jewellery by Verdura includes the 1947 cabochon ruby heart brooch wrapped in strings of diamonds.

The question for our jewellery historian of the future is whether the globalisation in the jewellery industry today will lessen the impact made by individuals or companies who move countries, or will the worldwide industry allow itself to be invigorated by the influences from the developing countries before it swamps them?

Fig.325: 'Ray' brooch in diamonds mounted in platinum and gold. Vedura, American, 20th century.
© Christie's Images Ltd. 1999

Surface textures came to the fore in gold jewellery during the last quarter of the twentieth century. Earlier goldsmiths, such as Fabergé for example, had experimented with gold surfaces and created a variety of intriguing textures – including rippling surfaces produced by almost heating sheet gold to melting point. However, the greater freedom of form in jewellery in the post Second World War years meant that irregular and asymmetric shapes could be produced with cast, chased or even electroformed surfaces to provide an infinite variety of imaginative ornaments.

The large 18 carat gold cuff bracelet here is by David Webb, an American jeweller who is famous for his bold, gold jewellery. In the 1950's he carried out commissions for the rich and famous – including Doris Duke – but perhaps became more widely known when he was discovered by Jacqueline Kennedy in the 1960's.

The hammered finish on this bracelet is just one of the many surface textures experimented with by recent goldsmiths. The deliberate application of a finish to make the object look unfinished is one of the paradoxes confronted by the jewellery historian, and is very much a twentieth century and later phenomenon. Through most of history, gold jewellery was usually surface finished in one of two ways. The surface could be treated with chemical etchants to leave an even and often slightly matt surface, or it could be polished to as bright a shine as possible. The nature of the object played a role in this choice, as did its composition. Intricately decorated surfaces, Etruscan granulation, say, could not be polished and was thus simply chemically cleaned to remove discoloration caused by soldering and such like. To talk of chemical cleaning might sound too loftily scientific for the ancient world, but the chemicals concerned included urine, vinegar and salt. The ultimate example of chemical cleaning of gold was the *tumbaga* surface finish of some Pre-Columbian goldwork (as described with fig. 204).

Smooth gold surfaces could be polished to a fine shine, but this was far more commonly carried out by rubbing the gold surface with a smooth metal tool, pebble or shell, rather than with a fine abrasive 'metal polish'. This rubbing with a smooth surface is termed 'burnishing' and provided a very shiny and compacted surface. Abrasive polishing was rarely used until quite recent times and this is why a modern jeweller raised on abrasive polishing finds it so hard to restore a damaged Victorian brooch, say, that would have had a burnished or chemically 'coloured' surface originally.

Since the surface of jewellery is the feature we see, we might expect significant changes here over the coming years. Perhaps there will be a new fuzziness in the distinction between surface and gem. For example, thin layers of synthetic diamond could be applied over gold surfaces to provide extra durability and, perhaps, interesting optical phenomena. Nanotechnology could be married with goldsmithing to provide gold or platinum structures of hitherto unimagined flexibility, springiness or colour.

Fig.326: 18 ct gold bracalet. David Webb, American, 1960s.
© *Christie's Images Ltd. 2004*

A pair of earrings in titanium, designed and made by Reema Pachachi in about 1979/1980 while a student at the Royal College of Art. At that time this use of titanium was a relatively new material, but a beautiful and durable one. That was quarter of a century ago. Titanium still hasn't hit the mainstream.

The introduction of a jewellery metal has been far rarer through history than the introduction of new gem materials. The uninitiated might thus suppose that a beautiful new metal would be greeted with far greater enthusiasm than a new gem. Strangely this is not so. Even traditional jewellery companies have embraced all manner of new gem materials with scarcely a murmur, even some synthetic gems and many treated ones. But, anything outside the usual range of gold, silver and platinum alloys is usually greeted with scorn. In the past, we might excuse this as an avoidance of base metals that might stain clothes or of plating that might flake off. But it is hard to substantiate this approach with something like titanium that is far less likely to stain clothing, or stimulate allergic reactions, than many 'precious' jewellery alloys. Indeed there are all manner of alloys today that would be perfect jewellery materials from a purely aesthetic point of view. Stainless steel, for example, has most of the properties of platinum, but is seldom seen in jewellery outside of body jewellery or some designer pieces. We can't blame it on cheapness, steel jewellery can cost more than silver jewellery.

This continued grasp by much of the conventional jewellery industry of what are very outdated views on the intrinsic preciousness of jewellery may not continue indefinitely. It will need some soul-searching to discover what jewellery really is, or should be, but change will happen. Then the jewellery playing field will become a more revolutionary battlefield. Presumably that is why conventional jewellers are instinctively resisting such change.

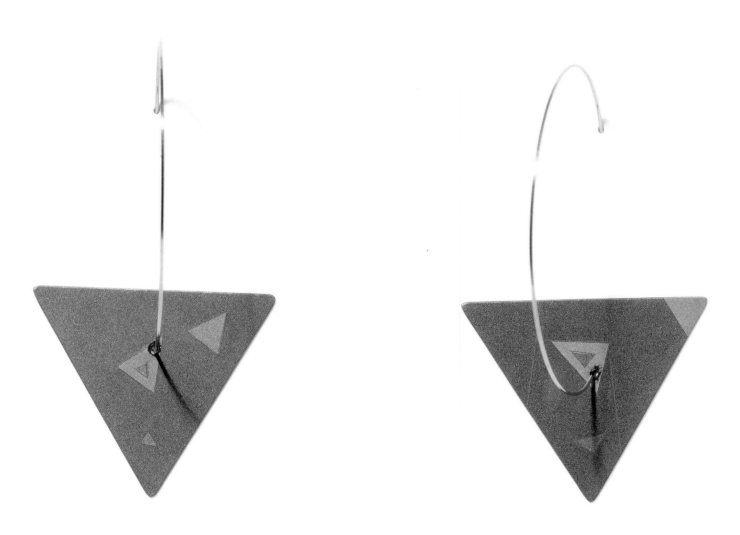

Fig.327: ' A pair of titanium earrings. Designed and made by Reema Pachachi, London, ca 1980. (Victoria and Albert Museum, London)
V&A Images / Victoria and Albert Museum

The term 'Bling' has been defined as 'a particular fashion of ostentatious displays of wealth, one where oversize jewelry is the norm.' That's from a scholarly thesis on the subject: 'Bling-Bling: The Economic Discourses of Hip-Hop' by Alf Rehn and David Skold, Stockholm, 2003.

Against the Bling phenomenon of the last decade or so, with its mass of glittering diamonds ('ice' or, more recently 'frosting') and, usually, more accent on flash than design, one name stands out - Jacob the Jeweler. This New York jeweller, Jacob Arabo, was born in Russia and started designing and making jewellery in his teens and then carved himself a niche among rich and famous celebrities as a designer of wonderfully over-the-top and often humorous jewellery. The piece shown here is a diamond-set ring in the form of a turntable record player.

The humorous aspects apparent in some jewellery of the last few decades is an interesting feature of post Second War World jewellery. There had been some playfulness in earlier times, including the imprisoned Eros in fig.287 and the not dissimilar class of depictions on some Roman intaglios, but there is little sign of jewellery that was deliberately intended to raise a smile. There was no lack of sense of humour in earlier cultures, whether we are looking at early Egyptian sketches on limestone fragments or a Mozart comic opera.

When jewellery historians of the future look back at our times they might well see jewellery intended to make us smile as just one manifestation of some need to demonstrate lack of aggression or as an antidote against seriousness, much as we encounter in tee-shirt texts and badges, but it will be interesting to see how much it, or the slightly anarchistic spirit it imples, enters the mainstream jewellery world. Is humorous jewellery the antithesis of luxury brand jewellery?

Fig.328: ' Diamond-set ring in the form of a turntable record player.
By Jacob Arabo - 'Jacob the Jeweler' - New York, 1990s.
Courtesy of JACOB & Co.

Body jewellery is a very ancient tradition that has become mainstream in recent decades. What probably began in the developed world as a counter-culture, a youthful rebellion against norms that grew out of a fusion between hippy culture and alternative sexual practices, has become a ubiquitous badge of youth. Studs and rings are inserted through an imaginative array of body parts and range from simple surgical steel or titanium studs to expensive diamond-set ornaments. Side by side with this fashion is the decoration of teeth – most often now an inset diamond. Here we see the American singer, songwriter and producer Mary J. Blige quite literally flashing a smile.

The common feature of this sort of jewellery is that it is body ornament that tags the body– it is jewellery that has largely lost connection with clothing, although it may compliment it. Is this because clothing has largely been democratised – even the rich wear jeans? Or is it because clothing is either too ornamental or too 'dressed down' to require or suit additional ornament? Or possibly clothing is now so disposable and ephemeral that it has become unsuitable as a repository for personal jewellery?

Body jewellery may well become increasingly mainstream and in the process lose its allure for rebellious youth, but how far will this go? Would Cartier, say, now publicly market a fine platinum and diamond nose or navel stud? Would they have done so eighty years ago, if such studs had been as publicly worn by celebrities then as they are now?

Fig.329: ' American singer, songwriter and producer Mary J. Blige flashes a diamond-set smile.
© Getty Images

At the beginning of this book I warned that it might well pose more questions than it answered. In the context of jewellery of the past that is fair enough – we are trying to reassemble the past from the meagre flotsam that the tides of time have washed up at our feet. Inevitably we have more questions than answers. But I also believe it to be right to pose questions about the present and future of jewellery? Every book about archaeology that I read as a child justified the science: only by understanding the past, it might explain the present and help steer the future. Noble sentiments, but perhaps as true with jewellery as with any other of man's endeavours. It is not simply that there are also questions to be posed about the jewellery of today and tomorrow. We need to pose those questions. We can learn much from the answers, and much from our inability to always know the answers.

Index